Stress in Psychotherapis

All psychotherapeutic work involves the practitioner in intimate emotional and mental contact with the client. Each session is shaped by different factors, including the client's problem, their perception of what they want from the treatment and the therapist's assessment of the client's needs. Responding to the client's immediate needs whilst making an appropriate intervention creates a delicate balance for the therapist to maintain. *Stress in Psychotherapists* highlights the pressures inherent in therapeutic practice and emphasises the need for therapists to find ways of managing stress, for themselves as well as for their clients.

Written by a team of experienced practitioners, this book looks at how stress experienced by psychotherapists varies according to the problems they treat, the settings in which they work and their professional and personal development. Practitioners are encouraged to think critically about how stress affects their practice and what can be done to benefit both themselves and their clients.

Before his retirement **Ved P. Varma** worked as psychotherapist and educational psychologist. He has edited many books, including *Anxiety in Children* and *The Secret Life of Vulnerable Children*.

Stress in Psychotherapists

Edited by Ved P. Varma

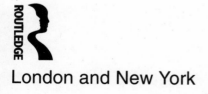

London and New York

First published 1997
by Routledge
11 New Fetter Lane, London EC4P 4EE

Simultaneously published in the USA and Canada
by Routledge
29 West 35th Street, New York, NY 10001

Typeset in Times by
Ponting–Green Publishing Services, Chesham,
Buckinghamshire

Printed and bound in Great Britain by
Redwood Books, Trowbridge, Wiltshire

British Library Cataloguing in Publication Data
A catalogue record for this book is available from the
British Library

Library of Congress Cataloguing in Publication Data
Stress in psychotherapists / edited by Ved P. Varma.
    Includes bibliographical references and index.
    1. Psychotherapists–Job stress.   I. Varma, Ved P.
    [DNLM: 1. Psychotherapy.   2. Stress, Psychological.
    3. Occupational Health.   WM 420 S915 1996]
    RC451.4.P79S77   1996
    616.89'14'023–dc20
    DNLM/DLC
    for Library of Congress   96–4647

ISBN   0–415–12174–4 (hbk)
ISBN   0–415–12175–2 (pbk)

Contents

Contributors

Philip Barker, Professor, Department of Psychiatry and Paediatrics, University of Calgary, Canada.

Irene Bloomfield, Psychotherapist in private practice, London.

Cassie Cooper, Senior Lecturer in Counselling and Psychotherapy, University of Westminster, Harrow Annex.

Delia Cushway, School of Psychology, University of Birmingham.

Francis Dale, Principal Child and Adult Psychotherapist, Devon.

Christopher Dare, Senior Lecturer in Psychotherapy, Department of Psychiatry, Institute of Psychiatry, University of London.

David Jones, Senior Lecturer in Psychology, Birkbeck College, University of London, Chartered Clinical Psychologist.

Frank Margison, Consultant Psychotherapist, Gaskell House, Swinton Grove, Manchester.

Louis Marteau, RC Priest, Founder of the Dympna Centre, London.

Meg Sharpe, The Group-Analytic Practice, London.

Valerie Sinason, Consultant Child Psychotherapist, Tavistock Clinic and St George's Hospital, London.

Andrew Skarbek, Consultant Psychotherapist, Runwell, Rochford and Basildon Hospitals, Essex.

Susan Wallbank, Co-ordinating Counsellor, Cruse, London.

Arthur Hyatt Williams, formerly Consultant Adolescent Psychiatrist, Tavistock Clinic, London.

Preface

Over the last twenty or so years psychotherapists have made a great contribution to the mental health problems of their fellow human beings and there has been a great need for them to do so. As Malcolm Pines wrote in 1974 (Varma 1974), rising living standards in underdeveloped countries often precede and may eventually lead to revolution. Similar conditions in advanced western societies lead to a demand for psychotherapy – the hungry mind replaces the empty belly; the emotional sickness shows.

Almost all of us in advanced western societies have experienced stress at one time or another, in our personal relationships, in our work, in our health, or in all of these and other areas as well. Psychotherapists have experienced more stress than other people because they deal with the stressed and the stressors.

The other reason why psychotherapists experience more stress is a result of the inherent complexity of their subject (Bloch 1982). This complexity is reflected in the vast array of different psycho-therapeutic approaches. The number of 'schools' of psychotherapy well exceeds 100 and a recent publication contained almost 1,000 pages describing no less than 64 'innovative' approaches (ibid.). In this book, rather than trying to represent this enormous field, I have taken what seems to me the more sensible course of showing how stress affects psychotherapists working with different aspects of three fundamental models of which virtually all the others are variations: the psychodynamic, the humanist–existential, and the behavioural.

During the last thirty years work has been done on stress in a wide range of occupations (Payne and Firth-Cozens 1987), but it is only recently that books have begun to appear which deal with stress in specific occupational groups. So far as I know, this is one of the first books to look at the question of stress in psychotherapists, although chapters on stress have appeared in books dealing with different aspects of psychotherapy, and papers have appeared in journals. Inevitably, I have had to be selective and it has not been possible to cover all aspects of the question as fully as one might have wished. Nevertheless, I believe that the subject is an important and neglected one and it is my hope that this book will not only prove helpful to those who read it, but will also act as a catalyst for further work.

REFERENCES

Bloch, Sidney (1982) *What is Psychotherapy?* Oxford: Oxford University Press.

Payne, Roy and Firth-Cozens, Jenny (1987) *Stress in Health Professionals*, Chichester: John Wiley.

Varma, Ved P. (1973) *Stresses in Children*, London: University of London Press.

Varma, Ved P. (ed.) (1974) *Psychotherapy Today*, London: Constable.

Ved P. Varma
London 1995

Chapter 1

The experience of being a psychotherapist

Christopher Dare

A recently appointed high-up official in a Mental Health Trust had courteously set up a meeting with me in pursuit of his conscientious wish to understand more of the services provided within his new responsibilities. He naturally wanted to know of what psychotherapy consisted. He displayed a genuine curiosity, a wish to learn and to place the psychotherapy business alongside his previous experience of other businesses. He had worked in industry and he wanted to make a parallel between the activity of the psychotherapist and his own experience of giving career advice to junior staff in his previous executive positions. At the same time, he displayed a characteristic fear: people could get an excess of advice and support and might grow to rely too much upon it. He feared that receiving psychotherapy might become an indulgence; it might create a risky dependence. He also displayed a belief that there could be something unhealthy about talking a lot about feelings. In saying such things he revealed all that characterises a very English attitude towards the subject. In many ways it is surprising that someone accepting a position in a Mental Health Trust in the United Kingdom at the present time would be comfortable with his own attitude. The field of psychodynamic psychotherapy owes a great deal to the British school of psychoanalytic thinking. It is also true that the subject, as a professional practice, is now undergoing a veritable explosion in the numbers of psychotherapists within Britain. The recently established register of psychotherapists demonstrates how many organisations are currently developing standards of practice and are training psychotherapists. At one time such trainings were almost exclusive to London (with one training each in Aberdeen and Edinburgh). Now psychotherapy courses are available in many centres throughout Britain, with, for the first time, an evolution of university-based diplomas and masters degrees in the subject. There is an even more marked development in the more 'sanitised', apparently cheaper form of talking treatments which are encompassed by the concepts and practices of counselling. In my discussion with this senior executive, I chose not to confront the inconsistency in his attitude and side-stepped the issues. I talked of the particular psychiatric conditions that interest me and for which 'psychological treatments' alone are the only ones that have been shown to work. (These are, specifically, the so-called eating disorders, especially those associated with self-starvation, which have been shown to be singularly unresponsive to pharmacological therapies, and for which effective residential treatments are expensive and scarce; see Dare *et al.* 1995). My response was tactical and I failed to talk with him about the origins of his beliefs about what is for me my life's work. Of course, his views are indeed common and representative and have an important place in any understanding of the phenomenon of psychotherapy. The common attitude to psychotherapy includes two persistent myths.

THE FIRST MYTH

Psychotherapy is nothing much more than an everyday matter of a cheerful and friendly chat, commonly available over the garden fence. Contrary to this belief, psychotherapy is a highly technical professional activity that uses a wide range of complex intellectual models, one class of which (that derived from the scientific psychology of learning and cognition) is justified by detailed and sophisticated psychological experiments. The other main class (psychodynamic or psychoanalytic psychotherapy) is sustained by a century-long process of changing and refining complex and subtle views of mental function through clinical experience with tens of thousands of patients. It is disheartening for those of us who work in this field that even apparently informed criticism of our subject addresses psychotherapy as though it were a unitary and essentially unchanging body of knowledge and practice. A 'sound-bite psychiatrist', much used by the media to comment upon the passing scene, derided psychotherapy because there were so many named varieties of the activity, as though it could not possibly be evidence of the multiplicity of practices in response to the multiplicity of problems and situations in which people need psychological help.

THE SECOND MYTH

Psychotherapy (specifically psychoanalytic psychotherapy) probably does not work to any beneficial ends but is potentially dangerous. Psychoanalytic psychotherapy, in particular, is portrayed as an implausible and futile mish-mash which has no claims to efficacy but which can cause dangerous dependence and even suicide. Again the facts are in opposition to this myth. Psychotherapy has been shown by large numbers of studies to be a powerful treatment. It has been shown that the common ingredient of all psychotherapies, the provision of warmth and empathic understanding, has such potency that it is technically quite difficult to show the specific ingredients of different forms of psychotherapy, the variance deriving from different techniques being swamped by the non-specific power of talking treatments (Luborsky *et al.* 1975). Studies of the changes people experience in the course of therapy show that there is a very rapid response indeed to the provision of a thoughtful, caring, professional listening (Howard *et al.* 1986). The proportion of people reporting marked improvement in their subjective feelings rapidly increases within a few sessions of treatment (in comparison with matched groups who are not getting help). This 'dose effect' has been shown in many studies. The rate of change of objective measures of psychological state, that is, of changes that an external investigator reports, is also quite steep, but not as much as that of the subjective feelings. Symptoms, anxieties, depressions and so on change quite quickly, whilst self-esteem difficulties and relationship problems take much longer to improve. Specific psychological treatments directed at a particular focus or target can produce rapid change, although it is not always well sustained. For example, in the field that I know best, that of eating disorder, we are some way along the path of showing just the sort of specific effects that different psychotherapies exert on different patients, in different contexts, with different sub-groups of the conditions. In addition, there is a beginning literature on the risks of psychotherapy, which, none the less, are often considerably less than the risks of not giving psychological treatment, in those situations where it is indicated. For example, in young adult patients with schizophrenia, whose families are critical of their diagnosed family member, the patient's risk of relapse is seriously heightened if specific psychological help is not given to the patient and family to help cope with the criticism.

THE ORIGINS OF PSYCHOTHERAPY

Psychiatry, as a medical sub-specialty, has existed for perhaps two centuries, although physicians have had a role in the care of those designated as mentally ill for very many centuries. (The psychiatric hospital at which I work, the Bethlem Royal Hospital, joined with the Maudsley Hospital, is shortly to celebrate its 750th anniversary). Some aspects of this medical help have had a psychological intent. For example, the moral treatment developed progressively in the first half of the nineteenth century, initiated by such as Philippe Pinel in Paris, and continued by Hack Tuke in York and John Connolly in Colchester, implied an essentially psychological approach. The giving up of constraint and the attempt at a moral reorientation constituted an early form of something like psychotherapy. Likewise, philosophers from Immanuel Kant onwards have believed that their special preoccupation with reason and morality offered an approach to mental disorder. The ideas of the philosophers and the human-isation of the hospital management of the mentally ill certainly have an honourable claim to the history of psychotherapy.

It is more often proposed that the likely antique origins of psychotherapy are the advice and support that pastors and priests have been offering since such roles became differentiated within human society. Such an idea is commonly offered in the somewhat derogatory manner that I had felt was behind the senior manager's conversation with myself reported above. I think that it is linked to the proposition that psychotherapy, particularly psychoanalytic psy-chotherapy, is in any case quasi-religious, the underlying ideas depending more on faith than on reason.

It is obvious that the activity now known as psychotherapy had some antecedents in age-old human concerns. Since time immemor-ial, it would seem, one person would offer another support and advice out of their own shared and different experiences of life's problems and their solutions. In a non-professional setting, a priest or a pastor has a greater duty towards his faith and the wider body of the flock, than to the one person alone. A friend or relative, likewise, will have responsibilities, when giving advice, to be concerned with other family members and mutual friends. There are limits imposed by tact, courtesy and convention within the informal setting that need not oblige the professional. A complementarity can be expected in the social give and take of supporting and advising. Love will provide an unconditional form of personal support and care, but the long-term nature of such a context makes it quite different from a professional activity. The care given will be part of the maintenance of the relationship concomitant with the expectation of the enduring future that is implicit in love relationships. Likewise a priest or family practitioner can offer personal psychological help, but everyone knows that if such occurs, it is only a part of the relationship, being offered alongside the principal project, priestly or medical. However, psychotherapy is, historically speaking, a new and distinctive activity. First, the personal support and psychological help is the purpose of the meeting. It is not incidental to the other things. Second, it is conducted professionally, that is to say, the one person, the client or patient, goes to the psychotherapist, expecting that the latter will be functioning as best he can in the patient's or client's interests. (It is probable that most psychotherapists are women. However, the present author is male and 'he' is used to mean 'he or she' when referring to a psychotherapist.) The psychotherapist tries to have a point of view that is specifically and only for the other. This is the problem of being a psychotherapist. However, the professional activity poses peculiar difficulties for its practitioners. The implication that psychotherapy is nothing new, except for its mumbo jumbo, is part of a suspicious response existing not only in the minds of intelligent members of the public, in academics, in doctors and in psychologists but also, I believe, in ourselves, the psychological therapists. I think that psychotherapy is beset by the uncertainties of its practitioners. The reasons for and consequences of this uncertainty are the main focus of the remainder of this chapter.

THE UNCERTAINTY OF THE PSYCHOTHERAPIST

For most occasions in which we meet with another person, we know the point of the contact. Meetings with friends and family may seem to be exceptions to this but the family is a social organisation, usually essential, existing for the support, nurturance and care of its members, but having a corporate as well as an individualistic function. Meetings with family members have a function, but one that is so intrinsic to our lives that we never need be aware of the purpose, except when there exists an obligation above our own active volition. We are so used to knowing what families are for, have been socialised to perform properly from such a young age, that we do not realise how precisely and accurately we fit in with our family role.

The strong tendency to fit in with the expected role is strong, something for which we are precisely, psychologically adapted. Indeed, it is clear that when we enter any new social situation, in our formal professional life or in the course of our social meetings, we carefully observe the rules of communication and the structure of the power and allegiances of the situation. We do this swiftly and outside of consciousness, in order that we do not offend and so that we can find out how we ourselves will fit with this new situation. It is with these highly refined and well learned social skills that a psychotherapist meets a patient or client. However, in the usual social situation of leisure, travel, work or play, we are trying to adapt and accommodate ourselves in as gracious and comfortable way as possible, so as not to challenge the given order, to intrude on private closeness or to offend those upon whom we depend in a novel setting. In the process of meeting with a group or an individual, family members as well as friends or acquaintances not only have an axe to grind – the fulfilment of their own purpose and role in the meeting – but this interest is accepted as having self-serving aspects since the social context acknowledges a process of mutually beneficial social exchange. A psychotherapist has to strive to be truly altruistic and this goes against the grain. Customarily, we are all highly orientated towards maintaining a social and family order derived from our own wider culture and the particular religious, political and family points of view. The professional activity of a psychotherapist requires attention to be paid to those things that are expected and to which social custom would require conformity, not in order to comply, but to use this as information about the problem to be faced. For example, it is quite natural, in a social situation, to ask for and obtain reassurance. A stranger on a station platform will ask of a passer-by whether or not the train that is about to leave is going to a particular destination. The passer-by will answer straightforwardly. A psychotherapist in response to a comparable request for reassurance, as to where things are going, may not simply give the automatically reassuring answer, but must question the process itself. Is the question realistic? Can anyone know where a particular psychological process is leading, or if the outcome will be satisfactory in relation to some as yet unknown, future psychological state?

The psychotherapist has to restrain the customary response, or, finding himself blurting out a social response, has to try to understand what the pressures are that led him so to do, to use the reaction as a piece of information about the processes that the patient or client tends to evoke. That is, the therapist has to treat with suspicion his own normal social reactions. The reaction must be taken as evidence of counter-transference acting out; not a forbidden process, for such enactments are inevitable, but as a phenomenon to be understood very specifically in context. Such events in the here-and-now can have a potential for usefulness but are also a source of possible error. For example, in a diagnostic interview with a patient with long-standing and distressing preoccupations for which many people had unavailingly tried to give help, I found myself feeling quite controlled and disconcerted. The patient repeatedly demanded that I tell him whether or not I could offer help, before I even knew what the problem was. I inadvertently showed my own responsive impatience. The patient burst into tears of anger and hurt, saying that he always upset people from whom he wanted advice. It slowly became apparent that he was someone who had had to look after himself from an early age, had managed to do so quite extraordinarily well, through many hard times, but he had never been able to form sustained, close love relationships. It was easy to see that he had a set, a tendency to prevent himself getting the closeness for which he so longed in relationships. Patients express the nature of their problems not only in their account of their history and their current life, but in the sort of incidents and processes that occur in their relationship with the psychotherapist. This discovery of the transference process that Freud made upwards of one hundred years ago has conflicting effects. On the one hand, it means that the psychotherapist can find himself being inducted into repeating the patient's problems in a very painful manner. On the other hand, the vivid quality of such events, occurring not as part of a reported experience but in the exact present in the therapy room, are especially powerful, showing the problem, facilitating an exploration of its accompaniments and suggesting possible routes for the avoidance of like difficulties. The psychotherapist has to take up a position that has many of the qualities of an intense closeness with the patient or client. This is necessary in order to know what the problem is for the patient or client, it enables appreciation of the feelings as accurately as possible, and is essential to make a therapeutic relationship with the patient. Within psychotherapy patients are usually confronted with difficult, often hidden parts of themselves. The revelations are embarrassing and painful. This is only likely to occur if patients feel respected and know that their pain is sensitively heard. However, in order to manage the tendency to enter into a relationship that is too social to be helpful, the psychotherapist has both to be an emotionally present and empathically effective presence for the patient but also has to preserve a distance. Some separation from the patient is required so that the professional scrutiny of the relationship is maintained. The psychotherapist cannot afford to become so involved as to be unable to make forceful therapeutic responses, if indicated and timely. For a specific patient, in a particular setting within which psychotherapy can occur, there is much variation of the precise nature of the balance of emotional directness and responsiveness within a professional framework, the psychotherapist assessing the meaning of what transpires and retaining the capacity to make helpful interventions.

EFFECTS OF THE AGE OF THE PATIENT

Working with children is quite different from working with adolescents and adults. It is very easy for children to feel very attacked in therapy. It is unusual, especially in the early phases of treatment, for children to believe that the therapy is for them. Commonly parents, teachers, social workers or courts recommend psychotherapy for a child because of worries about behaviour. Children are capable of communicating their own distress, but help can be experienced as being to do with misbehaviour or badness. Adolescents often believe that their problems are unique, and cannot be accepted or felt by others. The psychotherapist can be seen as both alien and intrusive. Adults, especially perhaps men, in our culture believe that there is shame in experiencing panic, in being overwhelmed and helpless.

The aim of life, and therefore of psychotherapy, differs with different age groups. An adolescent is trying to maintain a pathway that shows allegiance to the past, to childhood relationships, but which takes a track which specifies the adolescent's own needs and individuality. The elderly are usually engaged in a survey of their life achievements and how these fit with earlier hopes and expectations. The needs and therapeutic aims of a person with children and grandchildren are likely to be different from those of people who find their social support and companionship in non-family relationships.

CONJOINT RELATIONSHIP THERAPIES

In the last twenty-five years, effective forms of relationship psychotherapy have been devised. Some of these can be undertaken with the patient alone, but sometimes treatment for the problems of the individual are most quickly and efficaciously undertaken in the context of the person's natural psychological setting. Throughout life, the psychotherapist must consider the intimate personal relationships of the patient in order to ask what the aims of treatment are likely to be and to determine whether or not conjoint therapy (couple or family therapy) is more appropriate. The conduct of such conjoint treatments imposes additional intensity and potential for disturbing counter-transferences upon the psychotherapist, but at the same time can increase the range and effectiveness of such treatments.

GROUP PSYCHOTHERAPY

For some people, group therapy is a much more natural setting for psychological growth and for gaining mastery of frightening and difficult symptoms and relationship problems. Some patients are very supported by the finding that they have difficulties similar to those of others and that they can help others in a psychotherapeutic group, when they had believed themselves to be quite without resources. It can feel safer to reveal feelings at the slower pace that characterises group treatments. A vulnerable patient can feel protected from the scrutiny of the psychotherapist about whom a fantasy of psychological resourcefulness and invulnerability may be woven, leading the therapist to be seen as remote and unsympathetic. Other members of a group can debunk such a fantasy or can be a bulwark against the feared disparagement of the professional.

Psychotherapies differ in the intellectual framework and hence the technical preoccupations they embody, in the intensity of the therapy to be undertaken, and in the context (individual, couple, family or group). Different age groups have differing needs determined by the stage and the current course of their development: the aims of a particular psychotherapy are affected by the life-cycle location of the patient. Psychotherapy is shaped by the nature of the patients' problems and their own perceptions of what they want from the treatment, and, in addition, what form of psychotherapy that they can accept will be determined by their general expectations of what constitutes professional help. Although a psychotherapist may believe that what he is doing is determined by his own intellectual stance and by a professional assessment of the patient's needs, he will be unaware of the extent to which his apparently professional, self-determined activities are structured by the patient's contribution.

The uncertainty established by the subtle interaction between himself, his own unconscious mental processes, and the multi-layered processes with the patient, make the conduct of psychotherapy necessarily inclined often to be bewildering and unnerving.

REFERENCES

Dare, C., Eisler, I., Colahan, M., Crowther, C., Senior, R. and Asen, E. (1995) 'The listening heart and the Chi square: clinical and empirical perceptions in the family therapy of anorexia nervosa', *Journal of Family Therapy* 17: 19–45.

Howard, K. I., Kapta, S. M., Krause, M. S. and Orlinsky, D.E. (1986) 'The dose-effect relationship in psychotherapy', *American Psychologist* 41: 159–64.

Luborsky, l., Singer, B. and Luborsky, L. (1975) 'Comparative studies of psychotherapies: is it true that "everyone has one and almost all have prizes"?' *Archives of General Psychiatry* 32: 995–1008.

Chapter 2

Stress and the personality of the psychotherapist

Francis Dale

In this chapter, we will be looking at the relationship between the way stress is experienced and dealt with and the personality of the psychotherapist. The main contention will be that certain individual characteristics in the therapist's personality are helpful and of value in managing stress; and furthermore, while some of these may be innate, that these, and other traits *can* be aquired in the course of working as a therapist – because the nature of the work *requires them to be present.*

Bearing this in mind, before we can talk about the emotional and mental functioning of the psychotherapist, we need to explore those character traits in the personalities of psychotherapists which are most conducive to helping them deal with stress in a positive and constructive manner.

I will try to draw out some of the important characteristics in the personality of the psychotherapist by examining the role of the psychotherapist; the nature of the work that he is called on to do; and the emotional and mental stress that engaging in this kind of work invariably involves.

As there are so many varied forms of psychotherapy – each with its own theoretical, philosophical and clinical orientation – it will be important to deal with the more general and perhaps universally agreed characteristics which are generally thought to be a pre-requisite of all psychotherapists (regardless of their orientation) before dealing in more depth with those psychotherapies, and psychotherapists, where the very nature of the psychotherapeutic process, and the success or failure of treatment, may depend on the *kind of relationship* which develops between patient and therapist.

Implicit in the above notion is the idea that, in some forms

of psychotherapeutic intervention, the personality of the psychotherapist is of less relevance or importance for successful therapeutic
outcomes than is the particular technique used.

For example, if we were to construct a continuum or scale which
registered the extent to which the personality of the therapist was an
essential component of the treatment, it would become immediately
obvious that different models of psychotherapy require corres-
pondingly greater or lesser involvement of the psychotherapist's
whole personality.

At one end of the continuum we would find those psychotherapies
which are more symptom-based, time-limited and didactic – for
example, the behavioural, cognitive and systemic models – while at
the other, we would find those psychotherapies which deal with the
symptom as metaphor, are open-ended, person-centred and mutually
interactive. Amongst these are all those psychotherapies which
come under the umbrella of psychodynamic therapy.

ThE DEMANDS OF THE WORK

The characteristics which determine the personality traits of psychotherapists are, inevitably, shaped by the nature of the work involved
and the demands that such work places on those professionals
engaged in it.

It is a two-way process – therapeutic work attracts certain types
of individual, whilst the work itself – over time – brings about
changes in certain aspects of personality structure and functioning.

If we look first at the wide variety of underlying motivations for
wanting to work therapeutically with people we can begin to see how
complex and difficult an issue it is.

THE MOTIVATION OF THE
PSYCHOTHERAPIST

Although the following list is not exhaustive it will, I hope, give
some idea of the multi-determined and frequently unconscious
factors which lie behind a choice to work with disturbed and unhappy
individuals.

Making reparation

Many of us have, in our personal experience, been confronted with
pain, misery and despair in people we are close to, or love, but have

been unable to help them. This can sometimes be a very powerful motivating factor in the choice to be a therapist. I know, for example, of one person whose real reason for working with handicapped people stemmed from her experience of having a sister who was mentally handicapped.

Guilt

This can arise from the same kind of situation as described in the above example. The same therapist may have been equally motivated by guilt at being the normal child or because of angry or destructive emotions directed at the sister who took up so much of her parents' time or who caused so much trouble and anxiety.

Displacement

This refers to a psychical mechanism in which one defends oneself against having to acknowledge and suffer from one's own hidden pathology by displacing, projecting, or locating it in someone else.

Omnipotent control

This is frequently related to displacement and is based on a fear or even terror of whatever one is avoiding inside of oneself.

Sadism

This frequently occurs in tandem with omnipotent control and displacement. Not only are parts of the self that are experienced as threatening to one's stability split off and projected into someone else, but they are also cruelly manipulated, controlled, attacked and frequently denigrated.

Vicarious healing

Although this still relates to using the patient as a receptacle for an aspect of one's own mental and emotional functioning, it is less destructive and hence more benign. In this situation, the therapist *vicariously* heals himself through healing the part of the patient he is in unconscious identification with. He needs the patient, not so much to 'get rid of parts of the self' but in order to make contact with his own psyche – at a safe distance. In this scenario, the therapist *needs* the patient in order to maintain his psychic equilibrium.

Vicarious living

Here, the therapist has a vicarious relationship with his patients in which he experiences life, at its greatest intensity, 'through his relationship with his patients'. That is, he lives his life using his patients' life experiences rather than his own.

The challenge of the unknown/intellectual curiosity

In this situation, the therapist's prime motive is intellectual curiosity and the challenge and excitement of exploring, uncovering and investigating the problems and difficulties of his patients. Sometimes, the investigative nature of the therapeutic work is more important and rewarding than the personal relationship between patient and therapist.

A love of truth

For some people, the most significant motivating factor in becoming a therapist has its source in a love of truth and a concommitant search for meaning. Understanding the enigmas of life, seeking the causes and solutions to individual suffering are what motivates the therapist and which support him in managing and containing the 'painfulness' of truth.

Interest in other people

This characteristic is clearly allied to the above for, to be *really* interested in the problems of other, sometimes very disturbed people, sufficient to contain, work through and understand their suffering, implies the capacity to know the truth about oneself as well as about one's patients. One cannot be properly interested in the deeper significance of life *and* tolerate deception or half-truths.

Compassion

This relates to the desire to ease other people's psychic and emotional pain and offer them both a therapeutic relationship and a method for understanding themselves and those they relate to, and to manage their lives better in the here-and-now and to fulfil their innate potential as human beings in relationship with others.

Even a brief glance at the motivating factors outlined above reveals that some of them have very little to do with the needs of patients and far more with the sometimes pathological needs of the therapist. As I have already indicated, both conscious and unconscious motivations interact in an exceedingly complex way with the personality of the therapist, and one cannot realistically expect that every thought, feeling and impulse towards the patient is completely altruistic and has nothing to do with the needs of the therapist. The real questions are whether the patient *has* to meet the therapist's needs; whether these needs are antithetical to the patient's well-being; and the extent to which the therapist knows about, is willing to find out about, and can meet his needs outside the therapeutic relationship.

It is not difficult to see that with some of the more pathological personality needs of the therapist – particularly displacement, omnipotent control, sadism and vicarious healing – the therapist's capacity for being able to manage *his own stress*, let alone that of his patients, must be severely limited.

In drawing the reader's attention to the unconscious motivations that attract people to therapeutic work and the personality traits and needs they subserve, I am not suggesting that only those people with the purest and noblest of motives should consider training as psychotherapists. What I am attempting to do is to draw our attention to some of the less obvious and, sometimes negative character traits, which, if not questioned and understood, can impact on our capacity to relate to and manage the emotional disturbance in our patients in an appropriately professional and therapeutic manner.

WORKING WITH PEOPLE

All psychotherapeutic work involves the practitioner in intimate emotional and mental contact with other human beings. In a continuum from working with groups, families and couples, to work with individuals in intensive one-to-one psychoanalytic psychotherapy, there is an increasing exposure to intimacy, interaction, involvement and struggle with people in considerable pain, distress or emotional difficulty.

To *want* to work with individuals who are suffering, who are angry, depressed, emotionally cut off, suicidal, dependent, distrusting, immature and sometimes rejecting and hateful – and to be able to *do* so in a way that is beneficial to oneself and one's clients – requires, and sometimes demands, certain characteristics of temperament, mental functioning and emotional stability.

From this perspective, some of the more positive motivational factors outlined above – making reparation, curiosity and the intellectual challenge, the love of truth, interest in other people and compassion – may be helpful in determining those character traits which are useful in helping the therapist manage the stresses involved in therapeutic work.

THE PERSONALITY OF THE PSYCHOTHERAPIST

Rather than engage in a philosophical or semantic debate about what 'personality' means, or whether indeed such a concept exists in a useful and meaningful way, I am going to assume that all of us share a general view that personality relates to a set of characteristics – mental, emotional and behavioural – which exert a powerful and compelling influence on our behaviour in a unique and consistent manner over time. For the purposes of this chapter, I will be defining it as: 'Those unique and distinctive individual characteristics by which we are known by other people, and by way of which we define, recognise and know ourselves.'

Those characteristics of personality which are most helpful to both client and therapist and which bear on the therapist's capacity to manage stress can be subsumed under the following headings:

- Moral qualities
- Temperament
- Psychological mindedness

Moral qualities

Because they are dealing with vulnerable people who have often been disappointed and let down by those they trusted and on whom they were dependent, psychotherapists can, both in terms of their personalities as well as in terms of what they say or do, exert a tremendous influence for good or bad on their clients.

This influence cannot be avoided and is in fact essential to the work of most one-to-one therapies. Because of this factor, everything the therapist says, does, thinks, or feels has an impact at some level on the client.

Every therapist makes mistakes, gets things wrong or fails to understand his clients at times. The positive or negative impact of these inevitable mistakes or failures in technique will largely depend on certain moral qualities in the therapist – most important of which are truthfulness and honesty. If one is truthful (in so far as one is conscious of one's motives) mistakes will be borne more easily by one's patients and more readily forgiven than otherwise. Truthfulness – even if it involves from time to time owning one's ignorance – will not generally result in a negative therapeutic response and may even serve to increase the patient's confidence and trust in the therapist's humanity and openness.

Therapists also need to have a strong sense of who they are and what they believe in – for themselves, as much as for other people. They should be patient, non-directive (where the model of treatment allows this), open to, and tolerant of, different ideas, values and beliefs (even those which in private life they may disagree with), and not attempt to influence, coerce or persuade their patients to think, feel, believe or become anything other than what they should be, given their inborn potential.

The therapist should not set out to be a leader, a teacher, but a servant, a 'follower', a catalyst who releases, frees and liberates the potential that is hidden, blocked or lost within his patients.

This requires another important quality – patience. The therapist needs to be able to wait, to suppress his desire for more progress, speedier change, frequently for long periods of time – particularly when, on the surface, nothing much seems to be happening.

The above-mentioned attitudes of truthfulness and honesty coupled with a relatively benign super-ego, point to a personality that is unafraid, direct, resilient, flexible and tolerant – all qualities which have a direct bearing on one's capacity to manage stressful situations in a positive and therapeutic way.

Temperament

Particularly with respect to the non-directive forms of psycho-therapy, one either needs to possess a non-forceful or non-aggressive attitude towards one's patients, or to have the ability consciously to suppress the more aggressive aspects of one's personality.

Aggression or dynamism is not, *per se*, a personality trait to be avoided in a psychotherapist. A certain amount of aggression, as expressed in resilience, determination and perseverance, is probably necessary in order to meet challenges, attacks (verbal and physical) and omnipotence from clients. However, the therapist's aggression should be used – wherever possible – in the best interests of the client and never to punish, control or 'get one back' on the patient.

Another important attribute in the therapist is the ability to be able to listen, to really 'hear' what the patient is trying to say. Frequently this will not just be verbal listening but also *internal listening*; that is, paying attention to what is happening emotionally and mentally inside oneself as a result of being with a particular person who is wanting (at least in part) to be understood.

We all have our own needs, wishes and fantasies, and sometimes it is hard to differentiate between *our* fantasies and those of our patients. Knowing the difference, and not imposing our needs, wishes, anxieties on to our patients, is crucial if we are to be there for them and not just there for ourselves.

Other important qualities which are useful, if not essential, are: resourcefulness, sensitivity, the capacity to tolerate doubt, confusion and 'not knowing'; emotional flexibility and openness, being able to be non-judgemental and impartial – even, as mentioned above, in areas where one's own values and beliefs are in direct opposition to those of one's patient; possessing creativity and imagination (imaginative conjecture); and, finally, but not necessarily least, having some degree of optimism regarding human resourcefulness and a belief in an individual's capacity to change, to grow and to be able to suffer in a 'creative and constructive' way.

Psychological mindedness

In a general sense, psychological mindedness refers to those attributes of thinking and feeling which, taken together, help us in understanding ourselves and others from the point of view of our internal motives, desires, attitudes and beliefs.

Apart from having to be reasonably intelligent, one needs to have a highly developed sense of curiosity about what makes people act, think and behave as they do; positively to enjoy puzzling out and probing into areas of the mind where there are no maps and few signposts to guide you.

Introspection, intuition and the capacity to empathise with a wide range of people and personality types, are also essential.

However, perhaps the most important factor in assessing psychological mindedness refers to the extent to which someone is capable of understanding their *own* unconscious processes – and being able to manage the pain, uncertainty, fear and upset that this may cause at times.

THE THERAPEUTIC RELATIONSHIP

In those forms of psychotherapeutic treatment where the focus of the treatment is on the relationship between the therapist and patient, this becomes the main dynamic and the catalyst by way of which change is facilitated and made possible. The relationship which develops between patient and therapist has both conscious and unconscious elements to it. Those aspects which are readily available to consciousness can be reflected upon and thought about relatively easily, and without too much resistance. The unconscious elements, on the other hand, which are by definition not directly available to conscious awareness, are more difficult to get in touch with and may stir up resistance in both therapist and patient. In this case, the therapist becomes aware of the unconscious aspects of the relationship through reflecting on the transference (the feelings, thoughts and motives attributed to the therapist which have their origin in earlier, usually parent/child relationships) as well as on the emotions and thoughts which are activated inside the therapist as a consequence of both conscious and unconscious influences arising from the therapeutic relationship.

STRESS AND THE MODE OF INTERVENTION

Another factor which interacts with the personality of the psychotherapist relates to the mode or 'nature of the intervention'. This in itself, is linked to the degree of pathology, the diagnosis, and the type of symptomatology. Thus, for example, if the degree of pathology is mild, the diagnosis positive and hopeful – requiring short-term focused outpatient appointments – then the choices of intervention or treatment modalities will be less likely to be overly stressful for the therapist. In the above category we might find people suffering from bereavement, marital difficulties or mild anxiety or depression.

The nature of the intervention in these cases would not be likely to involve the therapist's personality, emotions or way of thinking or being with the patient in such a way as to create undue amounts of stress. This is because the focus would be more on *the symptom* and much less on *the relationship* between therapist and patient. This means that the model of treatment chosen is a significant factor in determining the degree of stress encountered by the therapist.

STRESS FACTORS IN PSYCHOTHERAPEUTIC WORK

As a general rule, one could say that the following factors have a direct bearing on the amount of stress experienced by the psychotherapist.

1 *The degree of pathology.* The more disturbed and emotionally and mentally unbalanced the patient is, the more disturbing it will potentially be for the therapist.
2 The more the focus of the treatment is on the *relationship* between patient and therapist, the greater the stress. Here, for example, I am thinking of those methods of treatment – principally the psychoanalytic or psychodynamic therapies – where the transference occupies the central role in the interaction between patient and therapist.
3 *The model of treatment.* This again relates to the extent to which the intervention involves the personality of the psychotherapist in the treatment.
4 The existence of a *supportive network for the patient.* Patients who have family or friends to whom they can turn for help and support are less likely to 'dump' on to the therapist or to rely on him as their only security or lifeline.
5 The existence of a *supportive network for the therapist.* It is perhaps even more important that the therapist – particularly when he is working with extremely disturbed and disturbing patients – has the support of: (a) colleagues who work in a similar way; (b) a working context which supports the style of working; and (c) the possibility of receiving appropriate supervision.
6 *Training analysis.* When one is working with patients who suffer from very poorly integrated personalities, some of the ways in which they make contact with the therapist can be very primitive, disturbing and frightening. Without one's own analysis and under-

standing and appreciation of unconscious processes, it can be difficult to disentangle one's own unconscious processes from those of one's patients.

7 *The therapist's unconscious pathology.* Every therapist will, over the course of his career, encounter a patient whose problem sufficiently mirrors a difficulty for the therapist which is still unresolved. In this situation, unless the therapist is aware of the existence of their own pathology and can take it into account, they may respond to the patient in a defensive, resistant or blaming manner. Technically, this would be called 'counter-transference resistance'.

8 *The intensity of the treatment regime.* This relates to the frequency and duration of patient contact. For example, someone who is working long hours in an institutional setting will be more likely to suffer from stress than someone seeing a patient on a less intensive basis.

9 Finally, and clearly associated with point 5 above, if the therapist has the support of a stable family background, this is of immense help in grounding them in healthy, positive, nurturing relationships which can act as an antidote to the sometimes very negative, pessimistic, bleak and hopeless situations which have brought patients to seek their help.

MANAGING STRESS – THE PERSONALITY OF THE PSYCHOTHERAPIST

Normally, one of the mechanisms of avoiding stress which is open to us in everyday life, is that of denial or avoidance. We choose to turn away from the stressful situation. However, this method of dealing with stress by avoiding it, is not open (legitimately) to the psychotherapist. This is because the existence of stress in both psychotherapist and patient is an inevitable consequence of the therapeutic process – particularly where (a) the patient is deeply disturbed; (b) the patient is 'acting out'; and, (c) where the transference is the medium within and by way of which therapeutic change occurs.

In order to manage stress, therefore, the therapist has to confront it and rise above it, and the following personality traits – which are also listed in chapter 4 ('Stresses in child psychotherapists') – make this a possible, rather than an impossible task. Not necessarily in order of importance, the therapist needs to be curious and interested in other people (in what makes them 'tick'), to have a capacity for empathy, a certain degree of toughness and resilience, sensitivity, imagination and realism, to be a good listener, and to have determination and persistence, composure 'under fire', flexibility and a sense of humour, and a positive outlook on life.

Whenever one experiences stress, it is always a warning sign that our coping mechanisms are beginning to fail in some way. The problem for psychotherapists is that not only do they have to manage their own stress, but also that of their clients. Therapists are confronted on a daily basis with people suffering from extreme stress, which, if they are to be effective and helpful, they cannot deny or turn away from.

Sometimes, as Anthony Storr points out in his book *The Art of Psychotherapy*, one has to make a choice regarding whether one has the motivation, interest or a sufficiently robust personality to be able to work effectively and safely with certain categories of patient or disturbance. In his own case, he decided not to work with psychotic patients, finding that 'close encounters with schizophrenics seemed perilously upsetting'.

For therapists to be able not merely to survive the stress that is inherent in their work, but to use it to further their understanding of themselves and their patients, they need to have the capacity to be both distant and engaged, both passive and active, and to be able to suppress temporarily their own needs, wishes, values and opinions:

> Understanding other human beings . . . requires that the observer does not simply note their behaviour as if they were machines or totally different from himself, but demands that he make use of his own understanding of himself, his own feelings, thoughts, intentions, and motives in order to understand others.
>
> (Storr 1993: 172)

It is only through having learned effective ways of recognising and dealing with their own anxieties – through their personal analysis and long training – that psychotherapists can be effective in helping their patients find new and more constructive ways of dealing with the stresses – internal and external – which brought them to seek help.

REFERENCES AND SELECT BIBLIOGRAPHY

Coltart, N. E. C. (1988) 'The assessment of psychological-mindedness in the diagnostic interview', *British Journal of Psychiatry* 153: 819–20.

Farber, L. H. (1968) *The Ways of the Will*, New York: Harper Colophon Books.

Fromm-Reichmann, F. (1960) *Principles of Intensive Psychotherapy*, Chicago: University of Chicago Press.

Greenson, R. R. (1994) *The Technique and Practice of Psycho-Analysis*, London: The Hogarth Press and the Institute of Psycho-Analysis.

Klauber, J. (1991) *Difficulties in the Analytic Encounter*, London: Free Association Books.

Ogden, T. H. (1992) *Projective Identification and Psychotherapeutic Technique*, London: Maresfield Library.

Storr, A. (1993) *The Art of Psychotherapy*, Oxford: Butterworth-Heinemann.

Thompson, C. (1988) 'The role of the analyst's personality in therapy', in *Essential Papers on Counter-transference*, New York and London: New York University Press.

Chapter 3

Stress in trainee psychotherapists

Delia Cushway

INTRODUCTION

The subject of this chapter is important to me for several reasons. Firstly, when I was a trainee I experienced a considerable degree of stress. Although not all the stress was negative and was mostly perceived as a challenge rather than a threat, I was surprised by the number of demands placed on me and the extent to which they stretched my coping resources. Later, when I became a (stressed!) trainer, I found that some of the pressures were related to my role in attempting to provide support for a number of stressed trainees. In my efforts to understand stress in training I have carried out research into stress and coping in both trainee and qualified clinical psychologists and have now extended my research interests into stress in trainee and qualified mental health professionals more generally. I am committed to the concept of psychotherapists taking care of themselves and this chapter will draw on relevant aspects of my research and experience.

Psychotherapist is a generic as well as a specific term. In the UK we have tended to use the word rather narrowly to apply to those who have undergone a specific training in psychotherapy. Recently the term has been used more generally to apply to those from a variety of disciplines practising psychotherapy. For the purposes of this chapter I am using the latter general definition of psychotherapist to include psychotherapists, clinical psychologists, counsellors, psychiatrists, mental health nurses and social workers. Clearly, much of my own experience and research relates to clinical psychology training. The chapter will mostly be concerned with the stresses of full-time training, although it is recognised that a considerable amount of psychotherapy training is part-time. Part-time training courses will, of course, create extra stressors when the pressures of training are combined with other occupational demands. Jensen (1995) has explored some of the difficulties for counsellors juggling these roles.

Any training is a time of transition and, as such, will at times be exciting and stimulating. It is also inevitably challenging and will often be experienced as stressful. Gopelrud (1980) studied a group of American graduate students and found that they experience severe life stress due to the many changes associated with graduate training. Those individuals embarking on psychotherapy training courses are mostly older than usual students. There is some evidence that this is a group at risk of psychological distress. In addition to the usual student stressors of fear of academic failure, loneliness and perceived powerlessness, older students may have developmental needs which can be frustrated within the standard university environment (Whitman, Spendlove and Clark 1984). One study showed that much of the distress of older students was related to financial hardship as well as to the psychological discomfort that this created (Winefield 1993).

Guy (1987) comments that students entering graduate school to become psychotherapists are subject to many of the same stressors, along with additional ones. As well as coping with the rigours of academic work, trainee psychotherapists are also required to focus on themselves as 'the person of the therapist', since this will be of primary importance in the therapeutic process. As Guy succinctly describes it: 'It is no longer what a person knows which is of primary concern, but what a person is, and is becoming' (1987; 39). Farber (1985) discusses the development of psychological-mindedness by trainee therapists and its implications for awareness of one's own psychological difficulties. At the same time as grappling with this, trainee therapists are exposed, maybe for the first time, to the suffering, pain and distress of others. As trainees they will be uncertain and inexperienced and may feel overwhelmed by the complexities and difficulties of the therapeutic role. If this is not enough for the trainee therapist, s/he is usually required to complete an array of academic and clinical assignments and is observed, evaluated and graded at every step of the way. It is therefore not difficult to imagine why trainee psychotherapists may be stressed.

This chapter will attempt to answer four questions and will be divided into sections corresponding to these questions. These questions are: (1) How stressed are trainee psychotherapists? (2) What stresses trainee psychotherapists? (3) What coping strategies do trainee psychotherapists use? and (4) How can the stresses of trainee psychotherapists be alleviated?

HOW STRESSED ARE TRAINEE PSYCHOTHERAPISTS?

There have been few studies which have directly addressed the amount of strain experienced by trainee psychotherapists compared to other graduate groups. However, several studies have found that older and more experienced therapists are less prone to stress and burn-out (e.g. Hellman, Morrison and Abramowitz 1987; Kwee 1990). A few studies have investigated stress in trainee psychiatrists. Merklin and Little (1967) coined the term 'Beginning Psychiatry Syndrome' to refer to transitory neurotic symptoms and psycho-somatic disturbances which were seen as distressing but necessary formative experiences in the development of a psychiatrist. The largest systematic survey of psychiatric trainees was by the task force of the American Association of Directors of Psychiatric Residency Training who studied emotional problems of residents in psychiatry in some detail using questionnaire methods (Russell, Pasnau and Traintor, 1975). Seven per cent of 3,737 psychiatry residents did not complete the study year and 26 per cent of these terminated because of what they described as emotional illness. A further 6 per cent of the sample were reported to have finished the year despite marginal performances and/or emotional difficulties. Margison (1987) comments that the suggestion of Zilboorg (1967) that minor anxiety and depressive symptoms are part of early career development and represent the negotiation of developmental tasks, may offer a useful explanation of minor difficulties. But this does not fully account for the serious psychiatric disturbance found in the Russell, Pasnau and Traintor study.

Since there were no systematic published studies investigating the issue of stress in trainee psychotherapists in Britain, I carried out a study of 287 trainee clinical psychologists in Britain (Cushway 1992). The study aimed to identify how much stress existed among clinical psychology trainees, to identify the major self-reported stressors for trainees and to investigate the coping strategies employed. I also looked at gender differences and found, in line with other studies (e.g. Cushway and Tyler 1994; Davidson and Cooper 1986), that female trainees reported higher levels of distress than male trainees. While it was not surprising to find small, but significant, gender differences – a finding not limited to psychotherapists – the overall level of distress for the whole group was more surprising.

I found that the estimated prevalence of distress, as measured by the General Health Questionnaire, was 59 per cent, which was higher than that shown by comparable data for junior house officers (50 per cent, Firth-Cozens 1987) and medical students (30 per cent, Firth 1986). According to the GHQ manual the threshold score for 'caseness' reflects the concept of a 'just significant clinical disturbance', although this does not necessarily mean that those scoring above threshold require intervention (Goldberg 1978). Nevertheless, this finding was a reason for concern. Later studies of qualified clinical psychologists found that the levels of distress for qualified groups were all considerably lower (29 per cent, Cushway and Tyler 1994; 24 per cent, Darongkamas, Burton and Cushway 1994; 33 per cent, Sampson 1990.) This difference between qualified groups and trainees may be because stress peaks during training. However, the number of qualified psychologists in my later study describing themselves as very, or moderately stressed was identical to the number in my trainee sample where 75 per cent said they had been moderately (48 per cent) or very (27 per cent) stressed as a result of training. One interpretation of these findings is that qualified clinical psychologists cope with stress without experiencing symptoms. Alternatively, qualified psychotherapists may be less willing to admit to psychological symptoms. The next two sections of the chapter will look in more detail at which stresses trainee psychotherapists report and how they cope with them.

WHAT STRESSES TRAINEE PSYCHOTHERAPISTS?

Before discussing the specific stressors which face trainee psychotherapists it is worth considering the possible self-selection factors of psychotherapists and their potential contribution to the stress process. In recent years there has been an increasing body of literature investigating the motives of therapists (e.g. Guy 1987; Sussman 1992). Although there are considerable methodological problems with researching this area, the consensus in this literature seems to be that a major determinant for becoming a therapist may be a conscious or unconscious wish to make good the unresolved difficulties of early childhood. One study compared psychotherapists (psychologists and psychiatrists) with family practice physicians, who acted as a non-mental health comparison group (Krenek and Zalewski 1993). The authors reported finding no significant difference between the groups in prevalence of reported familial psychopathology. However, this study also found that the presence of a psychiatrically disturbed relative within the family of origin, a close emotional relationship with that relative, and feelings of anger and guilt towards that relative were found to be associated with career choice as well as with self-perceived therapeutic effectiveness and empathy. Another study of psychotherapists found that over two-thirds of the women and one-third of the men had experienced some form of physical or sexual abuse (Pope and Feldman-Summers 1992). Although the authors acknowledged that their findings may not be generalisable to the population of psychotherapists as a whole, nor that psychotherapists report more abuse than the general population, they conclude that substantial numbers of psychotherapists may have suffered from abuse. Another study of female psychotherapists found that they reported a higher prevalence of physical and sexual abuse, parental alcoholism or psychiatric history, death of a family member and greater family dysfunction in their families of origin, than did other professionals (Elliott and Guy 1993).

As I have already cautioned, the studies reported above do suffer from considerable methodological difficulties including low response rates, self-selected samples and the self-report and retrospective nature of the studies. Nevertheless, the unsurprising findings that psychotherapists have had at least as much trauma in their early lives as the general population raise questions about the impact of this on stress for psychotherapists in training. By the time they are qualified, psychotherapists are reporting less distress, and it appears that they are also reporting that they feel moderately competent to provide services related to victims of abuse (Pope and Feldman-Summers 1992). The qualified female therapists in the Elliott and Guy (1993) study reported experiencing less disturbance than women in professions other than mental health. Clearly how, and to what extent, psychotherapists resolve their early difficulties is an exceedingly complex question. Nevertheless, it is probable that training is a crucial time when trainee psychotherapists, possibly for the first time, have to confront and deal with their own distress. This is stressful enough at any time but training causes particular difficulties and contradictions. On the one hand, trainees are expected to become more self-aware and to expose their frailties as a step towards greater client sensitivity. On the other hand, they are selected because of their personal, as well as their academic, qualities and they therefore have to live up to this in training and display no weakness. Thus it is possible that, for some trainees, training may present seemingly unresolvable dilemmas.

There have been few studies of what stresses trainee psycho- therapists. However, in a study of trainee psychiatrists, Margison and Germany (1987) found that the most frequently rated stressor was overwork. These researchers classified the stressors reported by their sample into 'relationships with other staff', 'performance-related' stressors, 'organisation problems', 'inadequate resources' and 'threats to self-esteem'. Margison (1987) comments that threats to self-esteem and personal threats are more complex than simply being exposed to noxious stimuli: 'These personally threatening events are frequently associated with a sense of isolation and powerlessness. On some occasions a disproportionate level of personal distress is linked to intense identification with earlier conflicts and echoes early patterns of object relationships' (p. 114). This comment perhaps illustrates how external stressors can interact with personal history to create felt stress among trainees.

In my own study of clinical trainees the most frequently reported stressors and the percentage of trainees reporting each stressor were, in rank order: (1) poor supervision (37 per cent); (2) travelling (23 per cent); (3) deadlines (22 per cent); (4=) lack of finance (19 per cent); (4=) moving house (19 per cent); (6=) separation from partner (17 per cent); (6=) amount of academic work (17 per cent); (8) uncertainty about own capabilities (16 per cent); (9=) too much to do (15 per cent); and (9=) changing placements (15 per cent). These results give a flavour of the variety of difficulties experienced by trainees as stressful. When the stress questionnaire was factor analysed, six underlying factors were suggested by the analysis. These factors were named: (a) course structure and organisation; (b) workload; (c) poor supervision; (d) disruption of social support; (e) self-doubt; and (f) client difficulties and distress. I will now discuss in more detail some of the stressors suggested by these results.

Selection and competition

Although there is little written about the competitive nature of the selection process, anyone in the field knows that a very stressful factor is the fierce competition to enter psychotherapy training programmes, of whatever discipline, both in Britain and in the US.

Many students embark on years of study and work in pursuit of their 'holy grail', which is entry on to a training programme. This often leads trainee psychotherapists to have unrealistically high expectations of their training courses. Stress and resentment can be created when courses fail, almost inevitably, to live up to trainees' expectations of them. The competitive nature of the selection process can also lead trainees to have unrealistically high expectations of themselves. While the requirements may be different for different professions, most trainee therapists have had to compete and achieve in academic settings. This can create a stressful and competitive atmosphere among trainees. In my study several clinical psychology trainees had become disillusioned by the whole process of training. One second-year trainee commented: 'Clinical psychology is a rat race. It seems incredible that such a so-called caring profession is so destructive of its own kind.' Trainee psychotherapists are also judged on their level of psychotherapeutic skill and their personal qualities and, perhaps for psychoanalytic candidates particularly, the subjectivity involved in such comparisons and evaluations is difficult to challenge or correct. The stresses involved in selection and competition on psychotherapy courses can be some of the most invidious to overcome.

Supervision

Much has been written about the importance of supervision in training. As Guy (1987: 51) has written:

> Relating successfully with on-site supervisors is an important rite of passage leading to the practice of psychotherapy. As such it is highly charged with emotion and meaning. The expectations of each party, along with the multiplicity of roles inherent in the relationship, set the stage for problems which must be overcome.

In my study of clinical trainees 'poor supervision' was by far the most frequently reported stressor as well as being one of the six underlying factors found in factor analysis of the questionnaire. In their written comments, trainees said that they would have liked less criticism from their supervisor, more support and understanding as well as more positive feedback and encouragement. Margison and Germany (1987), in their study of trainee psychiatrists, found that relationships with senior staff were stressful when trainees reported a perceived lack of support, lack of feedback, conflicting ideology and fear of disapproval. It is probably the role of supervisor as evaluator and critic of the trainee's therapeutic skill that creates most stress for trainees, who are often at their most vulnerable and uncertain when exposing their lack of clinical expertise to supervisors. Beuchler (1992) discusses the shame of self-exposure of the psychoanalytic candidate, whose work is subject to scrutiny by supervisors, not to mention the candidate's analyst who may also have a role in the training process. As a supervisor of trainee counsellors, I have found it a difficult task to balance support for the trainee with acting as a gatekeeper for the profession. Fortunately, as will be discussed later, the supervisory relationship, when it goes well, can also be a very rewarding one for the trainee.

Course structure and organisation

Most psychotherapy training courses are exceedingly complex structures. They have to provide an academic training and assessment programme rigorous enough to meet the stringent requirements of both their host university and their professional accrediting body. They also have to organise, assess and monitor a variety of clinical training placements. As well as this they may have to arrange and monitor supervision and personal therapy for their trainees. It is therefore not surprising that, with the variety and number of demands it places on trainees, the course structure and organisation is perceived to be a source of trainee stress. Despite having been selected for their academic ability, therapeutic potential and personal suitability, many trainees find jumping through the hoops of training an infantilising experience.

Course organisers are often criticised mainly for their lack of openness, support and understanding. Trainees may feel that they are treated in an autocratic way and in my study commented that they would like more participation and consultation and, in particular, better communication with course organisers. Some trainees commented that the stressful nature of training is largely unacknowledged by course organisers and that if they admitted to stress it would be seen as a sign of weakness. This was described by one trainee as follows:

A problem with the course is the way in which trainees' problems will be held against them. Certainly feeling under stress on my course has been used a sign of an inability to cope generally rather than realising that this is normal and helping us. A sad situation indeed! My feeling is that, for a bunch of people that are supposed to be perceptive and understanding, clinical psychologists often fall short.

From my experience of other psychotherapy training courses I do not think that this view is restricted to clinical psychology training. Of course it has to be recognised that course organisers are often the butt for the criticisms of strained and bitter trainees. But I also wonder if what I have called 'the consultant syndrome' may be operating. That is, that qualified psychotherapy trainers may, like medical consultants, have been trained under the same stressful conditions as their present trainees. Thus they may feel that if they survived then so will the trainee. They may view training as survival of the fittest and think that only those who survive will be able to cope with the stresses of professional practice.

In my study clinical psychology trainees also found a number of other aspects of course organisation and structure extremely stressful. They expressed frustration at the poor quality of some of the teaching, at the same time expressing anxiety about being required to be competent in the complexities of research design and statistics. The ongoing and unrelenting academic assessment, whether by continuous assessment or by examinations, is a constant source of stress for many. The process of psychotherapy training is so inextricably bound up with the person of the therapist that it is often difficult for the trainee to separate out the person from the body of knowledge or skill being assessed. Thus a failed assignment can feel like a devastating personal failure. On the clinical side, trainees may be exposed to a variety of clinical placements and supervisors who may have very divergent expectations of the trainee. Constantly changing placements and adapting to a different set of circumstances is experienced as very stressful.

Workload

In most studies of stress, as in Margison's and Germany's (1987) study of trainee psychiatrists, work overload appears as a frequent stressor and my own study was no exception. Many and varied demands must be met by trainees on any professional training course but it is perhaps the apparently conflicting demands required by psychotherapy training that creates most stress for these trainees.

The question over whether psychotherapy is an art or a science may symbolise the felt conflict. On the one hand, trainees are required to assimilate the rapidly expanding literature in the field of psychotherapy and to produce a number of academic assignments testing competence in essay writing, case reports, research design and statistics. These require the essentially rational qualities of critical analysis and evaluation. On the other hand, becoming a therapist is more than the acquisition of knowledge and skills. It also requires the trainee to focus on internal processing and awareness and to hone up intuitive and empathic skills. Thus the trainee becomes increasingly sensitised to the mental suffering of others as well as to his/her own dynamics. These two somewhat contradictory processes contribute to the stress of the workload for the psychotherapy trainee.

Disruption of social support and financial pressures

For some trainees, embarking on psychotherapy training can disrupt their existing social support mechanisms. Some may move location permanently while others may travel long distances for training, perhaps only returning home at weekends. Even for those who do not travel long distances the demands of training may mean that the trainee has little leisure time to spend with his/her partner or friends. Paradoxically, psychotherapy training can mean that the trainee has fewer resources to invest in an intimate relationship with a partner. This can create resentment in partners and family and social isolation for the trainee. Unfortunately, relationship breakdowns are all too familiar for psychotherapy trainees. The financial pressures often interact with these problems and exacerbate them. Psychotherapy training can be very expensive. Trainees often have to finance their own training, which can involve finding course fees as well as supervision and therapy costs. For those on small training grants, financing normal living can be a struggle. Trainees often have to make considerable sacrifices such as putting off starting a family or buying a house. The expense of running a reliable car, necessary when extensive travelling is involved, is often beyond the financial resources of the trainee. The financial and social sacrifices are thus not limited to the psychotherapy trainee but involve his/her immediate family. The paradox is that, while the trainee's own relationships may be severely stretched, the trainee is learning to lavish care and attention on his/her clients. The trainee's partner is usually only too aware of the irony of this.

Client distress and self-doubt

In the clinical trainee study two factors which emerged in the analysis of the stress questionnaire were labelled 'client distress' and 'self-doubt'. To some extent these may be similar to the stresses labelled by Margison and Germany (1987) as 'threats to self-esteem' and 'personal threats'. For many trainees, beginning therapeutic work with clients is enormously stressful and this is usually the time when self-doubt peaks. Firstly, the trainee is brought face-to-face, maybe for the first time, with the pain and mental suffering of others. The trainee will often be required during training to work with a variety of people ranging from abused children to older adults suffering from dementia, or from those suffering from a physical disability or terminal illness to those who perpetrate abuse on others. Trainees may also face the threat of emotional or physical attack from disturbed or difficult clients. Thus the trainee not only has to witness the distress and manage the difficulty as well as attempt to provide some relief for the sufferer, but has to deal with the effects on him/herself.

This is indeed a pretty daunting enterprise and it is not surprising that an important factor emerging from studies of therapists (e.g. Hellman, Morrison and Abramowitz 1987; Cushway and Tyler 1994), which does not appear so readily in studies of stress in other groups of health professionals, is that of self-doubt or uncertainty about our own capabilities. The literature suggests (e.g. Dryden and Spurling 1989) that a crucial factor affecting psychotherapy outcome is the quality of the relationship (therapeutic alliance) that the therapist is able to make with the client. Clearly then this suggests that effective therapy is an activity which involves the whole person of the therapist and in which s/he is emotionally engaged. The research findings, relating to the importance of the stressor I have called 'professional self-doubt' (Cushway, Tyler and Nolan, 1996), suggest that conducting therapy is an inherently stressful and emotionally demanding activity. Given the findings relating to psychotherapy outcome, it seems that this stressor may be an inevitable part of conducting therapy but may be particularly enhanced for the trainee.

HOW DO TRAINEE PSYCHOTHERAPISTS COPE WITH STRESS?

In this section I will be looking at what we have learnt about how trainee psychotherapists cope with stress. The findings on coping suggest that it is ultimately an individual affair and the approach that has been used by the majority of the researchers in the field, which is consistent with this view, is that of conceptualising coping in terms of specific methods and/or foci of coping (Cox 1987). The approach that I have found most helpful, and which I have used in my research, is that of Billings and Moos (1981) who distinguish three methods of coping. These are (1) active-cognitive coping, where the individual attempts to manage his or her appraisal of the situation (e.g. 'tried to see the positive side'); (2) active-behavioural coping, which refers to the actual behavioural attempts to deal with the situation (e.g. 'talked with partner'); and (3) avoidance coping, where the individual attempts to avoid confronting the stressful situation (e.g. 'avoided being with people in general').

There are very few published studies examining coping strategies in trainee psychotherapists. Frequently used coping behaviours reported in two studies of trainee psychiatrists and counsellors include emotional support from partner or loved one, informal support of colleagues, talking with friends or engaging in social activities, engaging in sports or other exercise and time off (Margison and Germany 1987; Jensen 1995). In my study of clinical psychology trainees the most frequent coping strategies reported were: (1) talking to other trainees (51 per cent); reducing tension by exercise (38 per cent); (3) talking to friends (30 per cent); (4) talking to partner (29 per cent); and talking to supervisor (25 per cent). In general the coping strategies used by trainee psychotherapists appear, not surprisingly, to be similar to those employed by qualified therapists and other groups of health professionals (Norcross and Prochaska 1986; Cushway and Tyler 1994; Tyler and Cushway 1992). It is possible to say with relative confidence that the coping strategy which is cited by health professionals and therapists as most effective for them is talking to a partner or colleague or friend at work. Thus the most frequently reported methods are active-behavioural, which include talking to loved ones, colleagues, and friends, or engaging in sporting, social or leisure activities.Almost as frequently reported are active-cognitive methods, which include active problem-solving or planning. However, in all the studies it has consistently been found that there is a positive relationship between psychological distress and avoidance coping. I will now look in a little more detail at the coping strategies used by trainee psychotherapists to see whether there are aspects of training which reduce the likelihood of trainees utilising active strategies and promote the use of avoidance strategies.

Active-behavioural and cognitive methods

For clinical psychology trainees the highest scale score on the Health and Daily Living Schedule (HDL) (Moos *et al.* 1984) was found for behavioural coping and probably reflects the fact that talking with others accounts for four out of the top five coping strategies reported by trainees. In general, research findings suggest that, as stress increases, so there is a more frequent use of active coping strategies reported. One explanation is that, as stress goes up, so one has to use more coping strategies to manage it. However, an alternative explanation suggested is that these are the strategies that do not work for coping, since as the coping behaviours increase, the stress also increases. One clue that favours the former explanation is that, in the trainee study as in others, the relationship between active coping and psychological distress was low. One interpretation could be that talking to people is effective in ameliorating distress. This is indeed a fortunate finding for psychotherapists who spend their professional lives engaging in this activity!

Psychotherapy trainees then, like others in helping professions, rate talking to their peers as a valuable coping strategy. This has implications for the organisation of courses, in providing facilities for, as well as encouraging, formal and informal support mechanisms. However, if as discussed above, there exists a competitive atmosphere among trainees on psychotherapy training courses, then trainees will be unwilling to use their colleagues for personal support. In fact a study of qualified psychotherapists has shown that, while they would have valued it, they were extremely reluctant to seek support at work for issues which revealed personal vulnerability even if these issues were undermining their ability to cope at work. These qualified psychotherapists were reluctant to seek support because they believed that they would be stigmatised for their lack of ability to cope, because they perceived their colleagues as generally untrustworthy and because they believed that the expression of support needs in the workplace would be a potential threat to their job security (Walsh, Nichols and Cormack 1991). If qualified psychotherapists view seeking support as a sign of weakness, then it is extremely likely that trainees also believe this. In the Walsh *et al.* study cited above the authors discussed two underlying reasons why psychotherapists found seeking personal support at work threatening. The first reason is the professional threat involved for psychotherapists who express vulnerability and 'weakness'. The second reason postulated by these authors lies in the psychotherapist's fear of becoming a client. Of course psychotherapy espouses the value of therapy and indeed the majority of psychotherapy professions insist on trainees undergoing therapy. However, a training analysis may be very different from a psychotherapist seeking therapy for personal distress. It also has to be acknowledged that therapy can cause the stressed trainee to become more distressed in the short term. Even if the trainee is undergoing therapy, this does not preclude the necessity for other forms of support.

The research findings cited above also suggest that talking to partners and friends is an extremely important source of support. Jensen (1995) discusses the value placed on this form of support by the counsellors in her study and suggests that this is consistent with Guy's (1987) view that the personal and intimate relationships with partner and friends are an important priority for the psychotherapist and that they can have a 'holding' capacity for stressed psychotherapists. However, for the reasons discussed under sources of stress, trainee psychotherapists may experience disrupted social relationships, and overwork and lack of finance may prevent them from fostering these relationships and from pursuing other active forms of coping such as exercise and leisure pursuits. In my study of trainees, 'relationships with supervisors' featured among the most frequently used coping strategies as well as among the most frequent sources of stress. What this may be indicating is the power of the relationship between the trainee and the supervisor both to punish and to reward. Clearly, if this relationship goes well it can be immensely supportive for the trainee. As one trainee commented, 'talking over uncertainty with my supervisor has provided me with a major coping strategy. All courses have their share of lousy supervisors but I've been lucky; I've been working with supervisors who have made great efforts to provide as much supervision as I've requested. I have found this to be a tremendous help.'

Avoidance coping strategies

As mentioned earlier, a consistent research finding in relation to coping is the positive relationship between psychological distress and avoidance coping. In her study, Jensen (1995) found that 72 per cent of her sample used food for comfort, 75 per cent drank alcohol and 38 per cent used painkillers. I also found that the trainees who were the most distressed favoured avoidance coping. Norcross and Prochaska (1986) found that wishful thinking and self-blame were negatively correlated with successful coping. Of course avoidance coping may not always be a negative strategy, since there may be instances where avoiding the problem by various means may be adaptive. For example, if the problem cannot be solved, then a realistic strategy, at least in the short term, may be to get away from things for a while. Often this is difficult for trainees who may, for reasons of lack of finance, lack of necessary power or overwork, be unable to do this. The demands of training often feel inexorable. We have found, moreover, that where the avoidance coping behaviours involve the defensive process of denial they are more likely to be maladaptive (Tyler and Cushway 1992). It is possible that covert attitudes and beliefs among both qualified psychotherapists and trainee psychotherapists that, for example, to show weakness is a sign of failure, combined with the trainee's uncertainty and self-doubt along with the conflicting demands for excellence, may actually encourage unhelpful denial and the use of maladaptive avoidance strategies.

HOW CAN THE STRESSES OF TRAINEE PSYCHOTHERAPISTS BE ALLEVIATED?

In the last section of this chapter I will look at ways that the stresses can be ameliorated and at strategies for promoting the use of adaptive coping strategies among psychotherapy trainees. This chapter has suggested some points that can usefully be summarised here. These are that:

1 Training of any kind can be stressful but psychotherapy training may be particularly stressful because of the varied and conflicting demands it can make on trainees.
2 Psychotherapy leads us to confront our own distress as well as the distress of others and its effective practice is inevitably stressful.
3 There may be some attitudes and beliefs among qualified psycho-therapists, as well as existing course practices, which make it difficult for trainees to acknowledge stress and to practise adaptive coping strategies.

So what can be done?

In my national survey of trainees their suggestions for alleviating stress centred around the provision of more support, better communication, improving the course structure and organisation, and lessening the workload. The information from this study, as well as my daily contacts with trainees, encouraged and informed us in our attempts to improve the support systems for trainee clinical psychologists on the Birmingham University doctoral training course (Cushway, Dent, Offen and Howells 1993). The model of the support systems can be found in Figure 1. Perhaps most important, tackling stress needs to be a coherent and central part of course philosophy. As psychotherapy practitioners and teachers we need to be able to present ourselves as ordinary, human, and sometimes vulnerable people struggling with stress in our own personal and professional lives. It is also important to model a coping rather than a mastery model. From the beginning of training we need to normalise and acknowledge stress as well as educating trainees in the need to look after themselves. Unless we believe in, and practise, what we preach our trainees will perceive receiving personal support as a weakness and will fail to incorporate preventive personal support into their working lives. To this end it is also important to raise awareness among qualified professionals and to provide training for supervisors and teachers. (See Figure 1.)

Another principle on which our support systems are based is the need to provide a network of different kinds of support, since individuals have different needs and preferences and can opt to use the methods of their choice. First, each trainee is allocated a personal tutor, who is not a member of course staff, to act as a guide, mentor, advocate and supporter throughout training. Some trainees find their personal tutor immensely supportive, while others, perhaps because of incompatibility or geographical distance, do not fully utilise this system. Each trainee also has an appraisal tutor, a member of course staff, who attempts to guide and advise trainees on their individual training needs. Thus each trainee has two tutors throughout training, providing, it is hoped, some continuity. The second part of our support network is a personal awareness group, which is available for trainees, weekly in term-time, throughout the course. The groups are run by outside facilitators and are entirely confidential. Thus there is no feedback of content to course staff. Although we think our groups are an enormously valuable educative resource, attendance is optional, since their primary aim is personal support. For about half of the psychotherapy professions, therapy while in training

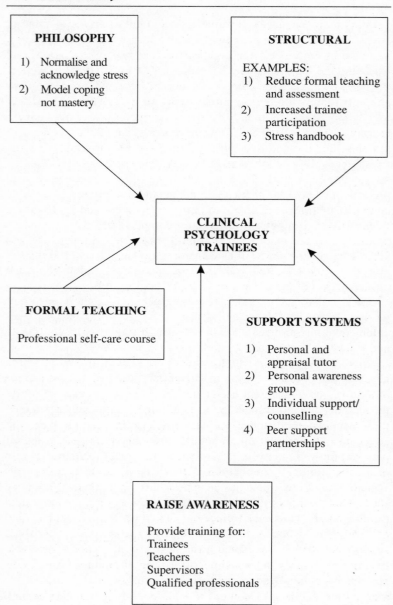

Figure 1 Model of support provision

is mandatory. Since this is not the case for clinical psychology training, we provide a list of individual clinical psychologists within the region who are available to give free, individual, confidential support ranging from crisis intervention and short-term counselling through to longer-term personal therapy or development. Trainees are able to access this list independently, although, in practice, many trainees do discuss their needs and choices with course staff. This is facilitated if trainees perceive obtaining personal support as a valued and legitimate activity.

The stress management literature (e.g. Cooper and Cartwright 1994) suggests that interventions focused at the individual should be accompanied by an organisational response to stress. My trainee survey also found that course organisation and structure was the highest loading factor in the analysis of the stress questionnaire. This has led us to some structural alterations to the Birmingham course, many of which were stimulated by trainees' suggestions. We have increased trainee participation in the course by altering the committee structure. We have also reduced formal teaching and assessment by 20 per cent and increased the number of private-study days. Another response to trainees' suggestions was the development of a stress handbook (Cushway, Dodd and Merian 1989). The most recent development was the introduction of the professional self-care course, which is part of the formal taught curriculum. It includes topics such as stress management training, assertiveness training, barriers to obtaining support, models of providing support, issues in the therapeutic relationship, working in teams, and personal issues in working with clients. The course is intended to provide a basis for preventive self-care, based on the belief that, unless we are able to care for ourselves, we will have little of substance to offer to others. I do not think that we have 'got it all right' at Birmingham – our systems are continually evolving – neither is this model necessarily suitable for other psychotherapy courses, which will have their own particular needs and preferences. But I do think that tackling the issue of stress in training presents an important challenge to all those involved in the practice and teaching of psychotherapy.

REFERENCES

Beuchler, S. (1992) 'Stress in the personal and professional development of a psychoanalyst', *Journal of the American Academy of Psychoanalysis* 20: 183–91.

Billings, A. G. and Moos, R. H. (1981) 'The role of coping resources and social resources in attenuating the stress of life events', *Journal of Behavioral Medicine* 4: 139–57.

Cooper, C. L. and Cartwright, S. (1994) 'Stress management interventions in the workplace: stress counselling and stress audits', *British Journal of Guidance and Counselling* 22: 65–73.

Cox, T. (1987) 'Stress, coping and problem solving', *Work and Stress* 1: 5–14.

Cushway, D. (1992) 'Stress in clinical psychology trainees', *British Journal of Clinical Psychology* 31: 169–79.

Cushway, D. and Tyler, P. (1994) 'Stress and coping in clinical psychologists', *Stress Medicine* 10: 35–42.

Cushway, D., Dodd. B. and Merian, S. (1989) *Coping with Stress: A Handbook for Clinical Psychology Trainees*, University of Birmingham.

Cushway, D., Tyler, P. and Nolan, P. (1996) 'Development of a stress scale for mental health professionals' *British Journal of Clinical Psychology* 35: 279–95.

Cushway D., Dent, H., Offen, L. and Howells, K. (1993) 'Providing personal support at Birmingham: answering the challenge to training courses', *Clinical Psychology Forum* 58: 20–3.

Darongkamas, J., Burton, M. V. and Cushway, D. (1994) 'The use of personal therapy by clinical psychologists working in the NHS in the United Kingdom', *Clinical Psychology and Psychotherapy* 1: 165–73.

Davidson, M. J. and Cooper, C. L. (1986) 'Executive women under pressure', *International Review of Applied Psychology* 35: 301–26.

Dryden, W. and Spurling, L. (1989) *On Becoming a Psychotherapist*, London: Routledge.

Elliott, D. M. and Guy, J. D. (1993) 'Mental health professionals versus non-mental health professionals: childhood trauma and adult functioning', *Professional Psychology, Research and Practice* 24: 83–90.

Farber, B. A. (1985) 'The genesis, development, and implications of psychological-mindedness in psychotherapists', *Psychotherapy* 22: 170–7.

Firth, J. (1986) 'Levels and sources of stress in medical students', *British Medical Journal* 292: 1177–80.

Firth-Cozens, J. (1987) 'Emotional distress in junior house officers', *British Medical Journal* 295: 533–6.

Goldberg, D. (1978) *Manual of the General Health Questionnaire*, Windsor: NFER-Nelson.

Gopelrud, E. N. (1980) 'Social support and stress during the first year of graduate school', *Professional Psychology* 11: 283–90.

Guy, J. D. (1987) *The Personal Life of the Psychotherapist*, New York: Wiley.

Hellman, J. D., Morrison, T. L. and Abramowitz, S. I. (1987) 'Therapist experience and the stresses of psychotherapeutic work', *Psychotherapy* 24: 171–5.

Jensen, K. (1995) 'The stresses of counsellors in training', in W. Dryden (ed.), *The Stresses of Counselling in Action*, London: Sage.

Krenek, R. J. and Zalewski, C. (1993) 'Psychiatric illness in families of mental health professionals: relationship to career choice and self-perceived therapeutic variables', *Journal of Social Behavior and Personality* 8: 439–52.

Kwee, M. G. T. (1990) 'Burnout among Dutch psychotherapists', *Psychological Reports* 67: 107–12.

Margison, F. R. (1987) 'Stress in psychiatrists', in R. Payne and J. Firth-Cozens (eds) (1984) *Stress in Health Professionals*, Chichester: Wiley.

Margison, F. R. and Germany, L. (1987) 'Stress in psychiatrists', in R. Payne and J. Firth-Cozens (eds), *Stress in Health Professionals*, Chichester: Wiley.

Merklin, L. and Little, R. B. (1967) 'Beginning psychiatry training syndrome', *American Journal of Psychiatry* 124: 193–97.

Moos, R. H., Cronkite, R. C., Billings, A. G. and Finney, J. W. (1984) *Health and Daily Living Form Manual*, Palo Alto, CA: R.-Moos, Social Ecology Laboratory, Veterans Administration and Stanford University Medical Centers.

Norcross, J. C. and Prochaska, J. O. (1986) 'Psychotherapist heal thyself-II. The self-initiated and therapy facilitated change of psychological distress', *Psychotherapy* 23: 345–56.

Pope, K. S. and Feldman-Summers, S. (1992) 'National survey of psychologists' sexual and physical abuse history and their evaluation of training and competence in these areas', *Professional Psychology, Research and Practice* 23: 353–61.

Russell, A. T., Pasnau, R. O. and Traintor, Z. C. (1975) 'Emotional problems of residents in psychiatry', *American Journal of Psychiatry* 132: 263–7.

Sampson, J. (1990) 'Stress survey of clinical psychologists in Scotland, 1989', *British Psychological Society Scottish Branch Newsletter* 11: 10–14.

Sussman, M. B. (1992) *A Curious Calling: Unconscious Motivation for Practicing Psychotherapy*, Northvale, NJ: Jason Aronson.

Tyler, P. and Cushway, D. (1992) 'Stress, coping and mental well-being in hospital nurses', *Stress Medicine* 8: 91–8.

Walsh, S., Nichols, K. and Cormack, M. (1991) 'Self-care and clinical psychologists: a threatening obligation?' *Clinical Psychology Forum* 37: 5–7.

Whitman, N. E., Spendlove, D. C. and Clark, C. H. (1984) *Student Stress: Effects and Solutions*, ASHE-ERIC Higher Education Research Report No. 2.

Winefield, H. R. (1993) 'Study-work satisfaction and psychological distress in older university students', *Work and Stress* 7: 221–8.

Zilboorg (1967) Cited by F. R. Margison in R. Payne and J. Firth-Cozens (eds) (1984) *Stress in Health Professionals*, Chichester: Wiley.

Chapter 4

Stresses in child psychotherapists

Francis Dale

INTRODUCTION

This chapter will look at the different kinds of stress which can be experienced by child psychotherapists in their work with disturbed children. Various stress reactions, their impact on the child psychotherapist, and the implications for treatment, will be examined. Particular emphasis will be given to understanding the dynamic significance of the developmental stages which children pass through and how these affect and determine their relationships with adults who interact with them.

The area of non-verbal communication, especially projective identification, will be examined with particular reference to the impact that such primitive forms of communication can have on the therapist. Factors in the personality of the child psychotherapist that may predispose him or her to emotional stress will also be discussed. Finally, the training of child psychotherapists will be explored to assess the extent to which it provides therapists working with disturbed children with the professional and personal resources to both recognise and manage the stresses which are an important aspect of their work with children.

DEVELOPMENTAL IMMATURITY

Although it would not be true to say that child psychotherapists inevitably experience more stress than therapists working with other client groups, it would probably be fair to say that some of the stresses generated by working with children create particular problems which are not met with so frequently or so intensively in other therapeutic contexts (with the notable exception of those therapists engaged in working with psychotic, borderline or narcissistic patients).

In order to understand the specific nature of these stresses – their aetiology and implications for clinical practice – it will be important to look at those factors which, in one's work with disturbed children, are likely to give rise to stress.

The developmental immaturity of children, their lengthy period of dependence on their carers, and the different demands of the various life stages they have to pass through and resolve on their way to mature adulthood, all make varying demands on the child psychotherapist.

One of the main differences between working with young children and the older child or adult, lies in the area of communication. Adults tend to communicate almost exclusively using the written or spoken word (as you are doing at this moment). The baby or young child, on the other hand, communicates much more through play and non-verbal means. Some of these non-verbal means of communication – by their very nature – can induce large amounts of stress and anxiety in the child psychotherapist. In order to understand this better, we will need to look at how very small babies communicate their needs.

PRIMITIVE FORMS OF COMMUNICATION

Given the complete and utter dependency of the young baby on its carers for every aspect of its survival, it stands to reason that being able to communicate effectively is not a question of choice but of life or death. The question we need to address is, 'How does the baby communicate its needs effectively when it has no language with which to convey them?'

In fact, babies have a very effective – if primitive – way of communicating their needs: by 'emotional contagion' or projection. In a way which is still not fully understood, the baby causes those on whom he is dependent to experience first hand – as though they were their *own* feelings – the baby's own primitive experiences of fear, anxiety, confusion, hatred and love.

This is a two-way process which depends as much on the mother's capacity to 'receive' her baby's projections and to respond to them appropriately, as it does on the baby's capacity to alert her to his emotional or mental state. Various attempts have been made to describe the mental/emotional state in which the mother is *maximally receptive* to the projective communications of her baby. Two psycho-analysts – Wilfred Bion and Donald Winnicott – described it respectively as 'Maternal Reverie' and 'Primary Maternal Pre-occupation'. Both of these terms refer to an attitude of receptiveness on the part of the mother towards her baby, in which she has a heightened sense of awareness of its internal experience.

In his book, *The Maturational Processes and the Facilitating Environment*, Winnicott talks about how 'mothers do in one way or another identify themselves with the baby growing within them, and in this way they achieve a very powerful sense of what the baby needs. This is a projective identification' (1976: 53), and, 'the mother through identification of herself with her infant knows what the infant needs in the way of holding and in the provision of an environment generally' (ibid.: 54).

When working with severely disturbed children, the same mechanism or process is directed on to the person of the therapist who is then the recipient of these primitive states of mind and emotion:

> The analyst who is meeting the needs of a patient who is reliving these very early stages in the transference undergoes similar changes of orientation; and the analyst, unlike the mother, needs to be aware of the sensitivity which develops in him or her in response to the patient's immaturity and dependence.
>
> (ibid.: 53)

The problem for the therapist is that he needs to be sufficiently open to receive these primitive projections from the child while at the same time being able to protect himself from being overwhelmed by them. Being on the receiving end of such powerful projections can both threaten one's emotional stability as well as one's capacity to think and reflect on what is happening.

I would like to give two examples to illustrate the disturbing, disorientating and stressful impact that such powerful projections can exert on one. The first relates to the mother of a newborn baby who had agreed to allow a trainee child psychotherapist observe the relationship between her and her baby for one hour a week over a two-year period.

When she was first observed in the latter stages of pregnancy, the mother in question was in a state of eager anticipation and could barely conceal both her excitement at the coming birth and her impatience to hold her baby in her arms. When her baby was born, she gave herself up entirely to the mothering experience, spending all of her waking hours watching, attending to, and anticipating her baby's needs. For her, becoming a mother was a revelation and she would frequently comment on the exaltation, awe and rapture she experienced when handling and feeding her baby.

However, this blissful intermingling of herself and her baby began to be replaced by anxiety, then panic, and finally, by a terrifying feeling that she was being 'taken over' by her baby and at risk of losing a sense of her own identity. She began to feel persecuted by her baby and his insatiable demands and to feel controlled and dominated by him. Fortunately, she had an understanding mother-in-law who was able to take over some of the care of the baby until she felt able to relate to him again, having re-established a sense of her own psychic boundaries.

It seemed that this mother had opened herself up to her baby to the extent that she had become completely identified with him and lost touch with herself as a separate entity. The problem would seem to be about how one attains a balance between being open and emotionally accessible whilst retaining a clear sense of one's personal boundaries and of having a differentiated self.

When working with children who have a clearly differentiated – if immature – ego there is less risk of being so completely overwhelmed by primitive projections. This is not the case when working with severely deprived or psychotic children where the therapist is frequently under intense pressure – sometimes even bombardment – from intrusive and invasive projections. The therapist, however, *cannot* protect himself by remaining emotionally or mentally detached because he would then be effectively shutting himself off from any meaningful contact or communication with his child patient.

The next example relates to the initial stages of therapy with a 3-year-old autistic boy who, prior to beginning therapy, had never spoken or shown any sign of understanding language – or any other kind of communication. He had been assessed as being either deaf, dumb or as having a congenital speech problem. It had also been suggested that he was suffering from some kind of brain damage.

I first saw him from behind a one-way screen during a diagnostic interview. Apart from his mother and grandmother, there were two other adults present who were carrying out the assessment. The little boy – whom I will call 'William' – appeared to have no 'connection' to his body, no sense of his or other peoples' physical/spatial boundaries. He moved around the room as though it were empty. If someone spoke to him or tried to gain his attention, he would ignore them and behave as though they were not there. There was a dream-like quality about him which seemed to place him in another dimension where no contact with 'reality' was possible.

In the very first session, I realised that there was no way in which I could understand or make contact with him, either by engaging him through his play, or by means of verbal interpretation in the way in which it was possible with other children. First, he didn't 'play'. It was like watching a robot which was randomly programmed and which failed to respond to external impingements or perceptions in any meaningful way. I might as well not have been there – and he didn't seem to be 'there' either. Second, and perhaps following on logically from the foregoing, he was either deaf, or language, speech, 'sounds', had no meaning or significance for him.

Being with someone you are supposed to be helping who fails to respond to you, who looks 'through' you and who seems to be completely unaware of your existence, is a profoundly disturbing and unsettling experience. It can make you feel confused, frustrated, 'empty', powerless, incapable of thinking, disorientated and frag-mented.

Being with this psychotic little boy rendered me incapable of thinking. It was as if there was no 'mind' there to think with – perhaps in part, because there was no 'object' (that is, person) out there to be 'thought about'. What I *could* do, though, was to observe. In stopping thinking about and trying to 'understand' him (that is, trying to understand him from the point of view of my 'world view' – *Weltanschauung* – and not his), a subtle but very significant change occurred in the way I began to relate to him.

I realised that the *process of 'thinking' itself* – in its logical, deductive mode – was placing a barrier between us and any pos-sibility of my understanding him. In the second session, I became completely absorbed in watching him, in following his every move-ment but without any attempt at trying to understand or think about what was happening. This 'intense watching' eventually brought about an altered sense of perception or reality – disembodiment – in which all I was aware of were my eyes, floating in space, watching him. There was no 'body' attached to them, no separate self, no observing ego.

After this session, I had to drive nearly fifteen miles across London to another appointment. That journey is lost to me forever. A part of me never made it. The first recollection I have, following that second session, is of coming back into my body and for several minutes not knowing who I was, where I was, how I got to where I was, what I was supposed to be doing or what this 'thing' (that is, the car I was sitting in) was.

Fortunately, I was able to regain my composure and recover the use of my mind – which I had temporarily given up in order to connect with my patient – to think about what had happened. My understanding of what happened is as follows. In order to understand William I had had to 'give up' my separate identity and, psychically, 'become him'.

In the process of identifying with someone as disturbed as William, or as undifferentiated as the baby in the previous example, one risks taking on board – in an undiluted, unprocessed way – the mental characteristics or emotional experiences of the person one is trying to understand or empathise with. It is important, therefore, when working with disturbed, and in particular psychotic, children, that we understand the nature of the primitive processes that may become activated in *both* therapist and child in the therapeutic interaction, and those aspects of theory and clinical practice which are most helpful in understanding and managing the sometimes extremely stressful emotional and mental states that are evoked in the therapist.

PROJECTIVE IDENTIFICATION

When Melanie Klein, a psychoanalyst who specialised in the psycho-analytic treatment of children, first introduced her concept of project-ive identification in her paper on schizoid mechanisms in 1946, it proved to be a major advance in our understanding of the kinds of primitive interaction which can occur between the therapist and the child or adult patient. In brief, it refers to a process of splitting whereby the immature ego disassociates from, and ejects, good or bad parts of the self which are then projected into another person (it may be a 'part' of the person, for example, the breast). Once 'inside' the other person, the ejected parts of the self become identified, or 'fused', with the external object (or person) which then, 'takes on the characteristics which have been projected into it'.

If loving feelings have been projected, then the object or person is experienced as good and loving and is actively sought after; if, however, more negative feelings such as hatred have been got rid of, then the object is experienced as persecuting and bad and every means is used to avoid or defend against it.

In individual therapy with psychotic, borderline or severely deprived children, child psychotherapists are frequently confronted with the kinds of intrusive and overwhelming projections described above. The therapist who receives these bad, split-off parts of the child, may then have to struggle to disengage his or her feelings from those of the child. However, as they are an essential component of one's work with such damaged and disturbed children, they cannot be avoided or denied, but equally they have to be 'managed' if only to preserve the therapist's equilibrium and therapeutic effectiveness.

CONTAINING THE UNCONTAINABLE

Wilfred Bion, an analyst who had himself been psychoanalysed by Melanie Klein, further extended and developed the notion of projective communication in an attempt to understand and to work with adult patients suffering from psychoses such as schizophrenia, manic depression and narcissistic disorders. He came to believe that, in addition to getting rid of parts of the self, projective identification was sometimes the only way in which some very fragmented patients could communicate. The problem lay in recognising, understanding and making sense of what was being communicated by the patient, in such a way that the patient could better understand what was happening in his internal world.

Before any of this can happen, however, the therapist has to be capable of receiving, and holding on to (that is, containing) 'inside of himself' what the patient has projected into him. These unprocessed, raw, fragmented, and sometimes 'unthinkable' thoughts and feelings were called by Bion, 'Beta Elements', and the capacity to process and think about them, was referred to as 'Alpha Function'. It follows from this that an increase in Alpha Function will also lead to a greater capacity in the therapist to contain and manage stress.

PSYCHOTHERAPY WITH SEVERELY DEPRIVED CHILDREN

Although there are areas of overlap between working with psychotic and borderline children and with severely deprived children, some of the stresses involved are different. Deprived children are generally more in touch with reality and able to use language more or less effectively to communicate their thoughts and feelings. Even if they shut you out and are silent and apparently unresponsive, there is often little doubt that there is 'someone there' whom you could make contact with should they allow it.

Because they generally have a greater degree of ego integration, when there is anger, hatred, despair, pain or sadness, it is more direct and more 'personal'. Frequently these children either have a 'false' way of relating in which they behave in a very placating and eager-to-please way, but where there is no real contact; or they present with a hard, impervious, shell-like persona which acts like a force field and which prevents you from making contact with the vulnerable 'child inside'.

Although these children still use the defences of splitting, denial and projection, it is less primitive and fragmented and tends to involve 'whole objects' and whole parts of the self. If, for example, it is the weak, defenceless, vulnerable part of the self which cannot be tolerated, than this will tend to be split off and projected *as a whole* into a suitable 'container' – usually an obviously weaker or more vulnerable child – where it can be attacked by the sadistic part of the self, but now 'inside someone else'.

Sometimes, it may be unacceptably aggressive and hostile feelings which get projected. In this case, the 'container', another child or perhaps the therapist, *becomes identified with* the projected qualities and is experienced as hostile and threatening and therefore to be defended against.

If the needy, vulnerable part of the child has been projected into the therapist, he may then be related to by the child as though the therapist were weak and helpless, and both the therapist and the therapeutic endeavour may be attacked, ridiculed and denigrated. This can be very stressful for the therapist, for not only are both he and his work being attacked and spurned, but the hopeful part of the child *inside the therapist* is also treated with contempt and rejected.

It may seem paradoxical, but the one thing which the severely deprived child most needs and wants – 'hope' and a loving, under-standing relationship – is at another level most fiercely resisted and defended against. This is because when one has been repeatedly hurt, battered, misunderstood and humiliated – sometimes since early infancy – owning one's neediness, vulnerability, dependency and hopefulness is experienced as a terrifying weakness and a threat to one's defensive mechanisms of omnipotence, denial, splitting and projection.

It is, therefore, frequently impossible for the deprived child to own his own hopefulness and need for help and understanding, sometimes for very long periods of time. The therapist, of course, has his own hopefulness but, in addition, it is sometimes the case that the child unconsciously projects *its* hopefulness, its loving feelings and infantile needs which have had to be shut away, *into the therapist for safekeeping.*

One adult patient whom I was seeing because of some difficulties she was experiencing in her relationship with her children, illustrates some of the points I have been making. Depending on the state of her 'internal relationship' with her infantile self, she would be either very positive and valuing of the help she was receiving from her therapy, or denigrating, attacking and abusive. She had been both physically and emotionally traumatised – even before birth (her father had violently assaulted her mother when she was heavily pregnant) – and learned to cope by identifying with her violent and sadistic father. At these times, she could be positively frightening in her rages, and if her anger could not be directed outwardly against other people, frequently with me as the 'victim', then she would internalise it and attack herself by cutting and mutilating her body.

In the positive and hopeful aspect of her relationship with me, however, she had entrusted the weak, needy and vulnerable part of her to me for safekeeping. Over time, this 'arrangement' became more substantial and permanent and I took on the role of keeping her infantile self, inside of me, safe from attack from the sadistic and denigrating part of her.

That she understood my role, as a kind of protective auxiliary ego, became clear in one session where she had launched into a lengthy and virulent attack on me and the therapeutic relationship. At one point she stopped railing at me and said: 'You know I can't leave without her [that is, the child part of her that she had projected into me for safekeeping]. Why won't you give her back to me?' I was then able to explain to her that my main responsibility was to the needy child part of her and that *she* did not want me to give up on her. I knew that if I did not keep hold of and protect the needy, vulnerable, infantile part of her inside of me, then the sadistic, denigrating part of her would attack and destroy it.

Working with children or parents who are filled with fear and loathing, and sometimes even hatred, for the vulnerable, needy and helpless child that is locked away inside of them, can be extremely stressful and disillusioning. It is not just the attacks on one's competence or on one's personal qualities that are so difficult to bear; it is the remorseless way in which the most hopeful, sensitive and 'valuable' part of the patient is subjected to cruelty and sadism which all too often mirrors the way they were treated by their parents in childhood.

> Almost all severely deprived children in the course of therapy repeat the emotional aspects of their original painful relationships, not only directly but also by reversal. They behave towards their therapists as they perceive themselves to have been treated by their absent parents. They make their therapists feel very fully what it is like to be discarded, ignored, despised, helpless or even unreal and non-existent. It is often a long time before the children can bear acknowledge any such feelings in themselves and dare to be aware of their dependency and needs.
>
> (Hoxter 1983: 128)

and:

> What needs to be understood in such situations is not that the child is perceiving the therapist as the insufficiently caring parent of his past experiences and revenging himself. Beyond this the child is also reversing the original situation. This time the child is identifying himself as the cruel, rejecting but powerful person and it is the therapist who is to feel rejected, hurt, helpless and . . . to feel the pangs of betrayal of trust and affection. In such situations the therapist cannot become genuinely trustworthy in the child's eyes until experience has shown that he has the strength to contain the projections of the feelings that the child finds intolerable.
>
> (ibid.: 129)

Sometimes, the stress and mental anguish of having to witness the repetition, in the here-and-now, of such destructive processes – particularly where young children are concerned – is almost unbearable. I once had a young mother referred to me because she couldn't tolerate her 3-year-old daughter's dependency on her and wanted her adopted. This mother had herself had the most awful childhood, being taken into care when she was eighteen months old because her schizophrenic mother was totally unable to care for her. She had spent the rest of her infancy, childhood and adolescence in various foster placements and children's homes, in all of which she created havoc and despair because of her destructive and out-of-control behaviour.

She had had two experiences of therapy, once at age 9, and again when she was 14. On both occasions, she sabotaged her therapy by walking out – no doubt leaving both of her therapists feeling impotent, useless, frustrated and guilty at becoming another in the long line of 'helping professionals' who had failed her.

She wanted to give up her child for adoption because, in the process of caring for her daughter, she was being constantly reminded of her own infantile deprivation – of the hurt, anger and longing still inside her. She was also terrified of identifying with her mother, and of the feelings of sadism which her daughter roused in her.

I was able to help her see that even though a part of her genuinely wanted to be helped, another part of her was terrified that her vulnerable infantile self might be exposed in therapy and that she couldn't afford to take the risk without a 'guarantee' of success. I predicted, accurately as it turned out, that she was still too frightened and untrusting to commit herself properly to do the necessary work. She did have her daughter adopted and decided not to undertake individual therapy. I really liked this woman – there was something courageous about her – and so it was particularly difficult for me on a personal level to watch her inflict so much pain on both herself and her daughter. (One year later, she contacted me again. I was able to offer her six months of therapy which she used to great effect.)

DEVELOPMENTAL STAGES

Latency

I would now like to continue with an examination of some of the difficulties with which therapists may be confronted given the developmental stage the child has reached.

From approximately the age of 5 or 6, and until the beginning of adolescence, there is what might descriptively be called 'a lull in the storm'; a period where the tempestuous feelings of infancy, the intense curiosity of the nursery child and the passionate intensity and urgency with which every waking moment of the day is invested, appears to wane and subside.

In psychoanalytic theory, this apparent diminishing of libido is thought to be due to a more sophisticated use of repression and sublimation and to energy being redirected to meet new challenges, notably school and the complex social learning which comes from interacting with other children.

Although latency children may appear to be more self-contained and compliant than the pre-school child, or the adolescent, they can be very difficult to make contact with because their emotions are so heavily defended against.

This can make therapeutic work with latency children slow, painstaking and frustrating. You may know from their parents or teachers that they have difficulties and need help, but they can stubbornly resist any attempt to get close to them or acknowledge that they need help. Frequently, the therapist only knows that there is an underlying problem by the feelings which such children provoke in them:

> We may find ourselves feeling hopeless, useless, rebuffed, un-wanted, confused or downright angry, or overwhelmed by pain and compassion while the child appears more placid, unconcerned, triumphant or detached than we experience ourselves to be.

(Hoxter 1983: 131)

Adolescence

By common consent, adolescence is recognised in all cultures as a difficult, trying and testing time for all concerned. There are several reasons why this should be so. Physically, emotionally and socially, changes of tremendous import are taking place. From being totally dependent on their parents, adolescents are having to define themselves in their own right, as well as preparing themselves for independent adult life. For many adolescents, their newly found status and maturity results in their questioning – and rejecting – many of the values and beliefs that they once took for granted. Frequently, this results in a turning away from the values inculcated by parents and teachers, and identifying with those of their own group.

In many ways, this rejection of adult values is – if it is temporary and not too deviant – healthy and normal. However, when working therapeutically with adolescents, it poses a serious problem in that the normal, developmental trend is towards identification with the youth culture and peers, and this can militate against the establishment of a close and trusting relationship with an adult.

Another factor which causes stress when working with adolescents, is their tendency to 'act out', rather than think about and process what may be troubling them internally. Like the pre-school child, they tend to rid themselves of unwanted thoughts or feelings by projecting them – sometimes violently – into the therapist: 'The pain which they cannot endure to experience within themselves they tend to expel in ways likely to hurt their care-givers, including of course, the therapist' (Hoxter 1983: 127). And, 'The difficult task of the Child Psychotherapist is to be able to receive, acknowledge, contain, process, think about and detoxify these feelings without denying them or being taken over and completely overwhelmed by them' (ibid.).

STRESS AND THE PERSONALITY OF THE CHILD PSYCHOTHERAPIST

In order to help the disturbed child the child psychotherapist has not only to be capable of thinking about and formulating hypotheses concerning the child's internal state and responding to it empathically, he must also be able to 'contain within himself' the child's inner turmoil (or deadness) – sometimes for long periods of time. This kind of work, therefore, requires certain characteristics, without which no meaningful contact can be made with the child. Curiosity and interest in other people – in what makes them 'tick' – the capacity for empathy, a certain degree of toughness and resilience, sensitivity, imagination, realism, being a good listener, determination and persistence, composure 'under fire', flexibility and, not least, a sense of humour and an optimistic outlook on life, are all part of the 'survival kit' of the child psychotherapist.

If one has a sufficient combination of the above qualities, or at least has the potential to aquire them, then one has a much better chance of both managing stressful situations *and* gaining therapeutic benefit from them.

THE ROLE OF TRAINING IN MANAGING STRESS

The training of child psychotherapists is specifically designed to help trainees develop their understanding of unconscious processes – both in themselves and in their patients. There are four main elements to the training: theory, clinical practice, supervision and personal training analysis.

If you knew that you were going to a strange country, the first thing which you would seek to aquire would probably be a map. You would need something which would give you a point of reference, the beginning of a conceptual framework, in relation to which you could orient yourself and begin your journey and exploration. Psychoanalytic theory is the map. It may not be completely accurate, and you may in time need to revise and update it; but without it, you will not know where you are going – or how to get back.

Clinical practice – working with patients – and personal analysis, are about learning from experience. You cannot get the taste of a lemon from a book. If you want to know what it is like to be a patient, to share your life, your hopes, fears, darkest secrets, to know the kind of intimacy which is the privilege of very few, you have to get on the couch yourself. This is the equivalent of exploring this unknown country on foot rather by car or aeroplane; it is a much more personal journey and you will not ever forget it or the lessons you learned on the way.

Supervision is the equivalent of having a guide who has been there before; who can indicate the signs that tell you when you are going in the right direction or have lost your bearings, and who knows the secret of finding one's way and surviving in uncharted territory.

In conclusion, the aim is not to avoid stress, but to *recognise when it is present*, to be able to manage and contain it, and to be able to understand what it is telling us about what is happening inside the child, inside ourselves, and in the interaction between the child and therapist.

REFERENCES

Bion, W. R. (1977) *Seven Servants*, New York: Jason Aronson.

Hoxter, S. (1983) 'Some feelings aroused in working with severely deprived children', Chapter 15 in M. Boston and R. Szur (eds), *Psychotherapy With Severely Deprived Children*, London: Routledge and Kegan Paul.

Klein, M. (1975) 'Notes on some schizoid mechanisms', Chapter 1 in *Envy and Gratitude and Other Works*, London: The Hogarth Press and The Institute of Psycho-Analysis.

Winnicott, D. W. (1976) *The Maturational Processes and the Facilitating Environment*, London: The Hogarth Press and The Institute of Psycho-Analysis.

Chapter 5

Risks to the worker with disturbed adolescents

Arthur Hyatt Williams

That some adolescents of both sexes pose difficulties to each other, to their parents, to educational and other authorities, not least of which are the forces of law and order, is wellknown. Part of their individual or, more frequently, group challenges to procedures which are established is creative, but when obstructed in this process, evoking responses which are partly idealistic and partly iconoclastic, there can be a resort to more clearly destructive behaviour.

In order to clarify how the adolescents, singly or in their peer groups, pose their challenge and introduce turbulence which has certain effects upon the adults whose 'cool sequestered way of life' is destabilised, is the subject of this chapter. One cannot deal with such a complicated problem in one chapter. Instead, we shall pick out one aspect of it, namely, the stress and risk involved particularly to workers with disturbed adolescents in or out of residential settings. Of course, this is not to disregard the other risks to the adolescents who have to deal with disturbed workers!

One of the essential features of the interpersonal transactions between worker and adolescent is the effect that they have upon each other. It is important that we should try to understand the problem and sort it out, at least to some extent. A good deal of illumination is necessary, particularly in the area of confused interaction with the person who is either in charge of the adolescent, or who attempts to give psychotherapy or group therapy to him or her. Let us consider the basic transactions which take place between the worker and the client or patient, their extent, limitations and, at times, perversions.

In the relationship which begins to develop between the client/ patient and the worker, it is necessary for us to distinguish and delineate two situations; first, the relationship as it exists in its own right; and second, transference proper in which elements of earlier relationships, including often very strong feelings, are mobilized from the unconscious mind so that an amount of previously un-metabolized emotional and psychic experience is transferred on to the worker and re-experienced in the relationship between the worker and the client. This is transference proper and a great deal depends upon the handling of that relationship. What makes the ordinary relationship between client and worker confused is the phenomenon familiar to most workers, namely the compulsion to repeat the past in the present, and to go on repeating it. I would tend to reserve the term 'transference' for the situation which develops when there is a mobilization of previously unfelt, that is, repressed or split off experience and its development in the therapeutic relationship.

The interactions of parents with their adolescent offspring show features similar to those between workers with adolescents who are disturbed by intrapsychic and/or interpersonal problems, followed by infringements of the law and hence conflict with those whose task it is to attempt to ensure that its measures are obeyed. Behaviour in the nuclear family may be the battleground for the conflicts, or they may be expressed mainly outside the family. These situations may be approached by the adolescent acting out in a solitary way, or within a peer group. These groups can be of any size, even amounting to a sub-culture. Sometimes, the turbulence appears to run a benign course and to be satisfactorily resolved, but sometimes quite the opposite takes place.

There are methods of communication which are non-verbal, but which convey states of mind and feeling. Melanie Klein (1946) described the means by which the process takes place. She named the mechanism 'projective identification'. The process is strongest during the pre-verbal stage of infancy, and takes place especially between the infant and its mother or, in the absence of the mother, with her surrogate. What the infant cannot express verbally and cannot digest psychically is communicated first as discomfort evacu-ated into the mother or her surrogate, who either finds within herself a way of remedying the distress or of comforting the infant and thus helps him or her to bear it, or fails to do that. This transaction takes place innumerable times with a good mother or her substitute in relationship to the child. Since Melanie Klein described projective identification phenomena, a great deal of work has been devoted to its study. For example, Wilfred Bion in *Second Thoughts* (1967) particularly, and elsewhere, describes the blocking of projective identification by the mother (or surrogate) which, over time, leads to an inhibited development, even a non-development, on the part of the infant or young person who is unable to develop an intrapsychic apparatus to cope with his or her own emotional needs – certainly as a result.

There are two main reactions to stress which cannot be psychically digested and metabolized. One is to act out in a way destructive to the adolescent himself and to other people, or to the conventional system. The other way is to look round for a person into whom to evacuate the destructiveness. That person may help or may block the communication, or may evacuate something back into the adolescent when he or she can least bear it. This evacuation nearly always has the characteristics of an over-severe super-ego. At any rate, the transactions are very likely to be anti-developmental.

Often, the evacuations by authorities into disturbed adolescents do more harm than good. But the adolescent does tend to use the unconscious projective identification mechanism and to put it into authority figures who become possessed by very uncomfortable feelings which really belong to the adolescent. These may be used, again unconsciously, but it is the adolescent's discomfort with the parent's feelings as different from his or her own which is decisive in determining the outcome.

On the other hand, the authority figure implementing established rules and procedures may retaliate in a punitive, super-egoish way. This usually acts as a goad rather than as a guide to the adolescent. Furthermore, the persons dealing with disturbed adolescents are often hardly trained at all in this aspect of their role. In practice, I have found that they do learn very quickly how to handle this kind of challenge. One example immediately springs to mind. Two adolescent girls in quest of an exciting thrill began to get friendly with two men who had bad criminal and prison records for sexual crimes. The warden of a probation hostel, a man with both courage and insight, saw this disturbing quartet in preliminary interaction. He challenged the two men and invited them to come into the probation hostel for a week or two until the risk had subsided, and also said that he was going to inform the parents of the two girls. This he did, and the escalation of risky relationships, which had been probable, did not take place.

There is often a confusion of roles of the worker and it might be helpful if we attempt to delineate three main roles, namely guardianship, caring and continuity. These terms are intended as working instruments and there is no magic about them. The guardianship role consists of ordering, setting limits and boundaries and the guardian acts as a leader with whom the adolescent finds it possible to identify, and by whom he or she feels protected and in some way controlled. It is a masculine role, a paternal one. Examples are headmasters, prison governors, etc. The carer on the other hand is a person who takes, receives and contains the communications of the adolescent. It is desirable for the carer to work upon what he or she takes in, if possible to improve, reconstrue and clarify that which has been taken in, and relay it back to the patient. Ideally the patient is thus enabled to handle, deal with, cope with what has been returned in somewhat improved form, and go on with the work, thus enabling psychic digestion and metabolism to proceed. If the carer is unable to work upon the communications sufficiently or if the patient is unable to deal with what is returned from the carer in the form in which it is returned, that particular unit of therapeutic transaction has failed. This procedure is by means of projective identification. There may arise a situation in which either the worker or the patient or both become frustrated. This pattern of the breakdown of progressive interaction and growth will be likely to follow the original path by which a young person became a patient. In understanding that pattern, the therapeutic situation may still be salved because one area of the unconscious compulsion to repeat what has happened before will have been re-experienced in a transference setting and worked through there, with more insight and less angry frustration than before.

The role of carer, it will be seen, is more feminine than that of guardian and derives from mother/child relationships. This is true despite the fact that as often as not the carer is biologically a male. Not all males are guardians and not all females carers. The female role is that of a container, but if there is no ability to work consciously or unconsciously upon that which has been taken or put back by the worker, the content remains unchanged. In such cases there has been an unloading and the transaction is one of psychic toilet only, the carer acting as a lavatory and the therapy being simply a disburdening and evacuation. Underlying many cases in which the adolescent patient becomes disillusioned and develops denigratory attitudes towards the therapist, is the hidden failure of the therapist to work sufficiently upon that which has been communicated to him or her, or the failure of the patient to accept back his or her own content somewhat modified by the pre-digestion of it carried out by the therapist.

There is, in addition, likely to be the unconscious or even

conscious expectation that history will repeat itself and events in therapy will necessarily follow the precise course followed by events in the previous history of the patient. The task of the carer is complicated and involves the ability to cope intellectually and emotionally with that which he or she is called upon to take in, work with and relay back to the patient. There can be no dissembling. He or she is forced to use himself or herself as the therapeutic instrument. Thus the worker brings to the task the weaknesses and strengths which stem from his or her own history, and ability depends not upon intellect or formal learning experience entirely, and certainly not upon intuitive gifts entirely, but upon an articulated balance between all three. To use such complex multiple skills, it is obvious that there are many points at which troubles and difficulties can arise. It would be a mistake to develop an heroic, ideal image of the carer. It is the hero and heroines who themselves are most at risk, particularly in dealing with disturbed adolescents. Usually there is an unconscious, automatic safety system which protects most workers with adolescents. People who do not have this safety system and who cannot develop it during their training should not involve themselves too deeply in this difficult field of work. The most common safety device consists of an *unconscious* opting out of a deep and deeply disturbing interaction in one way or another, that is, it sabotages the task which they have taken on. Sometimes the opting out is by means of an illness developing in the worker, which is unconsciously determined in order to halt a work situation in which there is considerable risk to the emotional stability of the worker. If a worker has structural difficulties of personality, he or she may press on with casework or therapy to his or her own detriment. When the problem of the worker is one of content, for example a disturbance in marriage or a bereavement, often this can be coped with by geting help from colleagues and support from the framework of the organisation or institution. Help in dealing with structural problems of personality in the worker is likely to take a great deal of time and may not meet the requirements of the emergency with which he or she may be confronted. In milder instances where the immediately available strength does not withstand the impact of what is taken in or forced into the worker, the problem may consist of a general state of inadequacy; or, in a relatively stable person, some specific communications of the patient might have found a particularly vulnerable point in the worker, and constitute the psychic Achilles' heel of that particular person at that particular time.

When a worker is in distress in dealing with the treatment situation, the signs of failure may consist of:

1 A simple denial and neither seeing nor feeling the communication relayed by the patient. The common outcome is either counter-denial on the part of the patient or, possibly, a breaking off of treatment or a crisis. In the neurotic patient, there is often the former and in the delinquent, the latter. Sometimes the obsessional patient and the therapist get into an unproductive relationship.

2 The worker may become extremely anxious, depressed or feel persecuted, may be unable to contain the situation and him or herself and act out, either in accordance with his or her own inner problems, or else on behalf of the patient. For example, in working with criminal adolescents, I have had many rows with the authorities on behalf of my patients in custody, and several times noticed that I have borrowed or was using the prisoner-/patient's own terms and attitudes.

3 The caseworker may become punitive and authoritarian. This is especially liable to happen if there is a guardianship role built into the job, as in the case of child-care officers, probation officers, staff of approved schools, etc.

4 The caseworker, provoked or burdened beyond his or her immediate capacity, may reverse the equation of container and contained, thus evacuating his or her own pre-existent or recently reactivated disturbances into the client or patient. The subsequent acting out of the client/patient, therefore, is dynamised not only by their own, but also by the caseworker's problems and difficulties. This situation is particularly dangerous in those with criminal personalities in whom there seems to occur not a simple addition of the two problems, but rather a multiplication. The ensuing crisis is akin to a chain reaction. But in any case it sabotages the task he or she has set out to do.

It will be realised that the situations just described are bewilderingly explosive and taxing to the worker. What happens depends so much upon the tension of the moment and the capacity of both caseworker and client to bear it. It will be clear that no rigid series of formulations can be made or learnt, but rather there should be a flexibility of interaction in which there is a tolerant acceptance of the patient's communication, which may be more difficult if the communication is made by actions rather than in words. *The reality sense of the worker should not be impaired.* Then should follow a response. Here the impatience of the patient may precipitate the worker into making mistakes, whereupon the patient responds in one or more of a number of different ways. I find that sometimes a way of avoiding this is to enlist if possible the co-operation of the patient by which they use that part of themselves which wishes to be helped by the therapy. I simply state that I am considering what they have said and that we should work together to try to understand what is happening. If this does not succeed in holding the situation, the response of the patient often gives a line regarding the main psychic current in operation at that particular moment, for example, mockery and triumph over my lack of therapeutic omnipotence, anxiety that I am not more powerful or competent, and sometimes relief at my lack of omniscience. At other times the patient shows relief that the problem is something which can be worked at and possibly resolved. Restoration of psychic equilibrium in the worker depends upon an ability to do internal work upon him or herself, especially upon the disturbance introduced by the adolescent.

Fortunately, in dealing with adolescents there is, as well as the provocation, hostility and all the destructive characteristics, often a very rewarding response and a utilization of what one gives in the way of help, clarification and understanding which carries the process forward in a way which is rarely found in the treatment of adult patients.

Confusion of caring and guardianship roles can cause trouble. One probation officer was confronted by a client who demanded whether she liked him, insisting on a yes or no answer. She said 'yes' waveringly and then he said, 'Come out with me tonight.' She then took refuge behind the guardianship aspect of her role and the patient in anger went out and burgled a house. Role-clarification has to be undertaken all the time. In this case, his burglary of the house was a lesser crime than the fantasized sexual assault upon the woman probation officer.

It is important that there should be minimal modification of the content of the patient's communication in the idiom of the case-worker or of the therapist's own personality and needs. If some modification has to take place, what is fed back into the patient should have been carefully considered and sorted out so that it does not contain what are best regarded as 'parts of the therapist'. It will be recognized that one part of the task of trainee workers is to grow to know their boundaries so that they do not become mixed up with the boundaries of their clients or patients. The problem is that too rigid boundaries of the self are inimical to meaningful communication between patient and therapist, whereas boundaries which are blurred must be suspect because of the confusions which arise.

How does one progress towards the balance between a rigidly stable structure which is unempathic and an open one which is muddled? The problem hinges in part upon the quality and amount of projective identification in the transactions from client to worker and the capacity of the worker to bear these communications without being possessed by them, or rejecting them, or giving them a twist and returning them to the client worsened rather than improved. Those who have had or are having personal analysis find that the tensions of dealing with the powerfully disturbing communications of the patient are better borne while the work upon them is being carried out. This is because they will have experienced similar, even if not such dramatically powerful situations, in their own analysis and are less likely to be thrown off balance, put to flight or goaded into an authoritarian fight which would set back progress considerably if not catastrophically. There are workers in all disciplines who are naturally gifted but even they are likely to benefit from personal analysis. Among the dangers with which the naturally intuitively gifted worker is confronted is that of hubris in the face of therapeutic success. I was told of a paper (written some thirty years ago) telling of the experience of some fifteenth-century monks who accidentally discovered the cures which could be effected by running very long confessionals and making interpretations. What caused this activity to be proscribed was the dangerous hubris, consisting of overwhelming pride and arrogance, which developed in the therapist monk or priest. This was regarded as more serious than the development of dependency in those who received the therapy. This story, which I am told is true, highlights a danger intrinsic in situations which foster power. One sees it in administration, but it is more dangerous in psychotherapists and caseworkers. When the feeling of power is intoxicating there is likely to be a manic process in operation, which, unchecked, will inevitably lead to a loss of sensitivity and balance in one's work and if developed further, to a corruption of it. What ensues is almost certainly a wishful assumption of omniscience in the defence against psychic pain. This does not mean that one should not get joy from the work which so often and for so long can be frustrating and unrewarding or extremely anxiety-producing. Somewhere there should be established within each caseworker/therapist, however, self-righting mechanisms which restore the balance of psychic equilibrium in the face both of external threats and of internal situations, the two often acting in relationship to each other either alternately or synergically like a see-saw or the compartments of an hourglass.

Some description of the role of the continuity figure is necessary at this point. Sometimes the person who offers continuity of relationship to the adolescent has a guardianship role and sometimes a caring role. Sometimes the continuity person is outside the guardianship or caring spectrum. Adolescents, particularly disturbed ones and those with delinquent tendencies, are extremely vulnerable to changes in relationships, and often there is a complete relapse when a worker who has been in close touch with them for some time leaves, retires or is posted elsewhere. Sometimes the continuity figure is required to do very little, apart from just being there. Sometimes he or she is called upon at a time of crisis. One sees the effects of disruption of continuity quite frequently in the probation service. The situation is now much better than it was when the first draft of this chapter was written. The continuity role of probation officers between the prison phase and post-prison time is a very great improvement on the split and divided care which made it impossible to exercise the continuity role. The recent break between child-care and the probation service, as far as the client is concerned, at the age of 17 years was a very anti-developmental administrative decision, as most probation officers would agree. When the adolescent is changing intrapsychically, it is important that some person in the environment should be constant and able to bridge the gap between successive developmental situations. As far as a simple example is concerned, I myself corresponded with one ex-prisoner who had relatively superficial psychotherapy from me, but the correspondence went on at three-weekly intervals for more than ten years. I also know a prison medical officer, known to be strict, who has a lively correspondence with a number of ex-prisoners. He even goes to see some of them and the continuity role he has taken upon himself is a very important one in helping to reinforce some deficiencies and facets of instability in the inner worlds of the former patients.

Every renunciation is paid for by depression, but such depression need not be unproductive, and if it is tolerated and worked through, psychic equilibrium can be restored in a constructive way. Failure to work through depression as the self-realisation process continues, often is followed by compensatory defence mechanisms. A manic process may intervene and mitigate or annul a healthy depressive feeling in the development of personal insight regarding one's work and this may lead to what amounts to a non-therapeutic situation with the patient, which is at best a stalemate and at worst a negative therapeutic reaction imposed upon the patient by the therapist. Sometimes this takes the form of a breaking-off of therapy. In the same category is the so-called 'wild analysis' in which sudden crash interpretations are given with no supporting linkages. The unconscious motivation of the therapist may be one of exhibitionism in a setting of omnipotence, or be even more dangerous if he or she envies the success of the therapy and the improvement of his or her own patient.

When the problem is the other way round and despite correctly given interpretations and a reasonable degree of humility on the part of the caseworker, the client's situation gets no better or even progressively worse, envy, in this case the patient's envy, is almost certainly the cause. There then arises an unconscious determination on the part of the patient to deny the therapist the fruits of his labours. There is of course a response from the therapist; sometimes tolerating a situation which should not be tolerated, sometimes becoming angry and rejecting or punitive, and this situation may unconsciously fit in with the masochistic needs of the patient whose requirement is punishment. This may be in order to mitigate an unconscious guilt-ridden situation manifesting itself as a need for punishment. This was all explained by Freud in 'The economic problem of masochism' as long ago as 1924. Capacity for favourable change depends on the patient's position within a spectrum ranging from a state dominated by persecutory anxiety at one end, to one dominated by depressive anxiety at the other. The Bion formula P/S = D (Paranoid–Schizoid position = Depressive position) helps us to clarify our thoughts about the situation. The concept of container and contained and of taking in a communication, working upon it and relaying it back in a more usable form are among Bion's formulations. Bion was referring to any interactions based mainly on projective identification. He was writing mainly about psychotic patients and young infants. In adolescence there is usually to be found a communication at several levels at once. Of these, the infantile level is the most important and the one which the adolescent usually denies most emphatically. The way in which the individual copes depends upon the way in which at the various relevant times in life he or she has negotiated the depressive position. Relevant, however, is the way in which the caseworker or the therapist is able to provide and facilitate another chance and a better negotiation of the depressive position than the original one.

I should like to add a few words about bad mothers, fathers, school teachers, army officers, prison officers, the police, etc. The do-gooders so enjoy a witch-hunt against the bad parent or parental surrogate that they tend to belittle the contribution of the adolescent himself or herself to the situation. Yet it is important to see the transactions as two-sided in which perhaps the worst service which can be done to a disturbed adolescent is to give him a justifiable grievance. The effect of the feeling of having been wronged enables the aggrieved adolescent to commit all kinds of offences while basking in the sunlight of his or she own self-righteousness, making no progress at all in taking personal responsibility for their share in the transaction. How many Richard IIIs are there among adolescent delinquents who, aggrieved by the unkindness of nature by being backward, neglected by parents, misunderstood by teachers and ill-treated by the police, feel themselves to be excused from the restrictions of behaviour which bind ordinary people! The adolescent may so threaten the stability of the worker that the latter reverses the evacuative process and the projective identification is from the worker into the patient. This reversal is, of course, much more frequently found from parent to adolescent. The latter may say of his or her mother, 'She drives me mad. She has no mercy on me!' The worker or the parent has temporary psychic indigestion and so the 'container and contained' are reversed. Freud described these people as the exceptions in his 1916 paper entitled 'Some character types met with in psycho-analysis'. It is not part of my intention to say that bad carers or guardians do not have a part in the aetiology of a no-growth condition or even-worsening disturbance, but rather to stress that there is a bipolar, two-sided situation, if not a multi-faceted one. The therapeutic setting provides a context which facilitates the repetition of the earlier sequence of events, but differs in that there is an opportunity afforded for alteration of the course of personal history of the patient. In that procedure there are risks to patient and worker. We have outlined the former but emphasized the latter, as it is with these somewhat neglected facets that we are dealing. Before the days of antibiotics, when medical powders had to be given when a horse became ill, the powder was put on the horse's tongue and blown down its throat by the vet. Often, however, the horse blew first. So also it is in the two-person relationship and it is not merely what was blown in which comes back.

How can the worker maintain an ongoing therapeutic situation, psychic poise and an increasing personal stability rather than worsening stress for him or herself with the risk of more serious breakdown? How can the intrapsychic situation of the worker be assessed if he or she is not having personal analysis? Certainly not all exacerbations of anxiety in the worker indicate that something is going wrong with him or her. Often an increase of anxiety in the worker indicates a dangerous situation in the near-future behaviour of the adolescent, which the worker has perceived unconsciously but has not yet been able to formulate clearly. I had a patient, not unduly depressed, who phoned to cancel a Saturday morning session. On the Monday morning I had a waking dream which consisted of a scene in which this patient, with a minute textbook dissection of his right axilla, was lying on a post-mortem slab. Three hours after this dream, his girlfriend arrived, knocked at my door and asked if I had seen her financé. One or two days later, he was found dead by the police, having taken an overdose of aspirin, alcohol and barbiturates. One's dreams indicate not only an unconscious contact with unconscious processes going on in the patient, but also how the worker is dealing with what has been taken in from the patient and how he or she is reacting to it. It is not necessary to have an exhaustive analysis of dreams to get an indication of the state of one's own psychic digestion and metabolism and whether one's resources and capacities are being taxed unduly.

Personal psychoanalysis often equips the worker with the skill to analyse most of his or her own dreams. I do not know how far this discipline can be of use and how far it might be dangerous for those who have not had personal analysis. Freud was able to accomplish his self-analysis by analysing his own dreams, but I am hesitant about making it a general recommendation. In addition, by means of dream analysis it is possible to see what role the worker is taking unconsciously, and sometimes that is quite different from conscious attitudes. For example, the worker may be identified with the adolescent in some dream episode, or with the establishment, possibly in a very authoritarian way. Early in my experience with delinquent youths, I was listening to a story about a criminal exploit which went wrong and before I realized what I was saying, I remarked that had he done this or that he would not have been caught. He said, 'Oh doctor, what are you telling me?' The more delinquent the adolescent, the more efforts are made to force the therapist into role-taking. These roles may vary from that of a punitive authoritarian to that of an accomplice, but in any case it is important not to have what invariably turns out to be an anti-therapeutic constellation of activity thrust upon one. Seduction into some compromising situation is used as a way in which to destroy an ongoing therapeutic process. This is particularly prevalent among delinquent adolescents. Sometimes the giving of presents, particularly by female adolescents, is used as a substitute for an improvement. Sometimes presents are given in order to inflate and eventually expose the greed of the therapist.

The whole business of therapy is about change and growth. The adolescent is usually more frank than the adult in resisting the efforts of those endeavouring to produce change and growth. The prototype of this state of affairs can be seen in young children who frankly want and need love and approval, *but on their own terms*, and sometimes those terms are quite impossible for adults and for society at large to accept. Also, the unconscious conscience of the young child (and adolescent and adult, for that matter) knows something about destructive or power-seeking motivation. Thus, if there is a soft yielding on the part of authority that does not touch the area of problem effectively, what seems to suit the child or adolescent does not do so, and the disturbed behaviour, particularly in rather un-integrated adolescents, tends to escalate. This is where the needs for limits and boundaries can be seen most clearly. In the adolescent, the child component is sometimes very strong, and when there is a regressive demand actually stemming from the child part – although ostensibly from the part which justifiably seeks for independence and freedom – yielding to the demand causes a worsening of the situation, perhaps after a brief interval of calm. The real need of the child part of the adolescent may be for limits and boundaries, and this may be more urgent than the need for freedom and independence which stems from the more adult part of the adolescent.

If the caseworker/therapist allows the role-taking to be imposed on him or her, the situation may end in a crisis either way. In the one case, the more adult part of the client may feel unjustly restricted and, in the other, the baby part may feel neglected, abandoned and not protected. I would attempt to interpret wide splitting, but sometimes the two extremes are frighteningly irreconcilable. It is important to outline both, even if one has to take the action necessary for the care and safety of the child part. The danger is that do-gooders try to do more good and pursue their policy to its limit. The authoritarians under stress become more authoritarian, restrictive and punitive and neither kind of authority is likely to succeed in restoring growth and a capacity for change. The adolescent at this point often turns to his or her peer group in an endeavour to regain some kind of equilibrium and then the usual troubles arise. The hard way of development up and down the spectrum of persecutory and depressive anxiety, bearing 'the fierce dispute betwixt damnation and impassioned clay' does not appeal to the adolescent in rebellion. He or she wants the rewards and gratifications but not the hard psychic work. At this point, the dangers are that there will be a turning towards drug-taking, to social philosophies which do not include good work, or even a move towards violence and crime. There is a peculiar appeal in some of the confused adolescent issues, not only to adolescents. Here again, in a group setting, the worker or therapist is at personal risk of being stirred up into a violent protagonism without previously clarifying the issues at stake and the motivations, conscious and unconscious, which dynamize them. The alternative is of being overwhelmed by the confusion and remaining in a dither, or else of resorting to anything without regard to its wisdom and likely outcome. The third possibility is a full retreat into authoritarianism, punitiveness and a stifling of young growth and vitality felt to be threatening.

Some of the younger authority figures deal with the problem by using their relative and apparent integration to adopt the aspirations and behaviour of the adolescent, individual or group, without realizing that the adolescents themselves, being usually far less mature and integrated, will not be able to emulate them. An example of this is the matter of drug-taking, especially cannabis but to some extent other drugs. When the worker in the adolescent field takes small quantities of these drugs, he or she becomes not only 'with it' but remains apparently safe and so says that the drugs are harmless. To a certain extent this may be true for him or her with soft drugs, but workers in the field of adolescent therapy are imitated, particularly in a therapeutic community, by their clients/patients. If for the worker there is an envious component in the identification, it is sure to be made unsuccessful. Therefore, one's public image should never be an irresponsible one and the inevitable identification with adolescent patients is safe only in a non-acted-out way.

What are the ways which are available to deal with the risks of working with adolescents?

1 Personal analysis is not available in most places in Great Britain. Clearly it is the most thorough and effective way of helping the worker to know him or herself and to develop the capacity to contain and work with adolescents and what is put into him or her by the adolescents, and to cut short by getting insight quickly into any dangerous acting out by himself.

2 Adequate pre-training and in-service training for the task include individual casework supervision, and training events in a peer-group setting help to give knowledge and confidence.

3 Ongoing training experiences, supervision, seminars, case conferences, staff meetings, sensitivity groups, etc., help the therapist develop skills and the confidence to proceed and get over any blockages and arrests that may have arisen.

4 Support from colleagues is essential for workers in residential settings but also very important in non-residential settings, particularly when working with delinquent adolescents where a semi-outsider may see more than the worker who is involved in a 'white-hot' situation with the adolescent himself.

5 An easily obtained early help service should be available when apparently insuperable difficulties arise, and more particularly when signs of stress or breakdown threaten the caseworker/therapist. Any loss of face should be avoided (nothing like the 'lack of moral fibre' label of the RAF in World War II should ever be used).

6 Adequate pre-service selection is necessary.

REFERENCES

Bion, Wilfred (1967) *Second Thoughts*, London: Heinemann Medical Books.
Freud, Sigmund (1916) 'Some character types met with in psycho-analysis', *Standard Edition* (1964) London: Hogarth Press, vol. 14: 332–3.
—— (1924) 'The economic problem of masochism', *Standard Edition* (1964) London: Hogarth Press, vol. 19: 159–70.
Klein, Melanie (1946) 'Notes on some schizoid mechanisms', *The Writings of Melanie Klein*, London: Hogarth Press and The Institute of Psycho-analysis (1975) vol. 3: 1–25.

Chapter 6

Stress in psychotherapists who work with adults

Cassie Cooper

Psychotherapists are not a breed apart. We bring with us in our work with patients a network of dependencies that are based on early experiences of our own formative relationships. To be sincerely and closely accepted by another person is a heady and seductive experience, something that one finds almost irresistible. Patient and psychotherapist present pathologies which are analogous to each other. This is, in some ways, an essential condition for the relationship.

If a patient has difficulties in relating to the therapist, then the therapist should become familiar with these hesitancies. It is only when the therapist is able to resonate to the presenting problem through the two-way mirror of his or her own stresses and difficulties, that a path is delineated to the reality of the psyche. In this way, the pain and distress caused to the psychotherapist becomes the basis for inquiry.

Inquiry is the necessary precondition for our profession.

During relationships it is the gaze of another which makes us feel alive and come alive. We feel alive if someone takes notice of us and takes us seriously. 'The child is conscious of himself only to the extent that the mother thinks about him. Thus feeling considered is equivalent to feeling alive' (Bion 1955).

An effective therapeutic relationship cannot be formed without an intense emotional involvement. The therapist can only invest psychic energy in a patient if there is a form of gratification in the relationship. This is stressful, particularly in view of the fact that the therapist, in making this emotional investment in a patient, does so not out of a sense of professional duty or even of material gain but rather because some aspect of that patient provides gratification.

Among laymen one frequently meets with the prejudice that psychotherapy is the easiest thing in the world and consists in the art of putting something over on people or wheedling money out of them. But actually it is a tricky and not undangerous calling.

(Jung 1935)

In a paper 'Therapist experience and the stresses of psychotherapeutic work' (Hellman, Morrison and Abramowitz 1987) the authors identified five stress factors which could be associated with psychotherapeutic work:

- How to maintain and sustain a therapeutic relationship.
- Identifying and scheduling the difficulties which may occur in the process.
- Professional doubts about the work.
- Involvement with the patient.
- Personal depletion and self-abnegation.

In addition the paper drew attention to five factors which could be seen to occur in patient behaviour, namely: negativity and contempt; resistance to interpretation and change; psychopathological symptoms; suicidal threats; passive–aggressive behaviour.

MAINTAINING AND SUSTAINING A PSYCHOTHERAPEUTIC RELATIONSHIP

It would be dishonest to put forward the theory that patient and therapist begin a symmetrical relationship – particularly since in the context of an educational institution (where I work) there are clearly defined hierarchical boundaries of ability and status. This is further complicated by the knowledge that our relationships, both personal and professional, are patterned and influenced by the significant others we have experienced in infancy and childhood.

We are told, furthermore, in every textbook and over and over again, that it is the responsibility of the therapist to avoid reacting to the patient in the terms of his or her own life experiences. This means that therapists should have enough sources of satisfaction and security in their own non-professional lives to forego the temptation of using patients as a means of securing their own personal well-being and security.

If the therapist is unfulfilled, lonely, lacking elements in his or her life which are wanted and needed, this can be recognized and understood – but it poses the question: who is to benefit from this relationship and what is its real purpose? If maintaining the relationship has become a source of satisfaction and security for the psychotherapist, dangers loom ahead. Is the therapist using in fantasy the material provided by the patient as a substitute for his or her own satisfactions?

Working with adults who bring to the therapist their experiences of success or failure in life and in prestige, of academic and financial success, of sexual prowess or impotence, vibrant self-esteem or the depths of depression, the therapist must resonate to these presentations, experiencing all too often his or her own wishes, longings, ambitions, feelings of envy and consciousness of failure, of age, and of lessening energy levels, and easily seduced by the patient's narrative into wishes to 'start again'. There is all of this to contend with and counteract in attempting to avoid the danger of using a patient's story as a starting point for a dream that never came true.

Learning to involve oneself in such a professional relationship and to expose oneself to the consequent dangers is not a once-and-for-all process, but rather is continuous since it can be seen to take place in various stages, representing the varying depths of the therapist's involvement.

The psychotherapist who has worked through the initial stages of engagement with a patient may then go through a period of over-involvement, wallowing in the joys of being found helpful and meaningful by another person. This can be followed by a period of almost paranoid sensitivity about the so-called 'slings and arrows of outrageous fortune' which have been perpetrated on the patient, who is beyond all reproach and criticism. At this time the psychotherapist needs all the supervisory help available to develop the capacity to withdraw at least intellectually from this quagmire, to look more realistically at the patient, at his or her situation, and at oneself as part of that situation.

The search for a patient suitable for psychodynamic psychotherapy is frequently a sign of resistance. One consideration is that the therapist assumes that this or that patient may be easy and well fitted for supervised work. This reflects the tendency (the rule rather than the exception) to fit the patient to the therapy and not to fit the therapy to the patient.

The need of an insecure therapist to draw security from a virtuous adjustment to the conventionalities of his time and from a quest for approval from the 'good and the great' may turn out to be another agent interfering with one's ability to listen in a therapeutically valid fashion.

This type of dependence on theory gives rise to the danger that the psychotherapist may consider the changeable man-made standards of the society in which we live to be eternal values to which he and his patients must conform.

Therefore the ability to listen and to help will be limited as his patients try to discover to what extent and in what way each of them needs to adjust to the cultural requirements of his time. He will become desensitized to the patients' personal needs because of preoccupation with his own dependency on the denizens of the group and the culture of his era and his modality and of its sometimes transitory values. This may render the psychotherapist practically incapable of guiding certain types of patients.

(Fromm 1941)

IDENTIFYING AND SCHEDULING THE DIFFICULTIES WHICH MAY OCCUR IN THE PROCESS OF PSYCHOTHERAPY WITH ADULT PATIENTS

Supervision provides many opportunities to broaden one's range of self-awareness, encouraging the therapist to be explicit about attitudes and difficulties which usually remain unexpressed. The supervisor may be helpful in recognizing competitive and prestige strivings for what they are, not as rationalizations for one's behaviour with a patient. Psychotherapists need support in accepting the fact that they are entitled not to know everything and to own up to occasional feelings of self-incrimination and sullen anger for having been found wanting.

Adult patients often present a wide range of, or frantic search for, sexual experiences through which they, in their deep distress, try to escape their loneliness and personal uncertainty. For the therapist, becoming familiar in a non-judgemental manner with the way of life lived by a patient is a broadening experience.

Therapists who could be called aggressively liberal in their sexual attitudes may need guidance in accepting that not every young woman who wishes to remain a virgin until she marries is repressed and narrow-minded, and that she may well deserve understanding for the decision which has prompted her to opt for traditional standards.

Therapists need support in their anxiety when progress is not dramatic and not as rewarding as their own need for reassurance demands. This is particularly so when declaring a patient to be 'untreatable' because the therapist feels that he or she has failed and wishes to recommend some organic treatment method as an alternative.

Such an example is the case of a client who may not be on the brink of disaster but whose therapist behaves as though it *is* a disaster. Somehow the therapist has become convinced that this patient must be treated in a special way, when more appropriate therapeutic interventions would not call for cautiousness. The therapist feels as though this patient is fragile and that unless one is extremely sensitive to the patient's feelings about practically anything, the patient will fall apart. This therapist has the feeling of walking on eggshells with the patient even though in reality the patient is not as delicate as the therapist contends.

In fact it could be that the patient is, in some ways, stronger and more manipulative than most. The patient is evoking feelings of helplessness and impotence within the therapist and the therapist responds to these feelings by becoming frustrated and angry at the unravelling tightrope on which both the patient and the therapist feel suspended.

In working with adult patients there may be a sense of confusion about what is transpiring in the relationship, and invariably anxiety is triggered – which may be a manifestation of a number of factors. The therapist's anxiety may be a function of his or her own experience if there is misunderstanding of how the patient is utilizing the sessions in order to maintain his or her neuroses.

The therapist, in interacting with a patient experiencing anxiety activated in the process of a relationship intended to be therapeutic, finds him or herself hopelessly trapped in the re-enactment of previous problematic encounters. He or she becomes immobilized by internal conflicts which relate less to the patient's apparent wiliness and ingenuity and more to features of the relationship which are significant to the therapist's own previous painful and problematic encounters with life.

It is this kind of unconscious collusion that leads to an impasse in the therapeutic process. The impasse occurs because the therapist has locked into and identified with a patient's problems. Identification with the patient is probably the most important single source of impasse in the therapeutic relationship.

The adult patient who presents to the adult psychotherapist brings into the session his or her 'messy jangle' (Freud 1935) of previous relationships – parents, education, marriage, work, sexuality – which are very different from the periods of development which preceded this stage in their lives. How easy it is then for the therapist to believe, and perhaps accurately, that he or she has the same un-resolved conflicts which beset the patient. The overwhelming sense of sameness that is felt towards the patient triggers anxiety in the therapist so that he or she feels unable to proceed with the therapy.

PROFESSIONAL DOUBTS ABOUT THE WORK

Every therapist, wanting to be liked, preoccupied by external status and with being considered authoritative and respected, fears that patients will not return. Some of the most far-reaching effects in the therapeutic relationship emanate from the patient's repeated efforts to test the therapist's adequacy. Patients test their therapists for a variety of reasons – ambivalence about changing, fears that the therapist may not be strong enough to combat the powerful feelings that confuse the patient, or just for the sheer joy of annoying an authority figure. These are just a few of the many motivations which compel the patient to chip away at the therapist to test his or her strength. This process of checking on the competence of the therapist continues throughout therapy.

At each stage in the relationship, as both therapist and patient work at deeper levels, the patient needs to check out the therapist before proceeding further. The testing processes vary depending on the previous life situation of the patient and his or her learned modes of checking on the motivation and strengths of previous significant others. In this way the patient defends against anxiety and the intensity of anxiety he senses in himself.

If, for example, a patient becomes unusually hostile during a particular session and the therapist feels puzzled by this hostility, it may reflect the patient's ability to reveal an aspect of his or her personality which has remained repressed. If the therapist responds by 'freezing', something has occurred which blocks off the creative associative process which can normally come to the rescue, enabling the therapist to penetrate the meaning of the patient's hostility. The therapist's ineffectiveness in making sense of a patient's behaviour is a measure of the anxiety which has been evoked within the therapist.

Inexperienced psychotherapists who may well be nurturant are astonished and hurt in their first encounters with hostile, angry and disturbed patients who do not seem properly to appreciate their warm, caring offers of help. Therapists can be bewildered and most confused when the previously accepting patient turns angry, rejecting or complaining. Sometimes it is this very willingness and eagerness to care that is in itself so deeply threatening to a patient. It is a hard lesson to learn that resistance to change is real in patients even though they may long to change their way of life. At this stage the therapist's anxiety may reflect past fears and experiences of hostile encounters. The patient has accidentally discovered the therapist's Achilles heel.

No one senses more deeply than the patient that his or her emotional life is held in a delicate pleasure–pain balance. In the therapeutic encounter, if some pattern of behaviour is offset by the experience of intense anxiety, at such times patients may strike back at the therapist to preserve their way of life and to resist change. An adult patient will have learned to react to implied threat (of anxiety and change) by falling back to ways in which anxiety was avoided in the past. Some reactions may be more dramatic than others. Patients may become violent and aggressive, become sexually provocative, withdraw from the session, or become tearful.

If the patient's hostility is a reaction to the therapist's punitive behaviour, then the therapist may – out of feelings of remorse and guilt – attempt to compensate in some way. Therapist and client may collude in simply sharing an insatiable punishment–expiation cycle which will continue until the therapist realizes what is happening, in that the process is perpetuating the cycle. When this is confronted by the therapist, who becomes aware of his or her punitive attitude and guilty responses to the patient, the cycle can, it is hoped, be broken. Only then can the therapist contend with some of the features of the patient's behaviour which may have contributed to setting the cycle in motion.

If the therapist has been punishing the patient for reasons other than those activated by the patient, an understanding of this situation may then lead to the discovery, as sometimes happens, that the patient had experienced punishment in the past, particularly in childhood, when seeking help and revealing his or her feelings.

Patients are, of course, ingenious in stimulating impasses so that they can continue in denial and avoidance to experience the anxiety which is necessary for change. But it is also true that therapists, with or without awareness, contribute to these deadlocks. Patients are astonishingly clever and effective in warding off their therapists when they wish to do so. The adult patient comes with considerable experience in warding off anxiety, so adroitness in this area comes as no surprise. But therapists take their work seriously – and they may well lose patience with their client's creativity in thinking up new ways of avoiding change and interpretation.

Perhaps more would be achieved if the therapist was enabled to sit back for a while in order to ponder on and even enjoy the ways in which a patient employs the unconscious, taking on board the fact that a patient's reaction time is an index of the anxiety level which the patient is experiencing.

As therapy proceeds, the patient becomes adept in locating suitable sore spots. Being with a therapist in close proximity week after week gives the patient ample time to diagnose the non-verbal clues given off by the therapist. In diagnosing (as it were) the therapist's reactions and locating the sore spots, the patient fulfils his or her continuing need. When anxiety is peaking, the threatened patient brings to bear useful defences with which to combat the intruder. What better defence is there than a hostile attack on the sensitivities and humanness of the therapist?

One of the central tasks in psychotherapy is to prepare the patient for the sight of him or herself, and therefore one of the central aspects of psychodynamic training is to prepare the therapist also for the sight of him or herself. Encountering a disruptive personality may bring to light those disruptive aspects of the therapist's personality which are usually hidden. However disruptive the patient may be, the experience for the therapist of catching sight of him or herself in this reflecting mirror can be a salutary experience.

A psychotherapist is always liable to feel insecure and sometimes this has the unfortunate result of using the patient as a test for the therapist's skills and power. Again, the therapist made aware of his or her own 'feelings' may be preoccupied with the idea that patients have to get well for the sake of the bubble 'reputation'. The therapist will listen to patients but conduct the therapy in such a way that it is deaf to and disregards the real needs and feelings with which the patient is struggling. A patient is well able to conclude that he or she is being used to strengthen the reputation of the therapist rather than being seen as an object of treatment in his or her own right. How can therapy succeed in this way?

INVOLVEMENT WITH THE PATIENT

In a social context alive with paradox, as psychotherapists we discern the anomie and nihilism which result from the process of institutional and societal control of our patients – a control whose purpose at times seems merely to be control for its own sake.

It is stressful to maintain in such a situation that the primary responsibility of a therapist is to have the 'patient's best interests at heart'. In making such a statement we are giving voice to a very complex problem, not to a resolution of it. It is not a resolution of the question as to what and to whom the therapist is morally and primarily tied. On the contrary, this statement erroneously suggests that we can resolve the grave moral problems our patients face.

Few will dispute the danger of a therapist who ruthlessly ignores professional boundaries, having sex with patients, exploiting them financially, hanging on to them as patients when they should be encouraged to terminate, violating confidentiality and fostering an unhealthy dependency. Our record in controlling these abuses is less than impressive. When it comes to mere incompetence, ineffectiveness or inappropriateness, who is there to tell the patient 'customer beware!'? Part of the problem is that while most professionals can recognize a 'good' therapist when they meet one it is difficult for the consumer to define excellence in any systematic way. It is of little help to shrug one's shoulders and say 'therapists are born not made'.

Psychotherapy is a stressful business. No amount of inner security and self-respect can protect the therapist from being as much a subject of and vulnerable to the inevitable vicissitudes of life as is everyone else. This being so, it is obvious that it is difficult for a psychotherapist to maintain the unadulterated role of the detached and impartial observer to patients. Psychotherapists know that the only valid means of acquainting oneself with the dynamic significance of their own early developmental history has to be their own personal analysis. This is essential in keeping the difficulties encountered in one's personal life separated and entirely apart from what is brought to attention and is in no way a part of one's professional life.

It is because of the relatedness between the psychotherapist and the adult patient that any attempt at intensive psychotherapy which helps patients reveal the disassociated and repressed elements of their personal life and to recognize transference and parataxic factors in their present interpersonal experiences with the therapist and others, must be fraught with danger where these allusions and experiences are not understood by the psychotherapist's own experience and hindsights of personal analysis.

Every therapist has this responsibility for self-evaluation and self-regulation. Continuous critical assessment of one's own performance is the best guarantee of an effective therapeutic process. To do this, analysis requires not only the will to engage in a critical self-evaluation but a knowledge of the standards and criteria that distinguish good practice from poor practice.

This questioning process can lead the therapist into two extremes. At one extreme is the therapist who loses him or herself in a fixed role as a therapist, hiding behind the strict professional façade. At the other is the therapist who strives too hard to prove that he or she, too, is human.

Veering towards either of these poles is a constant source of stress in therapeutic practice. The role functions of a therapist hide humanity, particularly when they are so bound up in maintaining stereotyped role expectations – nothing of the private person can be exhibited. Is it possible reasonably to perform our functions without burying our identities and becoming completely lost in a role? The more insecure, frightened and uncertain we are of our professional work the more we appear to cling to the defence offered by a pseudo-anonymity.

Once again our unrealistic expectations that as therapists we must be superhuman leads to our nervous ossification in fixed roles. We should always care, demonstrate warmth (whether we feel it or not), enjoy and like all our patients. We should know what is happening to us and them at all times, be all-understanding and fully empathetic. We are not acceptable to ourselves and others as therapists unless we are fully together ourselves. Any indication of a personal problem rules against therapeutic effectiveness. Therapists are the providers of answers for their patients, answers which patients have indicated they cannot find within themselves.

How readily psychotherapists deceive themselves into thinking they are that which they are really not. We are easily indoctrinated into the idea that we should behave in a certain way. The roles that are played are not always congruent with the ways we deeply feel. Finding boredom, we deny it and force attention. Discovering negative feelings toward a patient, we deny these in stressing the positive qualities we can identify. When we are uncaring at particular times, this feeling is intolerable and avoided.

We constantly wrestle with the issue of self-disclosure. How do we determine its appropriateness and relevance as a catalyst for growth and movement in our individual patients? Is disclosure a form of history-telling even if we are trying hard to be authentic? Is the therapist again trying to prove his or her own 'humanness'? Is the disclosure calculated to ensure that the patient goes away convinced that he or she has an 'open' therapist?

What has been said so far in this chapter could be summed up by saying that one of life's psychological problems for every individual – therapist and patient alike – is in finding, by trial and error, a comfortable and satisfying distance from other people in different relationships that are warm enough and not too intense – handling the basic conflict between the need for warmth and the need not to be hurt by the defending and narcissistic manoeuvres of ourselves and our patients. We could say that another of life's problems is knowing about boundaries, the thickness or the thinness of our 'psychological skin', and what we can hold to and keep to for ourselves and our patients within that boundary, including the basic conflict between self-expression and self-control.

PERSONAL DEPLETION AND SELF-ABNEGATION

The classic question 'What is happening between me and my patient?' is constantly brought into focus. Like the patient, the therapist faces the problem – should he or she reveal weaknesses in order to receive help? In supervision, the psychotherapist experiences the professional learning relationship as an emotional process in which full participation influences the way in which the therapist views him or herself 'for better or worse'. At this level the personal growth of therapists becomes characterized by a dependency–autonomy conflict in which they reflect on their character and how this is influencing their work whilst, at the same time, still struggling with dependency needs. The therapist is also struggling with insight, trying to differentiate more basic reactions from their cultural overlay. As a therapist, one varies from being over-confident with newly acquired skills, to being overwhelmed by the responsibility of the profession – often feeling ambivalent about relating, in the therapy relationship with the patient, to one's own persisting neurotic elements or with the discomforts of newly found self-awareness. This period is characterized also by huge fluctuations in motivation, veering from deep commitment to grave misgivings.

The fact is that patients need a therapist who is strong and adequate, so if patients sense that a therapist is concerned about his or her own adequacy to cope, they are stricken with terror and react with intense anxiety, sometimes expressed as random anger and lashing out, diffuse anxiety, confusion, withdrawal and depression, or – most difficult of all – as contempt. Events then can rapidly escalate and the relationship may deteriorate. It is very difficult indeed to cope with the hostile reactions of patients. Unleashed hostility is frightening because we fear its force and because we fear the strength of our need to retaliate. Hostility can be understood as a panic reaction. The frustrated and anxious adult patient can feel trapped and helpless, lonely and alienated from a productive society, self-esteem is bruised and it seems as if society conspires to render him or her powerless to alter the situation. Our patients may well have accepted procedures which can be viewed as demeaning, only to experience that the help desperately needed feels too little or too late. The patient who has known persistent deprivation feels alienated and diminished and tends to view the world as unjust and discriminatory. Small wonder then that distrust and suspicion colour attitudes towards the therapist. Because previous life experience has caused one to expect rejection, one can invite it by expressing anger and hostility at the anticipated or experienced rejection by the therapist.

Another, not infrequent, problem in this area is created when the patient improves, though the therapist exhibits, in supervision, no real progress in psychotherapeutic work, no growth in skill. The therapist (with qualms) may well point to the seeming progress in working with the patient as evidence of the adequacy of the work and as a resistance to his or her own need for insight and change. Yet this whole improvement on the part of the patient may be built on an intuitive, albeit static use of him or herself by the therapist who does not grow. It is the patient who adds insight and conscious control to latent levels of interest and warmth within the therapist which may have elicited an initial favourable response.

Being warm, curious and friendly are the therapist's central personality traits. Although he or she may become too involved with a patient, it is hoped that in personal analysis or by interaction and self-correction in the course of daily life and therapeutic work, it is possible to identify their own defensiveness and the reactions which may block independent movement of the patient.

Spontaneity is a part of the therapeutic interaction but beware the therapist who feels compelled to take the lead and restrict a patient's freedom, or to solve his or her own problems and seek fulfilment through the patient.

We have to learn from our own mistakes. We need to understand the patient's communications but not respond only to their manifest content. We can accept and understand unconscious processes and help to make them conscious, but in so doing we can see our connections in the patient's presentation, life history, fantasy and patterns of behaviour in life and in therapy.

In developing our own self-critical capacities we can come to accept – at times – our own rigidity and our need to think we know everything. On the other hand, if functioning becomes chaotic and lacking in surety we can recognize these 'flags' without becoming over-anxious. When patients become dependent we endeavour not to infantalize their needs by responding in an over-protective way. Patients are enabled to try to solve their problems in their own way, to gratify their own needs without having to satisfy the needs of a therapist seeking reassurance.

As therapists working with the adult patient, we need to have the humility to draw back from feeling compelled to treat patients outside our competence. Hostility and other feelings of a patient can be tolerated, but not every therapist can help every patient. We must be willing to let patients go elsewhere when we are convinced that we are no longer able to help.

There are continuing stressors for the psychotherapist in learning to handle his or her own hostility and problems with authority; in admitting the constant struggle with authority and power in the therapeutic relationship; in overcoming resistance to criticism and rejection and accepting it when it is constructive – while at the same time keeping hold of one's critical judgement and not accepting *all* criticism by authority as if it were a dictum.

There is one more reason why the psychotherapist's self-respect is of paramount significance for the therapeutic procedure. If it is true that one's ability to respect others is dependent upon the development of self-respect, then it follows that only a self-respecting psychotherapist is capable of respecting his patients and of meeting them on the basis of mutual human equality.

The psychotherapist should keep in mind that he is superior to his patients only by a special training and experience, and not necessarily in any other way. His patients may or may not have greater personal assets than he has. The fact that a person needs psychotherapeutic help in handling his difficulties in living by no means constitutes any basic inferiority. Only the therapist who realises this is able to listen to his patients in such a way that there may be a psychotherapeutic success. . . . If the therapist is self-respecting, has respect for his patients, his ability to listen will not be impaired by phantasies of omniscience or perfectionism. He will realise that he is not a magician who is expected to perform psychotherapeutic miracles, and will be able to admit mistakes, stress, distress, limitations and shortcomings, as they occur.

(Frieda Fromm-Reichmann 1950)

REFERENCES

Bion, W. R. (1965) *Transformations: Change from Learning to Growth*, London: Heinemann.

Freud, S. (1935) *A General Introduction to Psychoanalysis*, London: The Hogarth Press.

Fromm, E. (1941) *Escape from Freedom*, New York: Farrar & Rinehart.

Fromm-Reichmann, F. (1950) 'Notes on the personal and professional requirements of a psychotherapist', in *Principles of Intensive Psychotherapy*, Chicago: University of Chicago Press.

Hellman, J. D., Morrison, T. L. and Abramowitz, S. I. (1987) 'Therapist experience and the stresses of psychotherapeutic work', *Journal of Psychotherapy* 24 (2): 171–7.

Jung, C. G. (1935) 'What is psychotherapy?' in *Collected Works*, vol.16, Princeton: Princeton University Press (1954).

Chapter 7

Stress in psychotherapists who work with dysfunctional families

Philip Barker

While psychotherapists who are not family therapists may at times be faced with the task of working with dysfunctional families, this chapter will deal principally with the specific stresses family therapists are liable to face. Family therapy will be defined as psychotherapy which aims primarily to bring about changes in the functioning of family systems. While this may or may not involve meeting the whole family group at every therapy session, the focus is on promoting change in the family system, rather than on any particular member. Change in individual members of the family, which is what is often sought, may be expected to follow changes in the functioning of the family system as a whole.

Family therapy is a complex and usually challenging undertaking. Many family therapists would probably agree with Framo (1975: 18), who wrote: 'Speaking for myself, changing a family system is the ultimate professional challenge; it is perhaps the most difficult of all therapeutic tasks, but also has the greatest pay-off.' It is not surprising, therefore, that this activity can be stressful.

Wetchler and Piercy (1986) presented a wide-ranging review of the literature on how stress may affect family therapists, and in particular their own family lives. They quote Chessick (1978) and Fine (1980) who believed that listening to the problems of others 'takes its toll on the very wills and souls of therapists, leading to increased depression'. Among the possible stresses suggested in the literature are 'prima-donnahood', that is, when the lure of admiring clients tends to pull the therapist away from his or her family who do not bestow upon the therapist the same praise; and the use by family members of the therapist's profession by exploiting that member's weak spots, for example with reproachful phrases such as, 'And you call yourself a family therapist!'

Wetchler and Piercy (1986) point out that educators and super-visors in certain family therapy training programmes have recognized that the learning process can be stressful to beginning family therapists and their families and have recommended various forms of group, individual and family therapy as adjuncts to training. The necessity of such therapy is however by no means universally recognized, and many family therapy training programmes do not require their trainees to explore their own family of origin, or current family issues.

In addition to reviewing the literature, Wetchler and Piercy (1986) reported a survey of members of the Indiana Association for Marriage and Family Therapy. Respondents were asked to identify and rank in order various marital/family stressors and enhancers they believed emanated from their work with families. While the response rate was only 43 per cent, leaving the possibility that the more discontented did not reply, the good news is that significantly more enhancers than stressors were reported. The stressors checked by 10 per cent or more of the therapists who responded were:

- Little time left for own marriage/family (45 per cent)
- Little energy left for own family (44 per cent)
- Difficulty switching roles from therapist to family member (37 per cent)
- Personal development beyond that of own spouse/family (34 per cent)
- Difficulty listening to problems of own spouse/family (32 per cent)
- Spouse's family members' suspicion of being manipulated ('thera-pized') by the therapist (32 per cent)
- Setting unrealistic standards for own marriage/family (22 per cent)
- Tendency to look for marriage/family problems that do not exist (18 per cent)
- Spouse/family puts down my role as therapist (15 per cent)

The first two in the above list would not seem to be specific to family therapists, or even to therapists generally. They may be just the price anyone who works long hours and is deeply committed to his or her profession is liable to pay. Nevertheless it seems reasonable to suppose that work which daily brings one face to face with one's own past or present family issues may be especially stressful to some, especially those with unresolved family issues.

As mentioned above, however, the news in Wetchler's and Piercy's (1986) paper was not all bad. In fact the therapists responding to their questionnaire were more likely to identify enhancers of their marital/ family lives than stressors. There were also some interesting differences within the group of responders. Those earning more than $30,000 (the study was done in late 1984 and early 1985) were more likely to find it difficult to listen to their own spouses/families; and those spending more that 25 hours per week were more likely to look for problems in their marriages and families where none existed. These authors suggested that to be successful in this field it is necessary to spend more time away from home listening to the problems of others, making one less sensitive to one's own family, and/or prone to look for problems that do not exist. Wetchler and Piercy suggest that 'The challenge for family therapists appears to be one of balance. That is, how to benefit from the unique aspects of the practice of family therapy while planning for and lessening the impact of possible stressors' (ibid.: 106).

Kaslow and Schulman (1987) also discuss how the 'issues of the personal and professional life of the family therapist intertwine', and mention several of the problems listed above. Many of the factors they mention are not, however, specific to family therapy, for example, 'distressing syndromes', malpractice concerns, 'repeated terminations', confidentiality issues and 'the spectre of violence'.

THE SPECIAL STRESSES OF FAMILY THERAPY

Given that psychotherapy of any sort tends to be a challenging and complex undertaking, what is special or unique about family therapy, as distinct from other forms of psychotherapy? The following, singly or more often in some combination, seem to be the main features of family therapy which require consideration in answering this question. The list is derived partly from my overview of the literature and partly from my own experience, both as a therapist and as a supervisor of others learning or practising family therapy:

1 The added complexity, when family therapy is compared to therapy with individual clients, of having to interact with and be aware of several people at the same time.
2 The likelihood that the family members may not be in complete agreement about the changes they seek.
3 Differing degrees of motivation on the part of the various family members.

4 Attempts by family members to get the therapist to side with them, or with their sub-system of the family. The family may try to use the therapist as a sort of judge who is asked to give opinions on who is 'right' or 'wrong' or 'to blame'.
5 Feelings aroused in therapists which relate to their own past or current family situations. As the stresses and conflicts within the family under treatment become clear and, often, are acted out, the therapist may be confronted by his or her own family issues.
6 The sense of outrage which may be engendered by some of the things we learn of in the course of therapy, particularly the abuse and exploitation of children which sometimes comes to light or is reported.
7 The temptation to give advice, perhaps based on one's own personal life experiences, when it may be better to assist the family to find its own solutions to its problems.
8 Discrepancies between the personal, cultural, moral or religious values of the therapist and those of families being treated.

None of the above is entirely unique to family therapy and it might be argued that group therapy of other types can be as complex, and therefore potentially stressful, as family therapy. Nevertheless family therapy does present special challenges, and in striving to meet these many therapists undoubtedly feel under much stress. It is surprising, therefore, that few textbooks of family therapy have much to say about the stresses therapists may face. I have been unable to find it as a specific topic listed in any family therapy textbook, though there is some reference to the question of how far therapists should review, and perhaps come to terms with, their own past family experiences. The author who has written most about this is Bowen who, in a paper originally published anonymously (Anonymous 1972) but subsequently republished under his name, wrote of how:

the family therapist usually has the very same problems in his own family that are present in families he sees professionally, and . . . he has to define himself in his own family if he is to function adequately in his professional work.

(Bowen 1978: 468)

The implication of this statement would seem to be that, at least in Bowen's view, the therapist who has not 'defined himself' will not function optimally and may feel under stress, something we will return to shortly.

Next we will review each of the above possible sources of stress in turn and we will then consider how these may be avoided or alleviated.

SPECIFIC SOURCES OF POTENTIAL STRESS

1 The complexity of family therapy

It is not difficult to appreciate that having to attend to the behaviour and the communications, both verbal and non-verbal, of several people at the same time is more challenging than simply dealing with a single person. Indeed, the very process of establishing rapport, which is a vital foundation for any therapeutic relationship, is more complex. Many of the rapport-building techniques we may use (see Barker 1992: 91–4) involve matching one's behaviours, way of speaking and vocabulary with those of one's clients, and that is clearly more difficult when one has several people to consider. Another pitfall is that of being seen by family members as taking sides with one or more of the members. Avoiding this can be rather like walking a tightrope.

'Neutrality' is one of the three principles recommended by the Milan group of therapists in a classic paper (Palazzoli *et al.* 1980) on interviewing families. These authors suggest asking each family member in turn to give his or her views of how the family functions, using quite specific questions about who does what, or says what to whom, under various circumstances. This may seem like allying with the member who is being asked such questions, but the alliance shifts when the questioning moves to another person. Since the therapist allies in turn with each family member the end result aimed at 'is that the therapist is allied with everyone and no one at the same time'.

Keeping track of these things and maintaining objectivity and neutrality throughout the course of therapy, while at the same time being aware of all that is going on (or at least of as much as possible, for no therapist can be aware at all times of everything that is going on) is truly challenging, and thus may be stressful. This, no doubt, is why many therapists like to have one or more colleagues observing through a one-way screen, or on closed circuit television, and phoning in observations or suggestions, as therapy proceeds. It may also be why some professional fee schedules specify higher fees for family therapy than for individual therapy.

2 The likelihood that family members may not be in complete agreement about the changes they seek

I have pointed out elsewhere (Barker 1992: ch. 7), as also does Friedman (1985: 550), that it is important to establish treatment goals before embarking on a plan of treatment. With individuals this is usually a fairly straightforward process, but when we deal with families, it is by no means easy. Often some of the family members are concerned about, or are complaining of, the behaviour of one member, or sometimes more than one. This is frequently the case when help is sought by parents because of perceived problems in their children. The children, however, may be less concerned, or even quite unconcerned, about the behaviours or relationships of which their parents complain. This is often the case when the 'identified patient' (identified by the parents, that is) is an adolescent. Yet another, by no means uncommon, situation is that in which the parents are in disagreement about what the problem is, or even about whether there is one.

All these situations make for tensions in the therapy situation and tend to require the therapist to be a skilled negotiator in addition to possessing many other skills. Sometimes, even when you think you have reached agreement with the family about the goals of treatment, it emerges later that hidden disagreements persist. This can be frustrating for the therapist.

3 Differences in motivation between family members

This is closely related to (2). Again the therapist needs to be a skilled negotiator and must be willing to accept that limited motivation on the part of certain family members may restrict what can be achieved.

4 Attempts by family members to get the therapist on their side

Some family members seem to come to treatment, not so much to achieve any substantial change in how the family functions, but in the hope of having their opinion or point of view vindicated. Thus they may try to have the therapist take on the role of 'judge' and to say who is right and who wrong. Such situations can be difficult to deal with, especially when the therapist believes that certain family members are being more reasonable, or behaving more appropriately, than others. In these situations it is often necessary to bite one's tongue, at least for while, since delivering a judgement is usually a good way to lose the family. But biting one's tongue can be stressful!

5 Issues related to the therapist's own family history and background

Such issues can be a major source of stress, and there is extensive discussion in the literature, referred to briefly above, on this subject. It is inevitable that therapists will, from time to time and perhaps frequently, come face to face with family situations that bear a relationship to their own past experiences of family life, or to unresolved issues they are currently facing in their families. It was such a situation, concerning his own family of origin, that Bowen (1978) refers to in the article that was originally published anonymously. His solution was to go on what he described as a 'voyage of discovery'. In the paper he describes not only his family background, but also how he took a journey home and met and talked with family members with what he clearly felt were very productive results. As Bowen described this process, he felt he was able to differentiate himself from the 'undifferentiated ego mass' of his family. The paper is long and detailed and contains theoretical discussion as well as the 'clinical report' but is an important, and also courageous, contribution to our subject. It seems to carry the message that therapists who have not become properly differentiated from their families of origin carry a burden into their professional work that they need not have.

Since the publication of Bowen's paper there has been much discussion of how far it *is* necessary to explore one's own family issues while training for family therapy. In some family therapy training programmes this is considered essential, while in others it is not.

Aponte (1994) considers that therapy is 'a personal encounter within a professional frame'. While he acknowledges that theory and technique are essential he maintains that the process of therapy 'is effected wholly through the relationship between therapist and client' (1994: 3). Training needs, according to Aponte, to open therapists to themselves and teach them 'vulnerability, discipline and freedom within the relationship' (ibid.). To meet this need he and Winter have developed what they call the 'personal/practice model of training', a year-long programme at the Family Therapy Training Program of Philadelphia (Aponte and Winter 1987).

The idea that the therapist's own family life and experiences are relevant to the work the therapist does with families is not new. In 1968 Framo wrote about how, as he treated more and more families, he found himself reliving his own family life-cycle. He went on:

> While I am conducting a treatment session with my surface calm and importance, hiding behind my degrees and the trappings of my profession, evaluating the dynamics of the family before me, figuring out the strategy, avoiding the traps, I communicate to the family only a small portion of the emotional connections I make with them, the places where I touch.
>
> (Framo 1968: 19)

6 The sense of outrage that may be engendered by some of the things we learn of during family therapy

Depending to some extent on the setting in which we work, we are liable to be faced with highly dysfunctional families in which there has been, or may currently be, serious abuse, neglect or exploitation of children or even of adult family members. The abuse may be emotional, physical or sexual, or any combination of these. Such abuse may first come to light during the course of our work with a family, or it may have been revealed prior to our involvement. In the latter case the services of a family therapist may be requested by child welfare authorities who want to know what can be done to help restore the family to healthier functioning. Such families are among the most challenging of those that present to therapists. Not only is the degree of their dysfunction often so great as to make therapy both complex and difficult but the sheer enormity of the damage that has often been inflicted, on the children especially, can – certainly in my experience – be quite emotionally harrowing. This is related to the feelings of awe and even despair that we therapists may experience when faced with any clients who have been severely abused (Barker 1995). In these cases the support of colleagues, especially behind the one-way screen, can be particularly valuable.

7 The temptation to give advice rather that helping the family to find its own solutions to its problems

The temptation to advise rather than to engage the family in a constructive search for their own solutions is one that should have been dealt with and, ideally, laid to rest during the therapist's training. Family therapy is not primarily the giving of advice, though the use of injunctions, direct or indirect, is a well established technique (see Barker 1992: ch. 13). The question of when to use injunctions, especially direct ones, can be a difficult one for the therapist. Moreover, behavioural family therapy, which addresses more directly the environmental – that is, family – contingencies controlling or influencing behaviour, often does involve taking a more direct and directive role with the family.

Sometimes the tension resulting from the need to wait for the family to reach its own conclusions, rather than taking them straight to the conclusions you have reached, can be stressful for the therapist. This may be a particular problem when therapy has to be strictly time-limited because of financial considerations. In many situations the funding available for psychotherapy is limited. Third-party insurers usually limit the number of sessions, or the total sum payable over a period of time, to specific totals. This may lead the therapist to feel an entirely legitimate pressure to complete treatment in the time available. It can be hard to know whether it is better to try cutting corners by being more direct, rather than allowing the family time to adjust and find its own solutions. It is probably a result of the need to resolve this dilemma that techniques of short-term, 'solution-focused' therapy have come to the fore in recent years, pioneered to a large extent by de Shazer (1982).

8 Discrepancies between the personal, cultural, moral and religious values of the therapist and those of families being treated

We all have our own preconceived ideas, and even prejudices, about how families should be constituted and function. These tend to be limited and based on our own experiences of family life – both in our families of origin and in those of others of our acquaintance. But nowadays many 'non-traditional' families are coming for help – families of homosexual couples, families from immigrant cultures quite different from our own and, in North America as well as other parts of the world, the families of the aboriginal peoples who now represent a minority culture.

While dealing with families from radically different cultures clearly presents a challenge, it may be that those who belong to cultures nearer our own, but have different – or what we may consider deviant – values, can present even bigger challenges. How are we to deal with and provide constructive help to the criminal family – that is to say a family in which one or more members makes his or her living from activities that are illegal? And what about the family of the prostitute? Or the pimp? Or the drug dealer? Are we to judge them? We almost certainly have our own views on activities such as crime, prostitution and pimping, but should that stop us offering help to the families of such people? If there is abuse of children in such families, our duty to report this to the appropriate authorities is usually clearly set out in the child welfare legislation of the jurisdiction in which we practice. But what if there is no reportable abuse? And when does deviant behaviour become abusive?

Quite common, in my experience, are situations in which there is long-standing family dysfunction of a degree that seems to be determined by some combination of cultural factors and personal attitudes/problems of the individual family members. These factors are often multi-generational and the therapist is thus faced with the need to attempt to point the new generation in a different direction from that of its forebears. Sometimes it seems also that genetics is against one; indeed as more becomes known about the genetics of the disorders we treat, it becomes ever more clear that individuals may inherit factors that predispose them to learning difficulties, alcoholism and drug addiction, mood swings and personality problems of various sorts. Of course genetic factors are seldom if ever the sole cause of the problems our clients bring to us. Invariably they interact with environmental factors and it is with these that we can help the families we treat, something we need always to keep in mind. But our task as family therapists is challenging indeed!

POSSIBLE SOLUTIONS AND PREVENTION

How may we prevent or alleviate stress in family therapists?

First and foremost it is surely necessary for all concerned with the practice of family therapy and with the training of family therapists to be aware of the possible sources and types of stress that such therapists may face. This chapter has focused principally on stresses that are unique to, or at least more likely in, family therapists, but such therapists are also liable to be faced with the more 'generic' stresses discussed in other chapters of this book.

Prevention should surely start during training. It is important that those responsible for the training of family therapists are aware of the dangers that lie in wait for their trainees. Indeed, it is essential that all of us who supervise others who are carrying out family therapy have such an awareness.

Kaslow and Schulman (1987) suggest a series of 'recommendations for achieving balance':

Therapy for the therapist. This is undoubtedly sometimes needed although, as Kaslow and Schulman point out, 'sometimes a touch of narcissism, grandiosity, and/or omnipotence' makes it difficult for a therapist to turn to a colleague for help.

Treatment for the therapist's family. This is sometimes indicated and in some training programmes is encouraged.

Networking. It can be useful to have a network of colleagues to share the burden of difficult cases, to help bail out the therapist who has become enmeshed in a family system, or to break an impasse in the therapist/patient system. In hospitals and other institutions this may present little difficulty, but in private office practice the therapist may need to take active steps to establish a professional support network.

Transferring patients. This may be appropriate when a case proves extremely difficult. This may be because it is 'prolonged, chronic [or] falls outside the therapist's area of expertise'; or because of a poor 'therapist/patient match'.

Upgrading skills. This should be an ongoing process throughout our professional lives.

Personal care and replenishment. Taking care of oneself is certainly desirable for all those engaged in this often busy, challenging and responsible work.

Disengaging from one's professional role. One's work should not occupy one's entire life. A healthy life outside one's professional one is much to be desired.

Finally, Kaslow and Schulman list some 'warning signs' that may indicate that the therapist is 'entering a danger zone'. These are: not wanting to go to work; constant complaints about practice or feeling overwhelmed by it; a sense of foreboding or doom; feeling that life is dull, heavy and tedious; increasing experiences of negative counter-transference reactions; irritability, withdrawal, depression and/or intolerant behaviour at home; frequent illnesses of inexplicable origin; and wanting to 'run away' from it all, or suicidal ideation.

Friedman (1985) also suggests some ways of 'making family therapy easier for the therapist'. These are:

- Accepting that the major responsibility for positive change rests with the family, not with the therapist; the latter is generally a catalyst (with some exceptions, for example, extreme cases of suicidal or homicidal behaviour, or child or spouse abuse).
- Being clear about the expectations and goals of therapy.
- Role definition, including declining to accept the role of all-knowing, all-powerful expert.
- Using silence as a means of indicating to the family that theirs is the responsibility for deciding what will be discussed.
- Expressing one's feelings openly, in a non-hostile way, as a means of relieving tension and defining oneself as a 'real person with real feelings'.
- Judicious use of humour.
- Flexibility of scheduling. Sessions need not be weekly.
- Permitting the family to keep the problem when this is appropriate. Not every problem is soluble and 'an exaggerated need for success or unwillingness to accept an occasional treatment failure can place a tremendous strain on the therapist' (Friedman 1985: 552).

Finally, let us consider briefly how we may prevent or alleviate each of the specific potential sources of stress discussed earlier.

1 *The complexity of the process of family therapy.* A sound training, and the availability of support by supervisors and colleagues; the ready availability of consultation; and the use of teams and observers are relevant here.

2 and 3 *Disagreements about objectives, and varying motivation, among family members.* In these situations I find it important to bring these disagreements out into the open and discuss and, as far as possible, resolve them before going any further in therapy. It is generally unwise to proceed as long as any serious disagreements persist.

4 *Attempts to get the therapist to take sides.* This is a training issue and one of ongoing support and supervision. In such situations, as in most of those we are discussing, ongoing support from colleagues who can open our eyes to our blind spots is vital.

5 *Own family issues.* We have already considered how examining and coming to terms with our own family issues may be of help. A further discussion of this is to be found in Piercy and Wetchler (1987) who describe a 'didactic-experiential workshop' designed to assist therapists in this area.

6, 7, and 8 *Dealing with the sense of outrage we may feel, resisting*

*the temptation to give advice or use other short-cuts, and coming
to terms with personal, cultural and moral issues.* These all seem
to be matters which require the support of colleagues and consultation such as has been referred to above. Ross (1994) offers
some thoughtful reflections on how we may work within the
religious contexts of our patients. She reminds us that it may be
important to address the religious and spiritual aspects of our
patients' lives.

SUMMARY

Working with dysfunctional families is both a complex and a
challenging occupation. In addition to its very real inherent difficulties, it may arouse in therapists feelings related to issues in their
own families of origin or their families of procreation. Success with
certain families is likely to be limited and the therapist must work
within the limitations of what is realistic.

Sound, and ongoing, training; the support of colleagues; periods
of 'replenishment'; and taking proper care of one's body and soul,
are important in preventing and alleviating the stress this work
undoubtedly involves.

REFERENCES

Anonymous (1972) 'On the differentiation of self', in J. Framo (ed.),
    *Family Interaction: A Dialogue Between Family Researchers and Family
    Therapists*, New York: Springer.
Aponte, H. J. (1994) 'How personal can training get?' *Journal of Marital
    and Family Therapy* 20: 3–15.
Aponte, H.J. and Winter, J.E. (1987) 'Training the person of the therapist
    in structural family therapy', *Journal of Psychotherapy and the Family*,
    3: 85–111.
Barker, P. (1992) *Basic Family Therapy* (3rd edn), Oxford: Blackwell.
Barker, P. (1995) 'Foreword', in P. G. Ney and A. Peters, *Ending the Cycle
    of Abuse*, New York: Brunner/Mazel.
Bowen, M. (1978) 'On the differentiation of self', in *Family Therapy in
    Clinical Practice*, New York: Jason Aronson.
Chessick, R.D. (1978) 'The sad soul of the psychiatrist', *Bulletin of the
    Meninger Clinic* 42: 1–9.
de Shazer, S. (1982) *Patterns of Brief Family Therapy: An Ecosystemic
    Approach*, New York: Guilford.
Fine, H.J. (1980) 'Despair and depletion in the therapist', *Psychotherapy:
    Theory, Research and Practice* 17: 392–5.
Framo, J.L. (1975) 'Personal reflections of a family therapist', *Journal of
    Marriage and Family Counselling* 1: 15–28.

Friedman, R. (1985) 'Making family therapy easier for the therapist: burnout prevention', *Family Process* 24: 549–53.

Kaslow, F.W. and Schulman, N. (1987) 'How to be sane and happy as a family therapist or the reciprocal impact of family therapy teaching and practice and therapists' personal lives and mental health', *Journal of Psychotherapy and the Family* 3: 79–96.

Palazzoli, M.S., Boscolo, L., Cecchin, G. and Prata, G. (1980) 'Hypothesizing – circularity – neutrality: three guidelines for the conductor of the session', *Family Process* 19: 3–12.

Piercy, F.P. and Wetchler, J.L. (1987) *Journal of Psychotherapy and the Family* 3: 17–32.

Ross, J.L. (1994) 'Working with patients within their religious contexts: religion, spirituality, and the secular therapist', *Journal of Systemic Therapies* 13: 7–15.

Wetchler, J.L. and Piercy, F.P. (1986) 'The marital/family life of the family therapist: stressors and enhancers', *American Journal of Family Therapy* 14: 99–108.

Chapter 8

Stress in the therapist and the Bagshaw Syndrome

Valerie Sinason

'Stress' is one of those widely used words that appears to be generally understood and yet, when looked at more closely, proves to be a more complex concept. Coming from the Old French 'estresse' (from the Latin 'strictus') meaning narrowmindedness, straitness and oppression, it was used from the sixteenth century onwards to mean pressure from the outside exerted on either a physical object or a person. To stress a point is to make a point more emphatically, to bring more weight metaphorically to bear on a particular point. From the nineteenth century the term was also used architecturally and physically in terms of evaluating the amount of stress a load-bearing structure could manage before reaching breaking point.

Emotional stress is therefore generally understood to mean experiencing extra pressure which carries with it the fear of overloading one's psychic structure to breaking point, culminating in a nervous breakdown. However, the American Professor of Psychology and comedian, Dr Murray Banks (in 'How to live with yourself or what to do until the psychiatrist comes', LP Records), made the serious humorous point that nerves do not break down! In other words, the idea of a physical structure standing symbolically for mental structure is helpful, so long as it really is symbolical. However, it is hard to compare the mind to a physical substance that *could* break down under too much weight, without it concretely being experienced as a physical structure that *will* break down.

There is a way many of us, at times, subscribe to this concept of a mind with a physical, concrete checklist of stressors – from bereavement, disability, unemployment, etc. However, this could make us minimise the qualitative *meaning* of what the mental pain is that causes disturbances in order to underline the quantitative.

For example, Mrs T's life carries almost all the concrete external markers of stress. Indeed, she would find it hard to take out an insurance policy as insurance companies have been most assiduous in detailing the powerful external impingements upon healthy living. Her husband died at the age of 35 after being knocked over by a drunken driver whose car mounted the pavement. Mrs T was left with twin boys of 9, both of whom had a severe learning disability. She had violent, noisy neighbours on the council estate where she lived and was always struggling economically. In other words, she suffered enough adverse events to qualify for a prediction that her mind would not manage. However, in her once-weekly visits for supportive therapy as a parent with two disabled children, she showed herself to be a surprisingly resilient woman.

One morning, however, she arrived in great distress and anxiety and took a while to explain what had happened. I thought a child or close family member must have died as I had never seen her so distraught. She spoke initially in a very speedy, disjointed way. The content of her talk was about tidying up, cleaning her kitchen floor, and about a particular mess on the carpet from the remains of a crisp packet dropped by her children. I could not make sense of what she was talking about and her disjointed words were experienced by me as a mess in my mind. I felt useless, learning-disabled and messy, unable to help her tidy her mind up. Whilst I wondered about the meaning of that feeling projected into me, she became able to speak more clearly. She described how when she went to hoover the crisps it became clear the hoover bag was full. When she went to empty it, it had somehow burst open and the dust had fallen all over the floor.

This incident proved to be the visualisation of a previously unconscious fantasy that her insides had created her children's disability by contaminating and polluting them within her womb. Once this could be thought about by means of the counter-transference, her anxiety went. What was disturbing Mrs T in a way she found intolerable was not, therefore, the terrible list of experiences she had had to endure but an unconscious fantasy that had surfaced, making sense of a deeper anxiety. Mrs T provides a clear example of where the wider, unthinking use of the term 'stress' is not always helpful.

We cannot isolate ourselves from painful impingements either from the outside environment or from our own internal environment – it comes with the territory of being human. Some human beings can show resilience in peace and war, sickness and health. There are some emotionally gifted individuals, like Mrs T, who are perceived by others as walking Greek tragedies in terms of their external experiences or stressors – yet who have the mental capacity to retain a zest for life. The general health warning to 'avoid stress', and the research findings showing which illnesses are either caused by or worsened by stress, are, however well-meaning, in the end unhelpful.

'Physician heal thyself'

Professionals who make a space for the mental pain or projections of mental pain of others (psychoanalytic psychotherapists in particular), need to have a good understanding of their own vulnerable areas in order to provide the best service they can to their clients. Otherwise, the powerful feelings transferred from client to worker could lead to further problems.

For example, when I was a teacher, I was asked to offer 'sanctuary' time to children who could not learn or manage in the classroom. It was before I had begun personal psychoanalysis. I was aware, as teachers usually are, which children I felt internally well-resourced to deal with. Most people, without training or personal treatment, have some area or areas of competence that are there constitutionally and environmentally. Indeed, many people choose work that does not require abilities outside that zone of confidence.

However, knowing which areas are not internally well-resourced can be harder to come to terms with. I had just begun the observation course at the Tavistock Clinic, a pre-clinical course that is a necessary prerequisite for the child psychotherapy training but which also stands in its own right. The seminars I attended showed the unnecessary waste of human potential in children and adults when emotional blind spots carried on unchanged through lack of treatment.

I was therefore interested in evaluating, in difficult situations, what was my part in them, what was the child's, and what was the result of our particular combination. For example, just as some parents would do well with a quiet baby but experience difficulties if their baby was lively and demanding, other parents might experience a quiet baby as 'withdrawn'. The 'good' teacher who manages a noisy, deprived class might find she is lifeless when faced with a withdrawn, undemanding class. Of course, an adult who finds it hard to be with children would find any kind of child hard to be with. However, the good-enough professional, who has good-enough resources for most of his/her work, needs to pay close attention to where s/he is stressed.

I became aware that my emotional concerns focused on one group in particular. It consisted of five deprived, despairing and violent boys. Whilst I knew objectively that these boys were difficult for everybody to manage, I was concerned that what was preoccupying me went beyond that. One session, in particular, led me to take a different direction.

One of the boys entered the therapy room screaming and kicking. His sick grandmother had been refused an entry permit to come to England even though all his extended family had vouched that they would pay to look after her themselves. His fury and hurt about this racist rejection (as it seemed to me) stirred up in the other boys their own painful experiences of exclusion, from families, foster-families, schools and classrooms, and my words acknowledging their hurt and their anger with me could not be heard. Chairs were being thrown, tables kicked. For one powerful paralysed moment I realised I was frightened and, what felt worse, I did not know why I was frightened.

Was I frightened because I should be frightened because this group of boys was in a dangerous state? Was I frightened of how aggressive I might be if they did not stop? Or, was I feeling the boys' fears of their own potential violence that they had projected into me for safekeeping? In that moment the crucial knowledge came to me that I did not know! Knowing that I did not know gave me the energy to assert my authority and make the room safe again for the boys, for me and for our feelings. However, when writing up my thoughts on the session I realised that professionally and personally I needed to know why I was frightened. My own immigrant background and familial attitudes towards aggression were crucial to understand here.

While, as a teacher, my blind spots could make some problems worse, adhering to the teaching task could, on the whole, cushion the impact. However, as a therapist, the task is different, and unresolved personal issues hamper the treatment as powerfully as if a doctor who was scared of the sight of blood had to be on duty permanently in casualty.

ACP-registered (Association of Child Psychotherapists) child psychotherapists and adult psychoanalytic psychotherapists within the British Confederation of Psychotherapists have their own personal psychoanalysis during their training and the United Kingdom Standing Conference on Psychotherapy reports an increasing number of their registered practitioners who have had more intensive treatment as part of their training requirements. However, other professionals who are close to the feelings of vulnerable children and adults – hospital workers, teachers, social workers – do not include personal treatment as a necessary professional requirement. Even with the benefit of personal psychoanalysis and a rigorous training for therapists, the combination of particular clients and client groups and particular therapists may be complex.

I have personally noticed three specific areas of stress for psychotherapists.

1 When the particular problem of the client or client group stirs up something personally unresolved in the particular therapist.
2 When the extreme nature of suffering in the client or client group is overwhelming to most therapists.
3 When lack of external resources (whether legal, societal, economic or clinical) add to the difficulties of the therapist.

All my examples come from specific areas of work involving learning disability, abuse, chronic deprivation and trauma. Those who are working with such clients find they are having to get close to pain and loss on a level rarely encountered in other work. There are damaging consequences to this work if the worker is not adequately supported by supervision, a workshop, further training or their own therapy or analysis.

The sense of powerlessness experienced by an abuse victim is similar to that experienced by a child or adult with a severe learning disability. When the patient is both abused and disabled the worker also has to deal with a sense of powerlessness.

Every client group brings distinct counter-transference feelings to the therapists. Feelings in learning-disabled clients of being, for example, stupid, useless, uncomprehending, powerless, unattractive, socially denigrated and unwanted are projected into the workers. Where the therapist/counsellor/support-worker is unsupported, s/he can be taken over by these feelings, especially if such feelings resonate with similar feelings in the therapist.

STRESS RESULTING FROM UNRESOLVED PERSONAL ISSUES FOR THE THERAPIST

Mary, aged 40, came for a consultation about her patient, Emma. It was clear in the first few minutes that Emma was not the sole issue.

Settling into the armchair, Mary took a deep breath and said she did not know why she had come as she did not think she would stay in her job working therapeutically with disabled adults much longer. She said that there was no support, there was no sign of any change in the management structure, and she felt she was accomplishing nothing in her work.

It was certainly true, from what she described, that there was no support and there were no signs of change in the management structure. That was certainly depressing. However, once she began to speak about Emma, a despairing self-mutilating woman of 49, it became clear that she was empathically carrying Emma's projected feelings of uselessness and hopelessness.

Emma had been in her 'short-term' placement for fourteen years, waiting to go 'to the community', a promise regularly and tantalisingly made to her. It had never happened. The residential home in which she lived was going to close in four years but there were no plans for Emma yet. Emma had not been able to settle into what was beneficial in the residential programme because she was always waiting to be in this other community, which took on the fantasy aspects of a promised land of intellectual growth and cameradie. At the beginning of each once-weekly session, she harangued Mary about this community.

Whilst acknowledging the painful predicament Emma was in, we considered the bitter harvest she continued reaping. Emma, in fact, knew quite well that her staff-group was disorganised and had no coherent plans for her yet. However, there was a grievance deeper than the realistic grievance that was finding satisfaction when lodged in Mary.

Towards the end of the supervision Mary embarrassedly blurted out that she had been premature and her mother had expected her to be learning disabled. Her whole educational experience had been one of being observed by a disappointed parent who was sure she would prove defective. Was she too, she asked, clinging to a grievance by staying addicted to dead-end jobs? I suggested that Mary should go back into personal therapy. When she had been in therapy for her training she was not working with this client group so some of these issues had not been activated so powerfully.

Tom, aged 52, was taking more and more sick leave for backaches and colds. He was working in a unit for profoundly multiply-disabled clients who were injuring themselves. He said he loved his clients and felt deeply sorry for them. He just couldn't stand the way they hurt themselves. He then spoke of a once-weekly individual client, Eric, who regularly knocked himself unconscious. Eric's parents had died within six months of each other that year whilst only in their sixties. Their deaths were both sudden and shocking. Eric had lost his two main attachment figures and his home. As we spoke Tom could see how the emotional blows Eric had received had been translated into physical attacks and how the unspoken grief of Eric had been placed somatically inside him.

Further discussion revealed that Tom's father had committed suicide when he was 11, after which his mother became an alcoholic. The self-injury of his client group elicited his wish to repair what had happened to his parents but also reinforced his omnipotent feelings that he should have been able to stop their destructive behaviour. Underlying all of that was a powerful infantile sense of being bad, of having caused his parents to injure themselves. Inability to repair damage in his clients therefore stirred up primitive feelings of badness. Tom considered that in his past therapy he had dealt adequately with that subject but he had underestimated how a particular identification with Eric, as well as the power of Eric's projections, had temporarily impeded therapeutic work. He decided to join a supervision group.

Some therapists have sought supervision at moments where an identification with their client has taken them by surprise, impeding treatment. Mona, for example, whose 7-year-old had nearly died, found herself in difficulties when treating a mother with a dying child. Once she had understood her identification she was able to make use of the shared experience in an enriching way. Tony, whose wife had just left him, found it unbearable to work with Edward whose whole life seemed to have been spent in saying goodbye to people who mattered to him.

Such issues can crop up in therapy with all kinds of clients or patients but the therapist working with a population who are very different from his or her own family or friendship group might not recognise these identifications so quickly.

Another kind of difficulty that is rarely mentioned is that of a primitive biological response. Some patients who are profoundly multiply disabled are incontinent, smear faeces, cut themselves, dribble, smell, spit, bite, eat mucous, pull their hair, poke their eyes and are hard to understand. Shock at feeling a primitive response of disgust can make the therapist unable to think properly.

For example, when a patient of mine, Maureen, defecated and

urinated in my therapy room and rode her wheelchair over the deposit so that the smell and mess spread, I could not speak (Sinason 1993). All I could think about was opening the window, disinfecting the room and cleaning up. I could not speak until I was satisfied I could respond in a non-retaliatory way. I pointed out that maybe she felt like a piece of shit and wanted me and my room to know what that felt like but right now I was going to clean the room up and open the window because I could not think until I had done that.

Sexually abused children and adults who display eroticised behaviour in the therapy room – stripping, exposing themselves, masturbating – can also cause stress for the therapist, especially on the first such occasion. Sadly, we can become used to the sights and sounds of pain although we hope not to become anaesthetised.

STRESS IN CASES WHERE THE EXTREME NATURE OF SUFFERING IN THE CLIENT IS OVERWHELMING

In Coleridge's poem *The Ancient Mariner* we hear of a man who is desperate to tell his difficult tale to the wedding guest. The victim of trauma is also a witness who needs to pass on to others what he has witnessed, to share the pain and knowledge.

Those working with refugees, torture victims, victims of disasters, dying children (Judd 1989), patients who witnessed or were involved in murders, and satanist cult members, are bearing witness to unbearable matters. It changes your peacetime universe to take on board what people are currently doing to each other or experiencing.

When psychoanalyst Sira Dermen visited Armenia after the earthquake she spoke of the enormous sense of isolation she felt.

My plane landed at Heathrow but my own personal landing was in a series of stages. Each stage corresponded to a moment of communication when a friend or colleague who had been listening to me said something which made a bridge between the two worlds. I felt they had glimpsed that other world through my inadequate and inchoate account. I was not shut in or shut off. People wanted to know. This was my true homecoming. . . . If I needed help from others to tell my story after a short visit then we can see how for those there – what they need is an appreciation of how difficult it might be for them to tell or discover their individual narratives.

(Dermen 1991)

Hearing directly from a person who has been hurt in a profound way gives the listener a secondary trauma.

When a Swedish colleague, Anders Svensson, asked me to offer support and supervision (Sinason and Svensson 1994) it was because his patient, a severely learning-disabled patient, claimed she had been raped. As the therapy proceeded she began to provide details of rape, sadomasochistic activities, necrophilia, pornographic films, bestiality and, finally, the murder of a child. The police were called in and she was given extra security. Week by week a more harrowing tale evolved of night-time rituals, of men in masks, the drinking of blood and eating of faeces.

It took me over eight months to find the term 'ritual abuse'. Even living in another country, far from the patient's external world, I felt terrified. I carried that case with me morning and night. I worried for both Anders, his family, the patient and myself. I felt unable to speak in case I would be passing on something unbearable. After nine months, a colleague, Richard Davies, from the Portman Clinic, said 'What's the matter? Every time I see you you have had a long-distance call from Sweden and you look ill.' Only then did I realise the enormous toll this case was taking of me.

Sheila Youngson, an NHS Consultant Psychologist, conducted a survey of professionals working with ritual abuse survivors. She found that 97 per cent of her respondents had experienced stress – including disturbed sleep, headaches, sickness, nausea and volatile emotional states (Youngson 1994). Youngson's hypothesis, which was validated, was that direct work with children and adults involved in ritual abuse was 'more complex, more challenging and more professionally "draining" than clinical work with other client groups'.

STRESS CAUSED BY LACK OF EXTERNAL RESOURCES OR SUPPORT

The Bagshaw Syndrome

In *Crystal Rooms* Melvyn Bragg (1993) provides us with a concept that is extremely helpful in understanding iatrogenic stresses in the public services. Bagshaw is a rising executive with no creative skills who stands for all those who flourish at times of institutional insecurity. Mark, a creative film-maker wryly considers the depleted priorities of our current epoch:

A world made safe for Bagshaws, he thought, who manipulated it with Bagshaw precision for Bagshaw ends, which were what? The perpetuation of the Bagshaw of course, and to perpetuate the Bagshaw everything must be controlled by the Bagshaw, modelled on the Bagshaw, not allowed to deviate by any unBagshaw jot or tittle that might show initiative from the line laid down by Bagshaw, which was what? To please the Bagshaw superiors who wanted first, no trouble, and second, men beneath them who could deal with the departments and ministries of governmental Bagshaws on whom they depended . . . for the continuity of their own upper-Bagshaw existence. . . . And all of it declared to be pro bono publico. That was the rub.

A world of purchasers and providers and contracts is now the context for health service psychotherapy. New kinds of disturbances (which there will always be) and new disasters (which there will always be) do not fall into existing Bagshavian contracts. New theoretical understanding (which there will always be) and the creation of new specialisms (which there will always be) spoil the Bagshavian condomised state. Psychotherapists have already faced the stress of having to refuse referrals because the patients came from areas where there was no existing contract and where GPs were unwilling or unable to fund an extra-contractual referral.

In one of my clinical settings I made an initial illegitimate meeting with a mother from another part of England who rang in saying her little son had accused her respected local GP of being part of a paedophile ring that had hurt him. How could she ask him for an extra-contracted referral?

Bagshawism is particularly inimical to trauma. Where hurt is of an overwhelming kind it is untidy and demanding and it usually follows that there is a lack of adequate societal or legal resources. Where clients with severe learning disabilities are sexually abused there are particular stresses for the worker. As the law rarely considers an adult with a severe learning disability as a viable witness, very few cases get to court. In 1992, out of 140 sexually abused learning-disabled clients referred to me at the Tavistock only three cases got to court, where they failed. The wish to provide access to justice for a client (or indeed a relative or friend) is a basic one and where that fails there is considerable stress. It is due to organisations such as Voice and Napsac and the support of the Department of Health that Bagshawism in this area is beginning to be questioned.

On the D16 Child Protection course at the Tavistock Clinic (where I co-ran a study group with Portman psychotherapist and Senior Lecturer in Social Work, Richard Davies) we found that the biggest stress came, not just from the child's pain, but from the lack of justice and external resources. Week after week we would hear of cases where the adversarial system had put the child through further pain only for the case eventually to be dropped. Social workers on the course had the regular experience of seeing children returned to abusive parents because of failures in the legal system. An adversarial system is not the right context for delicate issues involving children and families.

Appearing in court on behalf of a child or adult client is a very difficult situation. It has not been part of psychoanalytic psychotherapy training, although psychoanalyst and child psychiatrist Dr Judith Trowell helpfully created a legal workshop in the Children's Department at the Tavistock. While psychoanalysts Dr Eileen Vizard, Dr Arnon Bentovim and Dr Judith Trowell have long experience in presenting their work to courts, and Dr Vizard is currently involved in clarifying the work of expert witnesses, most therapists are in need of further training. Appearing in court may rely on debating and logical skills that are not required for clinical practice. It can be very worrying to have to depend on an unresourced area in such a crucial arena. Being questioned in an adversarial way can also be very difficult at first.

On my first court appearance I was part of a multidisciplinary team where all five of us were called to give evidence. A 5-year-old girl had come to school regularly with worrying bruises, behaved in a sexualised way to teachers and other children and in therapy described abuse by both parents. Both parents denied it, although they agreed that her behaviour and her bruises were of concern. 'It could be anyone who did it', said her mother. I was expecting aggressive questioning and was initially lulled into a false sense of security during the following exchange:

BARRISTER: Do you think this little girl was abused by her mother?
ME: Yes.
BARRISTER: And do you think this little girl was abused by her father?
ME: Yes.
BARRISTER: And do you think this little girl was abused by her mother and father both singly and together?

ME (getting worried and not knowing where the crescendo would lead): Yes.

BARRISTER (accusingly): You thought this tiny little girl was being abused by her mother and her father and yet you let her go home to them each night for several weeks!

For a moment I was so successfully caught by his debating trick that I lost my mind. 'It's true', I thought. 'I did. I should be struck off! How could I have done that?' It took me quite a while to be able to think and then say something about how careful we had to be not to rush into precipitous action but to be as sure as we could be that the child's statements were correct.

My first significant experience of stress came in 1983 when I worked with Ali, a severely learning-disabled boy who revealed he had been abused (Sinason 1993). At that time, the Great Ormond Street Sexual Abuse Team was still new in the national psyche and psychotherapy with such a child was even newer. The combination of both factors meant that few colleagues were able to accept my account of his therapy, in which – as is now a shared piece of knowledge – once he had disclosed abuse his linguistic ability improved.

It is hard adequately to emphasise now, in a time when the Department of Health has lent its support to workers in the field of disability and abuse and when the high prevalence of abuse in this population is widely acknowledged, that over a decade ago comments about abuse and disability were seen as mad. A senior colleague did, in fact, gently wonder whether I might have hallucinated Ali's new-found language ability after disclosure.

The session in which Ali spoke of his abuse was in itself a disturbing one. I had realised for a while that many of the children I saw did not use their standard child psychotherapy toy kit. Rather nervously I added larger toys – dolls and bears and a six-million-dollar man. That week, every child I saw in three settings revealed abuse. I have written about that process (Sinason 1988) because doing anything new, being a non-Bagshaw, carries a fear of heresy with it! That case, which was also my first clinical work with an abused child, carried the strain of newness, of being close to a vulnerable child's internal and external life experience, and of facing professional disquiet or anger.

Beginnings are painful and enriching. New clinical experiences often call up in us our first experiences in other aspects of life, going back to early childhood. If we appreciate that newness will always be hard but that without newness our work is sterile and unchanging, we may refuel ourselves for the task ahead and get the Health Service and our own internal development out of a Bagshaw tyranny!

REFERENCES

Bragg, M. (1993) *Crystal Rooms*, London: Sceptre Books.

Dermen, S. (1991) 'Psychoanalytic Perspectives on the Armenian Earthquake,' talk given to the International Psychoanalytic Congress, Buenos Aires.

Judd, D. (1989) *Give Sorrow Words: Working with a Dying Child*, London: Free Association Books.

Sinason, V. (1988) 'Dolls and bears: from symbolic equation to symbol', *British Journal of Psychotherapy* 4 (4):

—— (1992) *Mental Handicap and the Human Condition*, London: Free Association Books.

Sinason, V. and Svensson, A. (1994) 'The fourth window', in V. Sinason (ed.), *Treating Survivors of Satanist Abuse*, London: Routledge.

Youngson, S. (1994) 'Ritual abuse; the personal and professional cost to workers', chapter 34 in *Treating Survivors of Satanist Abuse*, Valerie Sinason (ed.), London: Routledge.

Chapter 9

Stress in counsellors and therapists working with bereavement

Susan Wallbank

Dying, death and bereavement are an intrinsic part of human existence and counsellors and therapists encounter their effects in many different ways when working with clients. A death which happened a long time ago can unexpectedly emerge to become part of ongoing therapy; long-term clients may become seriously ill or suffer a major bereavement; a death can form part of a range of loss situations which prompt someone to seek out counselling support; the specialist bereavement counsellor, in offering an opportunity to focus on the repercussions of this particular form of loss, will be dealing with death again and again.

Counsellors' attitudes to death will affect their ability to work in what is a potentially high-stress area without becoming themselves the victims of stress. In the hierarchy of loss-creating life events, death is accorded top place in most societies. Therapists or counsellors working with a client who is facing his or her own death, that of a loved one, or who has recently suffered a major bereavement, may find themselves confronting issues of mortality. Whatever one's personal belief system, the transition from being alive to not being alive, from life to death, from having to not having, is thought-provoking and challenging. Many people have an unclear idea of what might lie ahead, and some have no belief at all in a life after death. It is hard not knowing, not understanding, not having a clear picture; a scientific society is used to having answers. Even spiritual and religious systems which offer a secure perception of the place of death within the cycle of life do not necessarily give total immunity against the threat that sudden, tragic deaths present.

Therapists' personal histories of loss and their attitude to death will contribute to their ability to work in what is a potentially high-stress area. Individuals, like societies, can be death-denying, death-defying, death-desiring and death-accepting. The individual, just like a society, will be constantly changing and developing an attitude to death as he or she comes under the influence of new ideas, or when major life events create the necessity to move from denial to acceptance or from defiant rage to a desire for an ending. Perhaps it is in that last area, the desire for death, that many counsellors and therapists have greatest experience. Dealing with a client who expresses the wish to end his or her own life is not unusual. Dealing with the client whose life is being ended through some definable terminal illness is less common for those working outside the hospital or hospice situation. It is often the rare experience, the unexpected happening that generates disturbance. If there is no bank of similar stories to draw upon from the work environment, the mind turns to the personal system and either draws from it, or projects on to it, as a way of making sense of the new.

The potentiality for stress in the counsellor or therapist working with dying, death and bereavement situations will be influenced by several factors. Perhaps the most obvious influence will be determined by the particular and unique circumstances surrounding the death that the client brings. Has it already happened? If the loss is still to come, who is dying becomes crucial. Is it someone close to the client, or the client him or herself? The specific circumstances of the illness and the ensuing practical implications will have a large effect on the ability of client and counsellor to continue working together. If the death has happened, then the influences that will affect work around it will be: When did it occur? Who was it that died? How did the death happen? The client wishing to explore the effects of an invalid parent dying eight years earlier will create a different response from that activated by the client who telephones to cancel the next appointment because a child has just died as a result of a car accident.

The death reported as happening very recently, perhaps yesterday or a couple of days ago, is likely to create a greater impact on the listener than a bereavement which happened some time ago. The receiver of the news immediately recognises that the teller has moved into a special place and, depending on the relationship between the teller and the deceased, accepts he or she is going through a unique and very special period of life. If the relationship was an important one, then the newly bereaved person may well be suffering from shock. They may be feeling sick, be experiencing palpitations or pains in their chest or stomach. They will be existing in that intensely concentrated period between the death and the funeral. Perhaps, in a life-span, there is no other time so packed with the need for things to be done. It is the numbing effects of shock that allow the business of death to take place; for information to be given and received; for forms to be completed and decisions made. Not all very newly bereaved people will be in a state of crisis but many will have moments where they feel overwhelmed by the emotions within them, by the thoughts running through their heads, and by the actions that need to be taken.

The counsellor or therapist may find that an ongoing client requires a different kind of support in the early days of bereavement. The client may request specific information, have a need to change appointment times, ask for additional support, cancel coming meetings or simply forget to turn up. The work which the client was engaged in during past sessions may appear meaningless. If that work involved any criticism of the person who has just died, the client may be confronting powerful feelings about therapy and the therapist.

Perhaps some of the potential for stress which exists for those working with people in this period of intense change rests in the importance that this time holds for the bereaved. Part of the work of grief involves the creation of a mental video, formed out of the events which lead up to and surround a death. This will be replayed time and again in the early months of grief and may be repeated for years to come. Thus, the kind gesture, the comforting remark, remain locked into the memory alongside the inappropriate comment, the rushed response, the dismissive sentence. Whilst it is possible to determine what is 'inappropriate' behaviour on the part of therapist, it is impossible to predict what the bereaved person will find appropriate to their unique situation; there will be those who value continuity above all else and those for whom any attempt at continuity seems an insult to the loss they have suffered.

There may appear to be no comparison between the grief experienced in the early days of loss and that which emerges years after the death. However, distant losses can be triggered and brought back by other life changes and the counsellor or therapist can be surprised by the intensity of reaction produced by a client who has reached a turning point in life where, once again, he or she needs to grieve for a long-past bereavement. Sadly, this natural need to re-experience grief is often wrongly perceived as unnatural, a product of a failure to grieve adequately in the past.

The death of a partner comes at the top of the scale which attempts to measure life events in terms of resultant stress. Most people who lose someone of great importance to them will define themselves, at some point in the lengthy process of grief, as feeling under extreme pressure and the counsellor or therapist working with a bereaved client is likely to encounter abnormally high levels of stress and distress. Of course counsellors and therapists are trained to work with client distress, and dying, death and bereavement are, after all, simply particular aspects of the many loss and letting-go situations whose examination forms the basis of most therapeutic relationships. Why should the losses which come as a result of death be fundamentally different from, or create greater stress than, those generated by divorce or redundancy? By what right does spouse death lay claim to that position at the very top of the stress scale? And why, when death is an inevitable consequence of the life process, a natural part of the normal human condition, should the threat of our own ending or the death of a loved one, generate periods of such acute disturbance?

Stress is generated when people are placed in high-affect situations which make large demands upon them but deny them an opportunity to affect the outcome. Excluding deaths resulting from murder, suicide or the switching off of a life-support machine, the ending of life is rarely controllable and many aspects of western society place high value on control, option and choice.

Death is often unwanted, unwelcome, untimely and seemingly unjustified. Where, how and when a life is ended usually allows for very little choice. What is most wanted, the continuation of a healthy life, is denied. Normal bargaining strategies such as tears, entreaty, pleading or threats fail dismally to affect the outcome. Such confrontation with the absolute of death is potentially stressful. There is no way the full meaning and implications that a death brings with it can be assimilated in a short period. Time and again people find their wishes confounded. People facing the ending of their own lives discover that their ability to make options and choices within their lives diminishes as the illness progresses and they become increasingly dependent on others to provide previously taken-for-granted acts of personal support and care.

In the first few months following the death a bereaved person can find that sleep and eating patterns are disturbed and he or she may well have diminished powers of memory and concentration. Long-assumed patterns of behaviour are no longer within their control.

Such loss of control can be stressful and the stress is likely to increase if there is fear of further losses – of job, income, or even of the family home. Those physical reactions often experienced in early grief – palpitations, sweating, constricted throat and nausea – may trigger thoughts of one's own death. The very assumption that life goes on suddenly becomes challenged.

A part of the work a counsellor or therapist may engage in with a client often includes an exploration of areas of potential for choice, an opening out of alternatives. When the absolute of death falls into the centre of an ongoing therapy it creates change, and the nature of that change is impossible to predict. Death is a catalyst; it may open doors previously closed or trigger regression. It can release emotion or activate withdrawal. It may bring client and therapist closer together or force a premature ending.

Many of the moral and religious codes used to instruct the young are based on the concept of 'fairness'. We are all led to believe that if we are good, good things will come to us; that if we work hard we will eventually succeed. Stories in films, television and theatre reflect these basic principles; in most fables, good triumphs over evil, the villain is discovered and punished. Perhaps no one is in a better position than the experienced counsellor and therapist to present a challenge to such myths; yet such is their power that they remain unassailably locked into society. It can be stressful to find one's belief in God challenged, to discover that the philosophy one accepted for so many years appears inappropriate or questionable. The newly bereaved client's exposure to an 'unfair' world may confront the vulnerability of the counsellor's own assumptive world, exposing him or her to new, uncomfortable concepts.

A death has the potential to change the lives of those closely attached to the deceased in a myriad of ways: emotionally, psychologically, spiritually, physically, socially and practically. The world the bereaved person previously inhabited has been shattered and changed for ever. The nature of that change is only slowly discovered as the long process of grief and recovery unfolds. With each discovery of a new aspect of change and loss there can be fresh pain and confusion before increased understanding. The counsellor or therapist used to seeing the therapeutic process as the most powerful instrument of change in a client's life may indeed find it hard to take second place, to put aside the current work, and allow clients the space they need to explore their new world.

The bereaved person in the early months of loss may be dealing with high levels of emotion – wildly fluctuating, often inexplicable and outside control. This is the important first strand of the work of grief, *the need to feel*. Such mood swings can threaten the very concept of self. 'I do not like the person I have become' is a remark made by many bereaved people. In order to survive the near unsurvivable, sacrifices have to be made. There may be little time for politeness, for humour, for patience with others' clumsiness. The tidy, controlled character may find him or herself in the midst of a world filled with emotional and practical chaos. Those who previously prided themselves on a careless happy-go-lucky attitude to life may find they can only cope with the disturbance of grief by careful planning. The bereaved will confront not only those new self-qualities gained through enforced knowledge of new situations and fresh challenges, but may also temporarily assume characteristics 'inherited' from the dead person.

The symptoms of grief can be almost identical with those associated with mental breakdown, only a thin borderline existing between the two. Perhaps the least recognised symptom of grief, but one of the most common, is fear. Fear of dying, fear of madness, fear of losing other beloved people, fear of having to live on alone without the deceased, fear of being out of control, fear of failing to grieve 'properly'. One of the greatest benefits a counsellor skilled in bereavement can offer clients is an opportunity to decrease unnecessary fear levels through an increased understanding of the process of grief. In order to do this the counsellor must possess the knowledge to determine the difference between necessary and unnecessary fear. He or she must have the skill to refer for specialist help where there is any risk to the client.

The investigation involved in reaching *an understanding of the reality of the death*, that cognitive second strand of the work of grief, initially focuses on the circumstances leading up to, and surrounding, the death, and necessitates an exploration of both the bereaved person's and others' failure to have ensured the survival of the deceased. The resultant emotions of anger and guilt often feature in early bereavement when, before the reality of the finality of the death has been fully accepted, alternative endings are still being explored. They can set the bereaved on a collision course with family, friends, professional carers and even with themselves.

Long-buried sibling rivalry, past deprivations and insecurities can be exposed by a death. Although bereavement draws some families closer together, others find they are dealing with explosive arguments, intense irritation and outbreaks of conflict in the immediate days following the death. The anger generated by such quarrels is not necessarily stressful in itself to the bereaved; in fact it may be easier to deal with than the pain, confusion and sense of helplessness of early grief. However, many people do find it stressful to be at odds with other people; it takes energy to defend a position, to justify a stance. The counsellor or therapist watching the expression of such anger may feel caught between the needs of their client to give vent to strong feelings and their own wish to make sense of the accusations, order them and allow the client an opportunity to grow through an understanding of what is happening and why. They may also wonder how they can continue to provide the safe place the bereaved client needs; how they can maintain a working relationship with a client who is likely to define someone as 'saviour' one day and 'destroyer' the next.

Death of a spouse is top of the scale of stress-inducing life events because it requires so much of the third strand of the work of grief, *the need to rebuild life without the deceased there as a part of it.* The closer the relationship, the harder this task will be. The bereaved husband or wife, the adult son who always lived with his mother, the sisters who have lived in a partnership for many years, all may have to work hard if they are to avoid the loneliness, the lack of focus and the disorientation which lies in wait for them as they move from the comparative safety of being one of a pair to the vulnerability of being single.

Of course, the fact that the life of a bereaved client may contain a great deal of stress does not necessarily mean this stress will automatically be passed on to the counsellor. However, there are many ways in which a bereaved person's stress may be carried into counselling and act as a potential trigger for stress in the counsellor or therapist. The newly bereaved person is close to the death situation. Their story is centred around that death experience which may also be re-activating memories of other deaths in their history. The work of early grief – expressing feelings and trying to reach an acceptance of the death – often flows out of the telling of the story; there is a need to describe events in minute detail. The events bereaved people describe are often painful and deeply distressing. The counsellor who specialises in bereavement will hear many stories of death; will know that dying can be painful and undignified as well as peaceful; that death is often unexpected; that almost any illness can, in extreme circumstances, lead to death and that no age group is immune from death.

The specialist pre-bereavement and bereavement counsellor faces continuous exposure to crisis. He or she will join those other workers involved with life-and-death situations: doctors and nurses, police and ambulance personnel, residential carers and funeral directors – those whose work brings them into daily contact with dying, death and bereavement. They may be a trench or two back from the front line of the hospital or the hospice, but, in listening, they are forced to follow their clients back into the theatre of pain. Such repeated immersion in death can activate a different kind of stress from that of the therapist or counsellor who suddenly and unexpectedly encounters death, dying or bereavement in a client. The cost of the creation of a system capable of tolerating such expressed pain can be high. The death of a beloved partner, a child, a much-loved parent, the loss of those most closely linked, who carried hopes, dreams, love, affection, defence against loneliness, humour, passion, creativity, history or the future, will leave behind a space and a need to grieve. Alongside those other volatile emotions of grief will ride from time to time a pure, almost unbearable sadness.

The other group of bereaved people who challenge the counsellor are those who define themselves as justifiably angry. These people might include those who have lost child or partner through murder; as a result of a drink/driving accident; through neglect or an alleged mistake by a doctor or hospital. If the bereaved feel that justice has not been done by society they carry a burden of anger, perhaps for a long time. This anger is often so intense that it is described by the bereaved as like a fire, capable of burning those within its reach. Such extreme, continuing anger is hard to work with and may create special pressure on the counsellor.

It can be hard to stay alongside the expression of pure despair. There are no solutions to grief, no answers. The wish to offer comfort can be as great for the counsellor as the friend; the desire to find a magic statement that brings temporary relief or captures some understanding of the pain; the search to produce the personal experience that links the client's suffering with a loss of one's own. Perhaps never more are the boundaries between the human being and the job description threatened than when dealing with death and bereavement.

There is another factor that can cause unexpected stress for the bereavement counsellor – the elitism of bereavement. Hierarchies exist in grief as in other fields. There is the hierarchy of *how the death occurred*. This is usually headed by the sudden violent deaths created through murder, suicide and disaster. Perhaps the greatest gift a counsellor offers a client is that of confidentiality. The price of this can be high for the counsellor or therapist working with clients who attract media attention. Then there is the hierarchy of *who is lost* where the death of a child usually takes first place. There is also that division perceived by the bereaved between those who have experienced a major bereavement and those who have not. It is impossible for someone who has not suffered a major bereavement to 'understand' the grief experienced after such a loss but then all counsellors are regularly confronted with pain outside their own experience and feelings are not transferable from person to person. No one can reach into another's head and feel their feelings or think their thoughts. Counsellors have to be wary of the traps planted by the bereaved which entice them into revelation of a shared loss experience only to find their loss denounced as insignificant by the client.

Those who have lost so much may have a great need to form new attachments. The last of the tasks of grief, *the need to re-invest the energy wrapped up in the deceased into new relationships or situations*, may increase the danger of inappropriate attachments by the client to his or her counsellor. Many counsellors recognise the privilege involved in working with people who are confronting personal tragedy and life crisis on this level. The boundaries of the contract will have to be carefully defined and the ending of a relationship which has travelled through time from despair to repair can be hard and stressful to both client and counsellor.

Many bereaved people will find themselves questioning the very meaning and purpose of their existence. 'I can see no point in going on', and 'Life has no point to it any longer.' They face that ultimate challenge, the restructuring of both their inner and outer worlds. The counsellor and therapist working with bereaved clients will need to monitor carefully the distinction which separates this appropriate response to a major loss from the expression of a serious threat of suicide. As the risk of suicide is greater in bereaved people it can be extremely stressful to assume this extra responsibility on behalf of one's clients.

So, to summarise, the counsellor and therapist working with bereavement will be exposed to scenes of death and dying. They may well be forced to confront the knowledge of their own mortality and that of those they love most. Counsellors and therapists are human. They love and are loved and those they care for may develop illnesses, be threatened with death, and even die. There will be times when the loss a client brings will affect the counsellor deeply, and bereavements locked into their past may be activated by exposure to a client's story. They will be working with people encountering high levels of emotional pain who are at a greater risk of suicide. All these factors lay the foundation for potential stress.

Although the counselling relationship is usually seen as taking place in a face-to-face situation it can, and does, take other forms. For instance, the national charity 'Cruse – Bereavement Care' primarily offers face-to-face counselling by trained volunteers to bereaved people in their own homes, but counselling is also offered by telephone, in small groups and by letter. When speculating which methods of contact have the greatest effect on the stress levels in a counsellor, it may be tempting to assume that the greater the distance between the client and the counsellor the less the stress! Working on this principle, counselling by letter ought to be the least stress-inducing mode of counselling. In this method of working, distance is translated into time. It takes time for the letter to work its way through the post to the counsellor and it may be some time for the reply to be written, posted and find its way back to the client. Letters once written, however, have a potential permanence. Clients may keep them to read many months later or to show to a friend or doctor. The passage of time may distort the emotional communication. By the time the counsellor reads the letter written in a period of despair in the small hours of the morning, the client may be feeling much better – in fact the mere pouring out of deep feeling can create a sense of release and peace. Having said that, the written word, as any avid reader knows, is capable of conveying great depths of feeling and a deep poignancy. The utter despair of loss, the fruitlessness of existence, anxiety over a child's welfare – all these may travel across land in an envelope. The counsellor cannot touch in comfort, cannot check the client for physical deterioration, has only the paper with which to work. When the counsellor is working in response to demand, there may be weeks or months between each letter, periods during which the counsellor will not know if the client is failing to write because of feeling better or much worse. Waiting can be stressful.

Counselling by telephone offers the bereaved client an opportunity for instant access and enables rapid emotional exposure. The client has control over initial access, although this may be controlled by an agreed contract subsequently. For the telephone counsellor his or her daily workload is unpredictable. It may contain a high proportion of initial contact calls resulting in referral, each call producing potent and disturbing histories, leaving the counsellor at the end of the day with a collection of powerful images. Such intense and concentrated listening can be stressful and it is essential that the telephone counsellor has time to debrief, as well as having regular supervision.

Short-term work, whether by telephone, face-to-face, by letter or in the time-limited, small-group situation, necessitates working at a level of high affect from the very first contact to the last. Such intensity of interaction takes its toll on the counsellor. Facilitators of Post-Traumatic Stress Debriefing programmes will face exposure to detailed accounts of traumatic events which took place very recently. The repetition of facts, which forms the core factor in helping the survivors of the disaster or trauma situation, becomes part of the facilitator's experience. The rapid intervention needed in such work means there is little time to prepare for it, and other, ongoing work may have to be rescheduled for it to take place in the necessary window of opportunity.

Bereaved people often express a wish to join up with others in a similar situation and find small groups valuable. However, it is easy to underestimate the confrontative qualities of such work. The group facilitators will need to monitor the various hierarchical layers within a 'mixed' group very carefully. Leaders have an obligation to ensure that those within it are not damaged by the experience, that each participant has an opportunity to contribute even if they do not wish to take advantage of that space. They also have a responsibility to themselves. The multiple tasks that face any group facilitator rest alongside the intake of different stories, each containing its own pain and sadness, each demanding acknowledgement as unique and special. Sharing the facilitation of any group enables co-leaders to carry the burden of responsibility for the group and to discuss particular difficulties after the end of a session.

For those working long-term with bereaved people there is the necessity of staying with the client's feelings over an extended period. Grief is long-term. The counsellor needs patience to stay at the pace of the client and has to be practised in maintaining a clearly defined role in the life of the bereaved person. The counsellor and therapist require good supervision to ensure they act as facilitator to grief in an appropriate way.

Counsellors and therapists who find that their work involves death, dying or bereavement will need to check their stress levels regularly. If these are high it is possible they need to look at their own past and current loss situations and examine how these relate to their work. They may also require more specialist understanding of the process of grief. The reassurance that the bereaved so often seek from those around them, that they are still on the right side of that line dividing the sane from the insane, can only be offered if those working with the bereaved have an understanding themselves of the length and the depth of normal grief and know when normal grief reactions become abnormal – for example when despair locks into chronic depression, when fear turns into phobia or becomes an anxiety state.

For those whose work requires a constant immersion in death and dying, there may be a need to ensure that stress levels fluctuate within given bands; that they remain neither at the very high position for any length of time nor at a very low level. The first indicates overload, the second may suggest the construction of heavy defence systems or an extreme level of exhaustion. Both states, if continuing for any length of time, will undermine the worker's ability to stay with the needs of those they are supporting.

Death is a natural consequence of living and normal grief is neither an illness nor a pathological state. It is perhaps fashionable at present to look for the burn-out in the working situation rather than the benefit, and there may seem to be something especially wrong about admitting to personal benefit when working with people who are confronting crisis and deep pain. However, there is evidence that many of those who work with the bereaved and the dying feel deeply enriched by the experience.

SELECT BIBLIOGRAPHY

Bowlby, John (1969) *Attachment and Loss* (vols 1, 2 and 3), London: Hogarth Press and The Institute of Psycho-analysis.
Disasters. Planning for a Caring Response. Report of the Disasters Working Party (1991), London: HMSO.
Johnston, Janet (1989) 'Haunted by memories', *Nursing Times* (15 March) 85 (11).
Murray Parkes, C. (1986) *Bereavement: Studies of Grief in Adult Life*, Harmondsworth: Penguin.
Parry, Glenys (1990) *Coping with Crisis*, London: The British Psychological Society and Routledge.
Raphael, B. (1984) *Anatomy of Bereavement*, New York: Basic Books.

Worden, J. W. (1983) *Grief Counselling and Grief Therapy*, London: Tavistock.

Wright, B. (1986) *Sudden Death. Intervention Skills for the Caring Professions*, Edinburgh: Churchill Livingstone.

Chapter 10

Therapeutic work as a minister

Louis Marteau

THEORETICAL BACKGROUND

From our earliest days as children we search for understanding. There is a constant questioning, a search for understanding about things, people, events and the connections between them. In each case the question is directed fundamentally at a deeper understanding of ourselves-in-the-world, our own existential. It is a voyage of discovery, the discovery of our own individual identity. The answers to some of these questions may even reach into the very depth of our personal security (Fraiberg 1968). This searching widens and deepens as the years roll on and the unfolding of life experience begins to impinge on us. We are then faced with the ultimate question.

At some point we are faced with questioning the very meaning of life itself. What is the purpose of it all? We live, we die, and time passes and all is forgotten. What is the meaning of this existence? Does it have any meaning in itself? What am I striving for? Is there any reason for the life I am living and the efforts I have somehow been programmed to make? It is the attempt to answer these questions which brings us into the realms of existential philosophy and its counterpart, existential psychology. The latter is, properly speaking, the study of the manner in which philosophical questions affect the behaviour of individuals. It is here in times of major crisis that the ministers of all the religious denominations find themselves challenged. Indeed, it might be said that it is their stock in trade – in their teaching and preaching, and in more specific terms in their pastoral work with those individuals who are faced with some crisis which has undermined their own personal existential (their individual and personal way of life) to such an extent that they can no longer find within it a reason-to-be.

The faith of each congregant or parishioner is contained within their life experience and their individual psychological response to it. We cannot separate the 'faith' from the person within whom it resides. Just as fluid takes the shape of the container, so faith is coloured by the individual into whom it is assumed.

Thus the individual's faith is appreciated at whatever depth the person has within their psychological capacity for such appreciation and is strengthened or damaged by the tests to which it has been put. We can apply the same criteria as we do to the physical nature of the human being. The human frame is made for physical stress and will develop through physical stress. The child will develop the ability to walk and then run as the muscles are gradually brought into stress and develop their capacity for these functions. Lack of that stress will be harmful. But if we are faced either with an unusual activity which calls for a different set of muscles, or with a muscular activity to which we are physically unsuited, we may suffer a physical crisis.

This is very much what will happen to those whose faith is for the first time tested by a challenge they find unusual or too great to integrate with the meaning in life, or personal faith, which they had up to that time accepted. It is here that the minister is faced with the individual's existential crisis.

While the minister of any religious organisation may have many responsibilities, it would also be true to say that he is primarily concerned with the existential – the reason-to-be – of the human condition. However it is also true that every single individual has his/her immediate personal concerns, professional status, expectations, and aims, the immediacy and vital importance of which may well take precedence over any examination of existential questions. In fact these may well become existential values. It is sometimes said that we are what we do and we do what we are. Our existential is a mixture of these two elements. When we suffer the loss of the ability to 'do' what we 'are' – to carry an activity which we perceive as a vital part of our professional self-image – then more fundamental questions may occur. Even our faith will have been assumed into these immediate present values and aims. In this chapter I am concerned with the stress of the existential both within the minister and with those who approach him at a time of their own existential crisis. To approach the stress on the minister we must first examine carefully the way in which the existential is built up in an individual and the way in which it fuses with the faith of that individual.

We begin by asking questions about the individual's existential –

not merely what makes the human being a human being, but what makes this human person human? Only at that point can we begin to examine the stress which will occur when that humanity itself is threatened – either in a general sense or for the particular human being. As Shakespeare put it, 'What is a man,/If his chief good and market of his time/Be but to sleep and feed? a beast, no more,' (*Hamlet*, IV. iv. 32).

There have been many definitions of existentialism. May (1958), with many others, sees it as ontological – rooted in our personal existence. Tillich (1984) sees it as relative in terms of our ongoing fate and absolute in terms of our death. He sees our spiritual existential anxiety arising relatively in terms of emptiness and absolutely in terms of meaninglessness. He sees our moral anxiety relatively in terms of guilt and absolutely in terms of condemnation. These concepts are played out vividly in both Heimler (1975) and Frankl (1969) who discuss how the whole ethos of the concentration camp was aimed at attacking the existential reality of the inmates and drove so many of them to suicide.

These distinctions by Tillich may help to clarify those areas which more properly belong to psychology and which belong to philosophy and religion. Thus we might consider that the absolute anxieties, such as death, meaninglessness and condemnation, might be the proper concern of religion, while the relative ones, such as ongoing fate, guilt and emptiness, are more properly the concern of the therapist.

This may be theoretically acceptable although my own distinction might appear to be rather more simplistic. I see the role of the therapist as being concerned with an inappropriate emotional re-action to events. Thus a state of anxiety or stress might be quite appropriate to any one of the above, or not. It would be the level of appropriateness which would determine whose concern it might be. The distinction has been somewhat fudged by the fact that we tend to use the same words to describe very different emotions. Thus the minister and the psychologist may both use the word 'guilt'. While this word is generally accepted as relating to moral or legal stand-ards, the psychologist relates it to an emotional 'sense of shame'. Normally it might be expected that a moral or legal transgression would also carry with it a sense of shame. The psychologist is concerned with the appropriateness of the depth of shame in relation to the actual guilt. The estimation of the seriousness of the crime relates to the moral law, while the estimate of the depth of the sense of shame rests with the psychologist. It may be that there is no sense of shame when the crime is very serious, or a great deal of shame when there is little or no crime involved.

The ultimate threat to our existential, our being, is in not-being – death. However, we have to go one step further and consider the individual's primary value scale. A particular individual may have placed a value on a given quality such that it has become synonymous with self. This is me, this is what I am, that is who I am, this is what makes me what I am, who I am. Without this – I am nothing. To lose this is to die. There are fates which may be seen as worse than death. This individual will be prepared to die rather than take this loss. This is the lot of the true suicide – life no longer has a meaning – s/he has already died. The physical death is an anticlimax. It is a statement that their death has already taken place.

While we may debate as to how far existential anxiety belongs to the realm of psychology or philosophy, and thus to the realms of psychotherapy or of religion, we have to bear in mind one fundamental reality. The anxiety does not exist in itself but resides in an individual. Thus it is the individual who will decide the appropriate agency to whom s/he should turn for help. In turn this decision will often be determined by the nature of the immediate occasion for the anxiety as well as personal relationships.

EXISTENTIAL CRISIS

The existential crisis occurs when the apparent 'reason for living' which has been accepted by an individual ceases to be satisfactory – has been blown apart by events beyond their control – events which, for them, have shattered the very 'essence' of their being. It may be true that they are facing a realistic existential crisis at this moment, but it may also be true that included within this will be the whole history of their past life. The present existential situation will have revived those events from the past which may also relate symbolically to the present. Every loss, every minor attack on their 'being', as it was at the time, will have been reactivated emotionally and will, in time, need to be worked through. The major event which has precipitated the existential crisis will contain within it all the conscious and unconscious material which in some way may relate to the present event. In the same way, any major emotional trauma will also have within it the seeds of the existential, and may need to be examined in the light of that individual's personal existential. Too often that personal basic existential may be taken for granted as the psychotherapist or minister concentrates on the presenting event.

The primary existential crisis occurs in the earliest days and weeks of life. Consider the world into which we are born, that strange new world so different from that which we have experienced in the womb. Every experience is a new experience, the world is completely foreign to us. In that condition we need to find some solid foundation if we are to have the courage to explore further. In those early months, and perhaps even years, we establish these solid points of reference, and an existential basis from which we can explore further. The first lesson for rock climbing is to accept that we have only four connections with the rock face, two hands and two feet. To move with security we need three in solid connection with the rock face before we can move the fourth. The child too finds these safe connections with its very being – but what happens if we choose the wrong ones, or the right ones suddenly let us down? This is a threat to the child's very existence. Already we have been presented with what I feel is enshrined in the story of Achilles' heel. This, I am sure, is an even more fundamental story that that of Oedipus.

We face a number of existential crises in our lives. Losses of every type are endemic to the human situation, while every gain we make in our lives implies a moving forward and thus a loss of what is past. Every choice we make in life implies a loss of the alternative. For every gain we must pay a price. Usually, we know the gain and we accept the price – rationally. However there may be occasions when we are unaware of the unconscious price, the hurt that will arise from our personal Achilles' heel. Here the apparently simple loss becomes an existential one. It has dredged up the primary existential threat.

There is a distinction here to be made between crisis intervention and psychotherapy. In a crisis there is a need for immediate action which may later be followed by some talking through the events which brought it about. In psychotherapy we begin with the talk and the therapist is the last one to resort to action. Thus the first need in an existential crisis will be in the form of some action which might allow the individual to regain sufficient emotional stability to begin to examine the situation at all.

Once the immediate crisis has subsided the individual may then be able to examine areas of the past, conscious or unconscious, which have combined with it to make the crisis so insupportable. But we have to bear in mind that the final existential reality – that of not-being – requires a vision that can accept non-being itself. This must surely be one of a life philosophy.

What happens when individuals are first faced with such a crisis? To whom do they turn? Indeed we may well ask what gives them, at that point in time, a reason for turning to anyone? What is that last glimmer of hope which is still hidden deep within them? For some it may be a relationship with an individual, or for some a deeper sense of reliance on their GP or their minister of religion. For others it may be that another person has seen the signs of that anxiety and has brought them to the person whom they felt would be able to help – once again this might be the GP or their own minister. This time it depends on how the friend sees the problem and its possible resolution. In turn the GP may see this as a problem for the psychiatrist, or a minister of religion, while the minister may see it as a problem for the GP or the psychiatrist. In the end the buck may stop with any one of these.

Stafford-Clark (1970) has outlined the difficulty encountered by psychiatry and medicine when faced with existential questions, questions which then call upon the doctor to become a philosopher rather than a practitioner of medical science. At the same time the minister may well feel that he is being called upon to be a therapist rather than a theological exponent, especially in the light of all the added conscious and unconscious material which will be involved in the crisis. The GP or the minister, presented with such an individual, may find their own fundamental existential challenged. Thus one existential crisis may be in danger of leading to another. Each may defend against this by redefining the problem according to their own categories, thus making it either an entirely medical or spiritual matter, so that they can then cope with it within their own existential. The difficulty is that the problem is often not as simple as this.

THE PASTORAL SITUATION

While the stress and the reaction to it may be similar for the GP, the psychiatrist or the psychotherapist, this chapter is concerned with the stress of the minister. For this reason I intend to examine it from the situation of the minister. In doing so I would also contend that working with the existential of the individual has been especially defined as a major part of the minister's role. This is supported by the definition of pastoral care given by Clebesch and Jaekle in 1964 (p. 36):

The ministry of the cure of souls, or pastoral care, consists of helping acts, done by representative Christian persons, directed toward the healing, sustaining, guiding and reconciling of troubled persons whose troubles arise in the context of ultimate meanings and concerns.

This defines as fundamental to the role of ministers their exercise of pastoral care directly in the existential field, dealing specifically with the areas of ultimate meanings. For this reason it is as well to examine more fully the stress of working with existential crisis which is experienced by the minister in his primary task. At the same time I note that the definition does not specify that the minister himself has to take on the total burden – there are other 'representative Christian persons' who may also become involved. This I will take up later. However, the primary burden will usually fall more immediately on the minister himself. It may well be that many will see such a crisis as the only reason ever to need to see a minister. Some may well see his whole role as a pastor as relating to such moments of crisis. The definition is one directed at the Christian minister. However I would see it as perfectly applicable to any religious ministers, be they Christians or not.

We must also remember that any real crisis will also have its reverberations within the unconscious. Not only will the unconscious often heighten any anxiety – it may also turn a simple crisis into an existential one. In doing so it will also increase the defence mechanisms. The closer the ego comes to interpreting the present crisis as a direct attack on its very being and as a danger of opening Pandora's Box, the firmer will the defences be against it. Thus we may well have to differentiate between a normal crisis, even of an existential nature, and one which, for this individual, has linked with it what Balint (1968) refers to as the Basic Fault, and what I prefer to call the Achilles' heel.

There are three ways in which a minister may experience stress in dealing with a person suffering from existential stress. These arise from the minister's professional and ministerial status as well as his personal one.

THE MINISTERIAL STRESS

I start from the minister's professional status as a minister. Here we have to regard the work of the minster as a sociological profession, even though many would prefer to consider it as a vocation. He has a set task within that body of professionals which relates to his theological stance and the congregation to whom he is appointed. There are for each a set of functions which are laid down by the religious body within which he is working and the situation of those for whom he is to work. These conditions may be more or less defined. They may also include quite a number of undefined tasks, some of which would be more in the realms of idealism, aims which are well beyond any realistic hope of accomplishment.

Among the tasks are those of a 'pastoral' nature. This is a somewhat undefined concept which on the one hand would seem to indicate a broad requirement for 'loving care', which may be likened to the situation of the shepherd with his flock. While there are some who would see this as demeaning to his parishioners – to be likened to sheep – it conveys something of the caring reality. At the same time his parishioners are adult, responsible and free members of his congregation with all the responsibility which this implies. In reality this pastoral responsibility should be shared with the whole of that religious group. However, it is also true that many would seem to operate on the principle that you do not keep a dog and bark yourself. The demands which individuals may make on the minister often have no clear boundaries. The relationship is often one-sided. The minister is expected to give everything, at any time, and for any length of time. This lack of any defined limits, even those of the individual human capacity of the minister, if fully internalised by the minister, can only lead to burn-out and final breakdown.

His role as pastor may also draw the minister into depths of counselling for which he may well be professionally unqualified. He may be called upon to deal with a crisis which not only involves an existential or theological problem, but which has now revealed the pathological areas in the parishioner's personality as well as all the past history of emotional trauma, both conscious and unconscious. He may not even be aware of the Pandora's Box which he may be opening. As he gets closer to these deeper feelings and to the unconscious, and as the parishioner's defence mechanisms harden, he may well begin to feel the stress himself without being able to identify it. Meanwhile he will continue to go on trying to understand, to do his best for the parishioner, but find himself more and more lost. All this time he may be unaware of the transference and counter-transference in which he is gradually becoming entangled. His lack of professional training then again leads to burn-out (Eadie 1972; Cherniss 1980; Stamford 1982).

It may not be surprising that the individual parishioner fantasises about the ability of the minister and his responsibility within the context of pastoral care. The problem really begins when the minister has introjected these expectations and then begins to see himself as a failure if not able to live them out. The more he has identified himself with his ministry, to the extent that it has become his reason to be, the more his stress becomes acute. His failure has now attacked his own very reason to be. He is now a victim of an existential crisis himself. He has slipped, so very easily, from matters which are concerned with crisis intervention, with which he should have some expertise, into the role of psychotherapist in which he may not. He has undertaken a task for which he is neither trained nor indeed has a right to expect himself to be so. But at the same time he is feeling a sense of guilt at having let the parishioner down, as well as betraying his vocation and perhaps even his very reason to be.

We now have to consider the situation of the minister who has had a deep training in counselling or psychotherapy and is faced with a parishioner who is in crisis. His training will tell him that all the vital structures of psychotherapy are in danger of being violated if he undertakes to try and help. He will now be undertaking an ongoing relationship in which he relates on two different planes – as therapist and as minister. Many would feel that these two relationships were, if not incompatible, at least liable to create grave stress for the minister. It will be difficult for him to make, as a therapist, a proper contract with suitable boundaries, since as a minister he is always available. He will be meeting the parishioner in the course of other ministerial duties and relating to that parishioner in a different way on those occasions where he is unable to relate as therapist. On each of these occasions he may become even more aware of the way in which the transference and counter-transference are having their effects. Then he is faced with the problem of supervision. If he does have a supervisor, as a therapist he is faced with the difficulty of deciding how far his ministerial role, which might even include knowledge arising from the confessional, can render the supervision less viable. He finds his ministerial role now in conflict with his professional one as therapist. At the same time his client is a member of the parish group, for which he also has responsibility, and he has to work now with the client in the matrix of the dynamics of the parish. The stress is one which resounds within his very person.

We have to remember the minister's relationship to the other members of the congregation, members who may be in some way related to this parishioner and to his or her problem. Thus the whole structure of this relationship is now contained within a matrix of formed relationships. This may make it stressful for the parishioner to admit the problem to one whom s/he knows and to whom s/he may have already built up a facade (true or false) of a strong and well based spiritual person who should not feel this way – it being seen as a lack of faith. At the same time the minister may feel a sense of guilt in not having been able to prepare this member of his congregation, at least in a broad sense, for facing such an existential crisis.

Even when he has completed his work with the parishioner there remains the relationship, and the transference which this has created, not to mention the counter-transference. If he has undertaken such counselling with several of his flock the minister will find himself in the stress of living in a matrix of transferences and counter-transferences. The process of therapy is generally greatly helped by the fact that the client is able to leave the therapist behind and does not have to live through the protraction which the transference may leave if there is a continuing relationship. Dealing with this, and the remaining counter-transference, may well place extra stress on the minister.

During the process of therapy, the minster might well become concerned as to whether this client needs a further referral. He is now faced with the stress of the decision as to whether he continues to try and help, or admits that he needs to refer to another. Whether he is highly qualified or not, his ministerial role may make him desperate to help in spite of all the elements which seem against it. How can he desert this parishioner just in his or her moment of need? To desert now, whether he is unsure how far he can help, or whether he is confident that he is highly qualified, would in either case militate against his view of himself in his ministerial role. He may begin to have doubts about his own status as a minister – for him an existential crisis has now arisen. He begins to work even harder, to wrestle with the problem which has now become his problem. He too is heading for burn-out in an existential crisis.

There are further problems arising from working with the individual who is not a parishioner. From the minister's point of view there may be a number of conflicting feelings. He may be glad that this individual has come into his orbit at this time. On the other hand, he may resent the time that he will have to spend with one who has been of little help to the parish or the community and is now demanding so much of it. There is a question of the role situation – is he taking on this person because he is a minister and sees in this contact an opportunity for leading a lost person into the supportive life of his religious convictions, or is he making a new contract of psychotherapy with a stranger? What are the roles here? Did this individual present to the minister because he is a minister, and if so, what did s/he expect of him? In the midst of the crisis there is little chance of working out the role before getting down to the counselling. If s/he has not been in any sort of touch with a minister before, how does s/he see the minister? What is s/he expecting of the minister? What is going to be the structure of the contract? Indeed, what is the contract? And without a contract how are the emotional situation and the transference going to be resolved?

THE PERSONAL STRESS

The personal stress can only be seen as a reflection of the individual personality of the minister, alongside his view of himself as a minister and as a counsellor. As a minister he may feel that it is his duty to respond 'without bounds' to this unfortunate child of God. He might even be inclined to bring the parishioner into his own home, to turn his back on the ninety-nine sheep to help the one that was lost. He might be inclined to bring that suffering individual into his own house to complete the work of 'sustaining, guiding and reconciling'. As his time devoted to this one person grows and as s/he becomes ever more demanding, what damage is this doing to his parish, or, if married, to his family? However, once started, how can he now reject that same troubled person?

THE ART OF REFERRAL COUNSELLING

There is a distinction between crisis intervention and crisis counselling. In many situations in which the minister is most likely to come into contact with an individual in a crisis, the crisis would be real, in the here-and-now. It may be a sudden death, an accident, a major illness, the loss of a child or parent, or one of the many severe problems which may suddenly strike the individual in the vicissitudes of daily life. The victim is in a state of confusion, stunned, feeling totally unable to cope, seeing nothing ahead and with his or her own personal world in tatters. There may indeed be truly an existential crisis. But it is also not the time to begin a process of counselling. Perhaps we might say that it is not even the right time for consoling, at least verbally. It is a time when all that we can do is to *be with them* in such a manner that they feel that we have entered their confusion rather than trying to pull them back into our world. It is often here that we may see the true role of the minister. It is here that the real stress of the situation has also to be accepted by the minister. The minister has to be able to enter the stress of the victim – not just to stand beside. The victim will soon be able to distinguish between one who stands beside, unmoved by the event, from the one who is able and willing to enter that distress with them. But this in itself means that the minister must accept the stress.

Any intervention may be more one of activity rather than words – not just the minister's activity, but also help for the individual to 'get moving' him or herself. It is the small practical matters which are now to be the minister's concern and his help for the victim is gradually to begin to undertake them. It may be useful here to reflect on the way in which we would help a little child, for the sufferer will have become like a little child whose world has become frightening. Here we would not discuss the realities of life, or even the spiritual dimension. Those in crisis need the warmth of feeling loved, the quiet and gentle distraction of the present practicalities.

So how are ministers to accept their role as pastors and yet be able to contain the stress? Thomas Klink (1962: 141) reminds us that 'Referral is not a pastoral failure. It is an important helping art. . . . I propose that we think about it as illustrative of the more generally useful skill of helping people to focus their needs and clarify their feelings.'

Howard Clinebell (1984) presents us with an overall view of the field of pastoral care and counselling in which I would see his most vital chapter as the one which deals with the art of referral. He sees it as an indispensable art in the minister's care of his parishioners. The minister has to ask himself if he is in fact prolonging the pain in his parishioner by trying to do the best he can, when that pain might well be less protracted in the hands of someone else. He would not think twice of referring someone to a medical practitioner if he was able to see that they were suffering from some form of disease which required medical intervention. It may well be more difficult for him to consider whether the individual is emotionally disturbed to the point where s/he needs professional counselling or psychotherapy. At the same time the parishioner may remain convinced that the problem is one of a spiritual nature, and may well be presenting it as such.

It is at this point that the delicate art of referral therapy comes into force. There are two major factors in this form of pastoral care. They are those of diagnosis and of correct referral. The minister needs to have some guidelines as to the interplay of the psyche and the soul, of the manner in which our spiritual life and aspirations are contained, and sometimes distorted, by our conscious or unconscious personality. There is no clear distinction between the four elements which make up the individual human being.

'We are a Bio-Psycho-Social-Being' (Marteau 1986: 141). We are what we are, as a unique individual, by the interaction of our physical chemistry and the environment in which we have been brought up within the family and culture of our lives. These together form our personality. Finally, we are a human being requiring to understand our existential – our reason to be. These four factors are fused together into a total unity. Changes in any one of them will have its effect on the others. However, the individual may well become aware of the changes taking place in one of these factors without realising that it has really been brought about in the first place by a change in one of the others. Thus a chemical change in the working of one of the ductless glands may well result in a feeling of depression. The change will present itself to the individual as a psychological problem of depression. In the same way a spiritual problem may present itself as such to an individual, but in fact arise from a change in one of the other three elements. Of course, the problem may well be a spiritual one, although the other elements may be having their effect. Thus the minister needs to have some yardstick for the diagnosis of the problem which this client is presenting to him. A simple guideline can be one of setting himself a limit on the time he feels it is right to give to this person to the detriment of his other responsibilities. Thus he may consider how far he has managed to help after seeing the person for four to six sessions. If he then finds no change, he has to consider referral. This is then an art in itself. He will need to have built up a resource file from the community – not just by compiling names and addresses, but by getting to know his resources personally, thus enabling him to make a personal introduction. Then he has to work towards helping the person to see that s/he needs such help. It is best if they take the first step themselves. He must also assure them that this is not a rejection and that he will continue to be interested in their progress, but will set limits.

I would maintain that ministers should relate to the group, to the parish, and only to the individual within that context. I feel that many are damaged by trying to be 'all things to all people' in so far as they attempt to be therapists as well as spiritual leaders. The primary task of ministers is to enable members of the group to take their full spiritual responsibility in relation to the rest of the group and to the world outside that group. The greatest stress arises when he identifies with the ideal of the Good Shepherd and sees the congregation as the sheep. It is also *their* responsibility to see themselves imitating the Good Shepherd to one another and especially to those in distress.

REFERENCES

Balint, M. (1968) *The Basic Fault*, London: Tavistock.
Caruso, I. (1964) *Existential Psychology*, London: Darton, Longman & Todd.
Cherniss, C. (1980) *Staff Burnout*, Beverley Hills: Sage.
Clebesch, W. A. and Jaekle, C. R. (1964) *Pastoral Care in Historical Perspective*, London: Harper & Row.
Clinebell, H. (1984) *Basic Types of Pastoral Care and Counselling*, London: SCM Press.
Eadie, H. A. (1972) 'Health of Scottish Clergymen', *Contact* 4.1: 24.
Fraiberg, S. (1968) *The Magic Years*, London: Methuen.
Frankl, V. (1969) *The Will to Meaning*, London: Souvenir Press.
Klink, T. W. (1962) 'The Referral', *Pastoral Psychology* (December): 10–15.
Heimler, E. (1975) *Survival in Society*, London: Weidenfeld & Nicholson.
Luijpen, W. (1969) *Existential Phenomenology*, Pittsburgh: Duquesne University Press.
Macquarrie, J. (1972) *Existentialism*, London: Hutchinson.
Marteau, Louis (1986) *Existential Short-Term Therapy*, London: Dympna Centre.
May, R. (1958) *Existence: A New Dimension in Psychiatry and Psychology*, New York: Basic Books.
Stafford-Clark, D. (1970) *Five Questions in Search of an Answer*, London: Thomas Nelson.
Stamford, J. A. (1982) *Ministry Burnout*, London: Arthur James.
Tillich, P. (1984) *The Courage to Be*, London: William Collins.
Van Kaam, A. (1966) *Existential Foundations of Psychology*, Pittsburgh: Duquesne University Press.

Chapter 11

Stresses in cognitive behavioural psychotherapists

David Jones

THE EVOLUTION OF COGNITIVE BEHAVIOURAL THERAPY

Even the title 'cognitive behavioural therapy' signals that we are dealing with a hybrid, or perhaps more accurately a collection of hybrids. There are still those who regard themselves as behaviour therapists and who have adhered strictly to the principles of learning theory in devising techniques for therapeutic intervention or the training of socially acceptable behaviours and skills. At the other extreme, there are cognitive therapists who base their interventions almost entirely on techniques to modify the client's patterns of thinking.

In a humorous speculation about the likely state of affairs a hundred years on, Franks (1981) posed the question about the therapists, 'Will we be many or one – or none?' Not many years later Mahoney (1988) identified seventeen cognitive therapies, although finding clear blue water between some of them would be a challenging task within itself. Haaga and Davison (1991) referred to more than twenty varieties of cognitive therapies. At the present time the many are still here, both in terms of variety in theoretical basis and in therapeutic practice. Also the many are increasing in terms of numbers of practising therapists. Nevertheless, there is a greater sense of unity in the confident eclecticism of the modern cognitive behaviour therapists.

Historically the major influences on the development of cognitive behavioural therapy were behaviourism and psychoanalytic theory – at first sight an unlikely combination, but there were those in both disciplines who felt the need for a more broadly based approach. Behaviourists had focused almost exclusively on events and actions which could be measured and recorded. Such internal constructs as intentions and beliefs had seemed outside the scope of study. Psychoanalysis had emphasised the importance of emotions, inner feelings and the unconscious which could not be readily observed objectively by the individual or by others. It was considered that change of these inner states was only possible through the intervention of a highly trained analyst.

Early exploration of the middle ground began at a non-clinical level with social learning theory and the attempts to explain imitative behaviour and modelling (Miller and Dollard 1941; Sears *et al.* 1957; Mowrer 1960). Within learning theory itself there was a growing interest in the role of intervening variables between stimuli and responses and on the importance of mediational processes to explain thinking and language (Osgood 1953). More recently, Bandura (1977) has demonstrated the importance of observational learning in the acquisition of a whole range of behaviours.

One of the first coherent cognitive theories was Kelly's (1955) Personal Construct Theory which drew attention to the way humans set up and test hypotheses about the meaning of the world. Personal Construct Theory has remained influential as a cognitive theory and has provided a theoretical base for aspects of both individual and couple therapy (Bannister 1970; Ryle 1975). It is a little surprising that the influence of this theory on cognitive behavioural therapy generally has not been more overtly recognised. There is a parallel in that recognition of the impact of George Kelly's theory on social constructionism in therapy has also been relatively low-key.

Probably the most influential of the theory-driven clinical approaches to therapy have been Ellis's Rational Emotive Therapy (RET), Beck's Cognitive Therapy and Meichenbaum's cognitive behaviour modification. A brief summary of these three approaches will serve as an outline of some of the theoretical principles of cognitive behavioural therapy. At different times authors refer to working with clients and working with patients. Mostly in what follows, the choice of term made by individual authors will be accepted.

RET (Ellis 1962) offers a cognitive approach to therapy and counselling based on a systematic evaluation of the client's pattern of rational and irrational beliefs. During therapy the client/patient is helped to develop techniques for challenging and subsequently modifying the experience of these irrational beliefs. More than most cognitive therapies, RET involves a direct element of verbal persuasion (Dryden 1987).

Beck, a psychiatrist with a background training in psycho-analytic methods, was the founder of Cognitive Therapy. The labelling can become confusing because there are more recent variations of treatment referred to as cognitive therapy which are not entirely based on Beck's work. In essence, Beck (1967, 1976) pioneered the application of Cognitive Therapy to depressive disorders and went on to extend the approach to the treatment of emotional disorders more generally. He is also famous for his development of measuring instruments to assess depression such as the Beck Depression Inventory (BDI) revised by Beck and Steer (1987) and the Beck Hopelessness Scale (Beck et al. 1974). Beck's model of unipolar depression acknowledged a vulnerability in some individuals to life stresses. He suggested that negative automatic thoughts disrupt mood, and if the individual fails to challenge them there may be a downward spiral of thoughts and affect. In the theory, a negative view of the self, of the world and of the future make up the cognitive triad of depressive thoughts. Beck also pointed out that depressed people are more likely than others to make systematic logical errors in their thinking both about life events and the behaviour of others. The therapeutic intervention is not the straightforward challenging of the negative thoughts but the much more difficult task of training the patient to recognise and challenge them herself or himself. The starting point for therapy is the identification of individual meaning systems followed by a rigorous and carefully planned intervention.

Meichenbaum (1977) came from a background training as a behaviourist. He set up a detailed theory of behaviour change which included careful and detailed manipulation of inner speech in self-instructional training. Meichenbaum (1985) further elaborated the use of stress inoculation training (SIT) in helping individuals modify a whole range of problem behaviours. Once again self-instructional training and SIT involve the therapist gaining an understanding of the individual patient's meaning system. The techniques have also been widely used with children and adolescents and in the training of individuals with developmental disorders.

It is not the purpose of this chapter to attempt an evaluation or comparison of the different cognitive behavioural approaches to therapy. Some behaviourists, such as Eysenck (1987) and Wolpe (1981), have been consistent in resisting what they perceive as attempts to merge two incompatible models, since they maintain that psychoanalytic therapy lacks validity. The emotive charge of pseudoscientific eclecticism has been made against the new cognitive movement, but the advance is much too far forward to be checked. This long-running dispute over the perceived weakening of behaviourist principles has been a source of stress for many therapists. However, the debate has been profitable despite some of the early expressions of anger. The healthy exchange of ideas between cognitive behavioural therapists continues.

THE COGNITIVE REVOLUTION

Another reason for the assertive advance of cognitive behavioural therapy can be traced to the cognitive revolution which has taken place in mainstream psychology over the past thirty years. It might be more accurate to say that there has been not just one but a series of cognitive revolutions. On the input side of the information processing model of cognitive functioning, enormous steps have been made in the understanding of processes involved in perception and attention. In the investigation of central functioning there has been an impressive progression of experimentation, theorising and model-building. Language, thinking, memory and imagery have all been studied in detail. The re-emergence of connectionism and the lure of neural networking has brought learning theorists closer to other cognitive psychologists.

The result of these developments in cognitive psychology is that of all the therapies, cognitive behavioural therapy probably now has the most extensive theoretical and experimental base. There is a clear challenge for the clinician/therapist to approach the modification of behaviours and cognitions in distressed individuals from a sound understanding of the cognitive functioning of normal individuals. For example, Watts (1986) demonstrated that spider phobics showed differences from others in their perceptual encoding of spider cues and in having poorly articulated cognitive structures for words related to their phobia.

THERAPIST FACTORS

Many attempts to evaluate outcome in psychotherapy research have reported that there appears to be a therapist factor. Typically, within any defined treatment condition, there is a tendency for reports of positive outcome to be more likely to be associated with some therapists and little improvement with others. An extensive review of therapist variables by Beutler, Machado and Neufeldt (1994) suggests that there is not evidence of a consistent pattern of characteristics associated with patient or client benefit. The importance of a warm and supportive therapeutic relationship gets support even though precise definition of the construct is difficult.

Conclusions on the importance of length of experience of the therapist were not found to be clear-cut in meta-analyses which combine the results of a range of studies. However, Beutler, Machado and Neufeldt (1994) point out that inspection of the more carefully controlled studies indicates the likelihood of a positive benefit to the client from being treated by experienced therapists. A major problem for the evaluation of non-experimental clinical studies is that experienced therapists tend to take on the more difficult cases.

Again there is some evidence that, on the whole, therapists who follow treatment manuals have a slightly higher level of success than those who do not. One problem for the interpretation of such findings is that the quality and use of manuals is by no means constant across the various types of therapy. Many therapists feel that whilst strict adherence to a manual is appropriate in a research project, it reduces flexibility in day-to-day clinical work.

This brief consideration of the complexity of some therapist variables which might be related to treatment outcome flags up two almost contradictory messages. First, there may well be similar therapist effects across different therapies. Second, comparisons between therapists employing different therapies may approach the meaningless when variables such as severity of patient disorder, extent of therapist training and the nature of the patient–therapist matching procedures (if any) are not carefully controlled.

All of these issues and many more need to be kept in mind when we turn to the question of what are the stresses which confront the cognitive behavioural therapist. Many will be similar to stresses experienced by therapists adhering to other methods of intervention. For individual therapists following any therapy there will be such questions as whether the training was adequate to meet the individual needs. Similarly, the availability of adequate supervision and peer contact are variables which potentially influence both quality of work and vulnerability to stress in most therapies.

At this stage of knowledge it would be pointless to claim that one type of therapy is inherently more stressful for its practitioners to follow than others. Even consideration of estimates of burn-out based on statistics of therapists giving up their profession is complicated by the need to evaluate a wider range of factors in the work context. For example, non-medically trained psychotherapists of various orientations working in multidisciplinary healthcare settings often experience challenges to their professional and personal self-esteem as a result of rivalry with medical colleagues.

Such issues as professional status and feeling professionally and financially undervalued are among the most frequently cited reasons for therapist burn-out. Since cognitive behavioural therapists often work in health-team contexts they have a high exposure to such professional status issue conflicts. Problems arising from hier-archical asymmetries in professional relationships occasionally arise for nurse therapists and for clinical psychologists working as cognit-ive behavioural therapists.

Professional identity, at least in part, arises from a sense of belonging to a clearly defined professional group. For many cognit-ive behavioural therapists there is a degree of role ambiguity to the extent that they hold employment contracts defined in terms of their profession of origin, which might be psychiatry, clinical psychology, counselling, nursing or education. Other therapists, such as family therapists, experience similar ambiguities in terms of professional affiliation and major work function.

A frequently voiced criticism of early behavioural therapy was that the techniques lacked an adequate theoretical foundation. Modifying the surface structure of the symptoms of distressed patients without addressing deep causes was a direct challenge to psychoanalysis. There was acrimony on both sides of the argument and the behaviour therapists were under pressure to justify their actions. If anything, this stress reinforced adherence to scientific rigour and a careful monitoring of outcome.

Nevertheless, within behaviour therapy there was an occasional sense of unease that the techniques were running ahead of theory. It was feelings such as these which made the merging of techniques with cognitive therapy an acceptable option. Cognitive behaviour therapy can no longer be accused of lacking in theory. As already indicated, if anything the stress now comes from the enormous breadth and complexity of cognitive theory which provides a poten-tial underpinning for therapy.

STRESS IN THE PRACTICE OF THERAPY

Critics of cognitive therapy display a failure to understand the complexity of the approach when they suggest that it is little more than a collection of useful techniques for modifying ways in which thought processes distort feelings and behaviour. Sadly, a similar lack of understanding is all too often encountered in reasonably well-disposed fellow healthcare professionals who make referrals to cognitive behavioural therapists. It is assumed that a few sessions of relaxation training or help with stress management can be tagged on to a broader treatment programme. Similar add-on packages might be requested for assertiveness training, improving concentration, help with impulse or temper control, and problems in children such as bed-wetting or soiling. The list could go on much further. One of the greatest unintentional insults I remember was when a psychiatrist made the request, 'Perhaps you could spare a few minutes to show my junior medical staff how to do cognitive therapy?'

In most situations involving individual therapy the cognitive behavioural therapists, in common with other psychotherapists, will share the wish to have an overall view of the patient before making an intervention. It would be fruitless to attempt to rate different schools of therapy for involvement or closeness between patient and therapist. Suffice it to say that cognitive behavioural therapy often involves the therapist developing an in-depth awareness of the world as construed by the patient.

A carefully conducted behavioural analysis, which is the pre-requisite for any serious treatment programme, involves the therapist in much more than just quantifying the antecedents of troublesome behaviour or disturbing emotions. The behavioural analysis is an essential starting point, but the therapist who wants to go on to help the patient modify thoughts and feelings will need to gain insight into the personal and special characteristics of each individual patient. In the space available some examples will be given of the range of client groups with which cognitive behavioural therapists work and of some of the different stresses encountered in these specialist areas.

WORKING WITH DEPRESSED PATIENTS

This is one of the most challenging areas for cognitive behavioural therapists. As already indicated, Beck's Cognitive Therapy provides both a theoretical basis and well-developed therapeutic techniques for this work. Therapists can also find further guidance from the work of Ellis on RET. It must be recognised that negative irrational thoughts which often underlie feelings of depression in the patient do not necessarily lack logic. From questioning and interaction with the patient, the therapist must recognise the negative spiral of thought processes and the feelings of lack of self-worth. Getting this far is intellectually challenging for the therapist but not unduly stressful. Demonstrating faults in the logic of the patients' reasoning and demonstrating that more optimistic outcomes are possible may bring temporary relief. Many concerned friends and relatives and sometimes lay counsellors get the patient this far.

The task for the cognitive therapist is the more complicated one of helping patients to recognise the negative thoughts for themselves. Helping the patient to develop techniques for challenging these depressive thoughts, despite the compelling logic behind them which is often a feature of the downward spiral, can involve the therapist in a complex self-reasoning exercise. Training and supervision are key elements in helping the therapist to retain professional objectivity in these interactions. Unfortunately, too often opportunities for peer supervision are lacking for senior members of the profession. Frequent contact with gloomy and pessimistic styles of thinking in a range of patients is a challenging experience. Therapists working day after day with depressed patients, endlessly wrestling with complex logical but irrational negative thoughts do experience stress and emotional strain.

EMOTIONAL DISORDERS AND PHOBIAS

The early success of behaviour therapy as a treatment technique was largely based on its speed and effectiveness in the alleviation of anxiety disorders. Wolpe (1981) demonstrated the effectiveness of relaxation and systematic desensitisation in the treatment of specific phobias. Eysenck (1987) developed a detailed theory of neurotic behaviour which took account both of individual differences in biological constitution and variations in normal learning and conditioning processes. Arguably, the pure behaviourist therapist was detached from the therapeutic process although able to show appropriate empathy to the patient.

With the move to more cognitive forms of intervention, the therapist becomes involved in the task of understanding the thoughts and feelings of the individual patient in a way similar to that described above for the patient with a depressive disorder. Rarely are thoughts and fears expressed by patients totally irrational. There is often a compelling logic to anxieties and fears as indicated by Ellis (1962) and Beck (1976). Many situations in life involve danger and threat but often the interpretation of threat can be greatly exaggerated.

The therapist needs to be able to understand the rationality of fears and to gain insights into the hierarchical arrangement of anxiety-arousing stimuli and situations. It is not the task of the therapist to offer the patient a better logic to challenge anxieties and fears. Rather, the patient has to be trained through the use of controlled exposure, practised relaxation, distraction and a range of other techniques to gain control over his or her feelings.

One potential stress for the therapist working with patients experiencing irrational fears or phobias can be explained in terms of Pavlovian conditioning. The patient frequently gives detailed descriptions of situations in which they have experienced acute distress. The therapist, however well trained, will experience some degree of empathy with the patient's recalled distress. A specific example will illustrate the sort of occasional hazard which can have negative consequences even for experienced cognitive behavioural therapists.

The patient was a middle-aged man complaining of agoraphobia, social anxiety and an unusually troublesome fear of heights. The therapist took a careful case history and was given a particularly vivid description of the circumstances surrounding the onset of the phobia about two years earlier. The patient had been on holiday with his wife on the South Coast taking a scenic cliff-top walk. Unexpectedly his wife chose that moment to tell him that she wanted to end the marriage. Later there had been a great deal of anger, legal battles and squabbling over property. The therapist successfully employed training in insight and desensitisation to enable the patient to overcome his fear of high places and significantly reduced the social anxieties.

Unfortunately, the following year the therapist also took a holiday on the South Coast and without conscious planning took his family on the same scenic walk as that taken by the patient. The location was recognised from the memory of the vivid description by the patient. Sadly, the therapist experienced a sense of nausea and needed to be helped away from the cliff-top. The feelings generalised to other similar situations involving heights. The therapist recognised the irrationality of the feelings and was not too proud to seek independent help to address the problem by desensitisation.

A slight diversion is justified here to emphasise the proper distinction between supervision and therapy for the therapist. Supervision should be available to support the therapist if necessary at the level of training and guidance but also to provide support and insight when the work is emotionally stressing. Problems in the therapist arising from past difficulties or life experiences generally become too complex for peer or trainee supervision situations and external support or therapy is indicated.

BORDERLINE PERSONALITY DISORDER

Increasingly, cognitive behavioural therapists are taking on the task of working with patients with Borderline Personality Disorder (BPD). The popular image of BPD patients is one of angry and threatening individuals frequently exhibiting symptoms of anxiety and depression. An additional stress for their carers is that BPD patients indulge in self-harm behaviours and are often at risk of suicide attempts. One of the greatest sources of stress for all therapists is experiencing the death by suicide of a patient in active treatment. The more common experiences of having patients who make repeated parasuicide gestures is also distressing for therapists.

Working with the BPD client-group can be regarded as an example of cognitive behavioural work at the level of crisis intervention as outlined by Turner, Becker and DeLoach (1994). In addition to regular therapy sessions, the therapist makes a considerable personal commitment and is available for telephone contact. Unfortunately for both patient and therapist the crisis situation can go on and on. The therapist can rarely feel confident that the situation is under control.

Linehan (1993) has theorised that BPD is primarily a dysfunction of the emotion regulation system and long-term interaction with adverse environmental conditions. Dialectical Behaviour Therapy (DBT) is a cognitive behavioural psychotherapy for parasuicidal BPD patients based on Linehan's biosocial theory. A recent application of DBT reported by Shearin and Linehan (1994) is particularly revealing in drawing attention to stresses on the therapists and to the importance of some therapist variables on patient behaviour.

The results of the Shearin and Linehan (1994) study have to be treated with caution because the critical findings were based on only four patient–therapist dyads studied over thirty-one weeks of DBT treatment. Patient and therapist ratings of each other were measured weekly and the dependent variable was the amount of patient ideation about suicide recorded daily. The authors report that when the patients rated the therapists as instructing, controlling and providing autonomy there was decreased suicidal behaviour in the following week. It was also found that increased therapist ratings that the patient liked the therapist were followed by decreased suicidal behaviour in the patients as a whole in the following week. The task and stress for the therapist is to achieve the right balance of control and acceptance to minimise suicide ideation.

PATIENTS WITH CHALLENGING BEHAVIOUR

This is an extremely difficult group of patients to work with and to date cognitive behavioural therapists offer the best prospects of providing a degree of behaviour modification. The pioneering work of Meichenbaum (1985) on SIT has already been mentioned. SIT was used in a number of studies to modify the behaviour of impulsive or aggressive adolescents. Variations of the techniques are still being employed. The disappointment for the therapists as well as for the adolescents themselves and their families is that the improvements in behaviour are not always long-lasting.

Attempting to conduct therapeutic work with the perpetrators of intra-familial aggression or sexual abuse is a particularly demanding task for cognitive behavioural therapists. Assessing risk and the degree of danger to the victims is never an easy task and if possible it should be a team decision rather than one for individual therapists. The consequences of underestimating the problem or failing to insist on full opportunity for disclosure are potentially devastating. The danger of physical assault on the therapist by the offender is always a possibility to be kept in mind, although fortunately the incidence of such assaults seems to be rare.

Direct work with violent and aggressive patients on psychiatric wards or in other forms of institutional care confronts the therapist with yet another variation of stress and a concern for personal safety. Many therapists find it difficult or unpleasant to acquire the skills for restraining a violent patient with the minimum amount of force.

A strict code of practice should always be followed when making home visits, particularly if there are likely to be known psychotic patients present or individuals known to exhibit challenging behaviour. If there is the slightest doubt, the therapist should not make a home visit unescorted. Social workers and community psychiatric nurses have the most frequent contact with in-home violence.

WORKING WITH INDIVIDUALS WITH LEARNING DISABILITIES

Behaviour modification has a long and successful involvement in the areas of training and improving the quality of life of both children and adults with learning disabilities. There are some well-established programmes for training children to use self-help skills in feeding, dressing and toileting. The parents of children with learning disabilities are usually encouraged to be active participants in the training processes. There has also been a lot of work in the training of children with language delay in the use of communication skills. Many of these tasks are demanding in terms of both time and concentration. The frequent reversals in progress can be a considerable disappointment for therapists.

Therapists cannot fail to be influenced by the distress and bewilderment experienced by some parents of children with learning disabilities. Some parents express great anger because they feel the care system is letting their children down. It is never an easy task to help families come to terms with disabilities.

In the area of working with adults with learning disabilities, there have been tremendous challenges in the move to community care and the provision of sheltered housing. Therapists have been involved in the direct training of individual clients in some of the life skills needed to cope with the greater independence and to support their self-esteem when faced with adversity and social rejection. The training and support of relatively unskilled staff groups in the provision of community care for adults with learning disabilities is particularly demanding.

WORKING WITH CHILDREN AND ADOLESCENTS

The question of what constitutes informed consent to treatment is a very real issue for cognitive behavioural therapists working with children and adolescents. Behavioural abnormality is often defined by teachers or parents. Yet we know from the evidence of systemic family therapists that the child is very frequently the symptom-carrier for marital problems between the parents or more general problems of decision-taking, communication and control within the family (see for example Minuchin and Fishman 1981; Barker 1986). Both cognitive behavioural therapists and psychoanalytical therapists need to exercise great care before being seen by the family to accept the child as the declared patient.

Behaviour analysis and providing advice on parenting skills can be one of the most rewarding areas of work for cognitive behavioural therapists when dramatic changes in a child's behaviour and family happiness come about very quickly. On the negative side, therapists encounter situations where the distress in the child is a consequence of parental abuse or neglect.

The question of informed consent to treatment arises in work with behaviourally disturbed children and adolescents who have high levels of aggression and destructiveness. Enlisting parents and teachers in behavioural control programmes for these children is an attempt to make them more like the rest of society.

THE MORAL MAZE

There are probably times when all therapists experience anxieties about the morality of their interventions. Occasionally the concern is around the justification of beginning therapy with a particular patient. Issues around whether the potential gains from treatment justify the expenditure by the patient are of relevance when private treatment is being contemplated. When the treatment is funded by the public health service the cost issue often takes the form of whether scarce therapeutic resources are being more effectively used if allocated to one patient rather than others.

Similar and sometimes more complex decisions have to be taken by therapists when there is a sense of stuckness or lack of progress in therapy. Clearly the nature and urgency of such decisions vary according to the length of the course of therapy and the frequency of the sessions. From the point of view of health service economy or the patient's bank balance, cognitive behavioural therapy offers a good deal when compared to psychoanalytic therapy. The time-scale of treatment is shorter, often markedly so, and sometimes even the therapy sessions themselves are shorter. To this extent the cognitive behavioural therapist has less of a moral dilemma on cost grounds about starting or continuing treatment. Usually it is worth a try. Whenever possible the patient should be given full information on the likelihood of relapse and be allowed to join in the decision-taking.

There may still be issues around whether a particular patient is suitable for the form of therapy on offer from the therapist. Does the therapist think the patient understands what is on offer and what the treatment will entail? Does the therapist mind whether or not the patient properly understands what is on offer? Some therapists may well ask what is 'properly understands'? Some may feel that if the therapy has a good prospect of benefiting the patient or the patient's family it is not necessary to give detailed explanations. What if the explanations might inhibit the client from opting to receive therapy which in the view of the therapist would be beneficial?

These questions and other similar ethical issues are not peculiar to cognitive behavioural therapy and they are not new. Increasingly there are voices being raised in sociology, philosophy and psychology for therapists to stop regarding themselves as experts. The suggestion is that the medical illness model of emotional distress or unhappiness has nearly run its course.

Naturally enough the practitioners of most therapies feel that their own version of intervention has got the balance about right in ethical terms. Generally, cognitive behavioural therapists are disposed to share their goals with their clients. This is particularly true of some of the cognitive therapies which involve intensive verbal interaction between client and therapist. Explanation is an essential part of the therapeutic process.

Traditional behaviour therapists faced a number of dilemmas around what was ethically acceptable as an intervention. Many labelled themselves as behavioural engineers, feeling they had the technology to bring about change in most behavioural characteristics. The problem is to define an acceptable line between forceful behaviour modification and the violation of individual liberties by the imposition of the therapist's value system. Even when the therapist and the majority of society share a value system, there is still a moral dilemma attached to the visitation of these values on those who might in some way be regarded as deviant.

A few examples will serve to illustrate the social and political implications of what were regarded as exciting advances in behaviour modification thirty to forty years ago. Raymond (1956) reported a case study involving the use of aversion therapy to treat a man who had a fetishism for perambulators. The outcome of treatment was that he took avoidance behaviour when he encountered a perambulator rather than attack it. Similar aversive training was used with men exhibiting fetishist behaviour towards women's underwear, usually in the form of stealing from washing lines. It was a small step further to use aversion techniques to modify what was defined in the early 1960s as sexual deviance. Most of the men in these early studies were voluntary patients who had requested help. Such were the pressures of society for them to conform.

In contrast, the use of behaviour modification techniques to treat alcoholics and substance abusers has been seen as more socially acceptable. Even here there is a grey area over what should be seen as fully informed voluntary consent from the patient. The therapist takes an uneasy position as the agent of society. Also, once again, in working in these areas therapists run the risk of physical assault.

For whatever reason, therapists have mostly stopped short of using aversive and other harsh techniques to modify aggressive and criminal behaviour. Relatively crude adaptations of these techniques have been used in the so-called short, sharp shock approaches to young offenders and the more recent experiments in boot camp environments. These schemes do not appear to have involved therapists designing control programmes for individual offenders.

Even when we evaluate more widely used behaviour modification techniques in the area of social skills training, it can be seen that there are often situations in which the therapist is making difficult value judgements about appropriate levels of functioning for the patient's well-being. Shyness can be an endearing characteristic. We might well tremble at the prospect of a world in which everyone has had a course in assertiveness training.

A recent dilemma for therapists is what stand to take on what is being referred to as the authenticity of recovered memories. A small number of cases has been reported of individuals who apparently recover memories of earlier abuse in the context of therapy. For the therapist there is the potential legal threat of being accused of implanting false memories during therapy. The British Psychological Society has published a survey and statement on the subject (1995).

There are many broader moral issues over the application of cognitive behavioural psychology in non-clinical situations. Crowd control, advertising, film and television-mediated aggression and management approaches to wage-bargaining are obvious examples. They go far beyond the scope of the present discussion.

WILL WE EVER BE ONE?

A personal guess is – not for some considerable time. The general move towards registration of practising psychotherapists is less of an urgent issue for psychiatrists and clinical psychologists. They tend to practise and receive supervision as appropriate within their own professions of origin. Perris (1993) points out that there are still inconsistencies and a lack of clear standards in the supervision of cognitive psychotherapy. Many of his remarks could also apply to the supervision of behavioural psychotherapists.

A paper by O'Hanlon (1994) suggests that psychotherapy is experiencing a Third Wave. The First Wave according to O'Hanlon was dominated by psychoanalytic theories and biological psychiatry. The Second Wave is described as the problem-focused therapies which include cognitive behavioural therapy and family therapy. The Third Wave includes narrative approaches to therapy and has been greatly influenced by social constructionism and post-modernism. Many of the techniques being claimed as part of the Third Wave are not new to cognitive behavioural therapy. Perhaps there is nothing quite like the stress of a good challenge to induce a rallying tendency.

REFERENCES

Bandura, A. (1977) *Social Learning Theory*, Englewood Cliffs, NJ: Prentice-Hall.
Bannister, D. (1970) *Perspectives in Personal Construct Theory*, London: Academic Press.
Barker, P. (1986) *Basic Family Therapy* (2nd edn), Oxford: Blackwell.
Beck, A. T. (1967) *Depression: Clinical, Experimental and Theoretical Aspects*, New York: Harper & Row.
—— (1976) *Cognitive Therapy and the Emotional Disorders*, New York: New American Library.
Beck, A. T. and Steer, R. A. (1987) *Manual for the Revised Beck Depression Inventory*, San Antonio, Tx: Psychological Corporation.
Beck, A. T., Weissman, A., Lester, D. and Trexler, L. (1974) 'The measurement of pessimism: the hopelessness scale', *Journal of Consulting and Clinical Psychology* 42: 861–5.
Beutler, L. E., Machado, P. P. and Neufeldt, S. A. (1994) *Handbook of Psychotherapy and Behavior Change* (4th edn), New York: John Wiley & Sons.
British Psychological Society (1995) *Recovered Memories*, Leicester: Report of the Working Party of the British Psychological Society.
Dryden, W. (1987) *Counselling Individuals: The Rational Emotive Approach*, London: Whurr.
Ellis, A. (1962) *Reason and Emotion in Psychotherapy*, New York: Lyle Stuart.
Eysenck, H. J. (1987) 'Behavior therapy', in H. J. Eysenck and I. Martin, *Theoretical Foundations of Behavior Therapy*, New York: Plenum Press, pp. 3–35.

Franks, C. M. (1981) '2081: Will we be many or one – or none?', *Behavioural Psychotherapy* 9: 287–90.

Haaga, D. A. F. and Davison, G. C. (1991) 'Cognitive change methods', in F. H. Kanfer and A. P. Goldstein (eds), *Helping People Change: A Textbook of Methods* (4th edn), Elmsford, NY: Pergamon.

Kelly, G. (1955) *The Psychology of Personal Constructs*, New York: Norton.

Linehan, M. (1993) *Cognitive-behavioral Treatment of Borderline Personality Disorder*, New York: Guilford Press.

Mahoney, M. J. (1988) 'The cognitive sciences and psychotherapy: patterns in a developing relationship', in K. Dobson (ed.), *Handbook of Cognitive-behavioral Therapies*, New York: Guilford Press, pp. 357–86.

Meichenbaum, D. (1977) *Cognitive-behavior Modification: An Integrative Approach*, New York: Plenum Press.

—— (1985) *Stress Inoculation Training*, New York: Pergamon Press.

Miller, N. E. and Dollard, J. (1941) *Social learning and imitation*, New Haven: Yale University Press.

Minuchin, S. and Fishman, H. C. (1981) *Family Therapy Techniques*, Cambridge, Mass.: Harvard University Press.

Mowrer, O. H. (1960) *Learning Theory and Behavior*, New York: Wiley.

O'Hanlon, B. (1994) 'The third wave', *The Family Therapy Networker*, November/December: 18–29.

Osgood, C. E. (1953) *Method and Theory in Experimental Psychology*, New York: Oxford University Press.

Perris, C. (1993) 'Stumbling blocks in the supervision of cognitive psychotherapy', *Clinical Psychology and Psychotherapy* 1: 29–43.

Raymond, M. J. (1956) 'Case of fetishism treated by aversion therapy', *British Medical Journal* 2: 854–7.

Ryle, A. (1975) *Frames and Cages: The Repertory Grid Approach to Human Understanding*, London: Chatto & Windus for Sussex University Press.

Sears, R. L., Maccoby, E. E. and Levin, H. (1957) *Patterns of Child Rearing*, Evanston, Ill.: Row, Peterson.

Shearin, E. N. and Linehan, M. (1994) 'Dialectical behaviour therapy for borderline personality disorder: theoretical and empirical foundations', *Acta Psychiatrica Scandinavica* 89, suppl. 379: 61–8.

Turner, R. M., Becker, L. and DeLoach, C. (1994) 'Borderline personality', in F. M. Dattilio and A. Freeman (eds), *Cognitive-behavioral Strategies in Crisis Intervention*, New York: Guilford Press.

Watts, F. (1986) 'Cognitive processing in phobias', *Behavioural Psychotherapy* 14: 278–82.

Weishaar, M. E. (1993) *Aaron T. Beck*, London: Sage.

Wolpe, J. (1981) 'Behavior therapy versus psychoanalysis' *American Psychologist* 36: 159–64.

Chapter 12

Stress in group psychotherapy

Meg Sharpe

Digging in the dirt
Stay with me I need support
I'm digging in the dirt
To find the places I got hurt
Open up the places I got hurt
('Digging in the Dirt'; Peter Gabriel, US Real World)

INTRODUCTION

The group psychotherapy I will be alluding to is that originated by
S. H. Foulkes during and after the Second World War. Its roots are
in sociology and psychoanalysis as opposed to medicine. Members
of analytic groups can come from a wider population than 'patients'
needing 'treatment'. Foulksian group analysis is treatment of the
individual *in* the group, *of* the group, and *by* the group, including its
conductor. Group therapists work in many situations, including
hospitals, private practices, industrial organisations, support or
charitable organisations, and with groups of varying sizes, from the
analytic small group of eight to median groups of around twenty and
large groups of sixty to 200 people.

In his song 'Digging in the Dirt' Peter Gabriel, the international
musician and rock star, evocatively describes the process of putting
one's psyche under the group microscope. The group therapist also
has to dig alongside the group, both into his/her own trials and
tribulations as well as into those of the members.

What stresses does the group therapist encounter in the daily life
of the group – stresses that may have similarities to, but also
differences from, those of individual practitioners?

In our work, inner personal experiences and suffering are constructive if they are acknowledged and utilised. Reflection on

motivations, limitations and expectations, and the personal and collective experiences from which they originate, can be useful. At the start of therapy, negative and positive experiences are evident in the circular interplay between the therapist, the group as a whole and its individual members. Patients tend to come for *cure*. The therapist has no power to do this and the sooner one disillusions the patient the better. Sheldon Kopp in his book *If You Meet the Buddha on the Road, Kill Him!* talks about a patient coming to therapy like a small child going to a good parent whom he insists must take care of him:

> My only goals as I begin work are to take care of myself and have *fun*. The patient must provide the motive power of our interaction. It is as if I stand in the doorway of my office waiting. The patient steps aside. The patient falls to the floor, disappointed and bewildered.
>
> (1974: 2)

It is similar in group therapy, and for the patient this may be a difficult experience, but Kopp says he offers 'a reflection that life is just what it seems to be, a changing, ambiguous, ephemeral mixed bag' (ibid.). The group therapist must cope with the 'expectation stress' of having to disappoint or disillusion not one, but several.

Kopp quotes Richard Wilhems: '"Everything good is costly and development of the personality is one of the most costly of all things." It will cost you your innocence, your illusions, your certainty' (ibid.: 6).

The group therapist covers a wide range of group work often in highly stressed environments – for example, intensive staff support, crisis intervention groups, bereavement groups, groups of survivors, alcoholics, drug dependency, eating disorders, etc. Similar processes appear in all these settings and I shall identify particular areas of potential stress in the daily life of a group therapist in relation to the average outpatient group. Although these situations occur also in inpatient groups, the support structure (for example, presence of nursing staff, co-therapists) may mitigate the stress.

AREAS OF POTENTIAL STRESS FOR THE GROUP THERAPIST

Starting a group

This is a critical time. The group therapist who is about to conduct his or her first group finds it unbelievably stressful. In the therapist's mind the group starts when it is put together. Fantasies, thoughts and feelings run riot. Why should this therapist and eight other people be grouped together? How? By chance? By design? What unconscious forces are already at work in all participants? Where will this experience lead? What personal change will it bring about? Will it be worth it? These are the universal feelings and thoughts of the therapist at this time, particularly with novices who have yet to develop enough confidence in their own ability. A common nightmare is that no one will turn up, and sometimes that happens. How to survive, how to ensure the group's survival, is the pre-eminent thought. And on The Night, the pulse rate is up, early tense moments focus on wondering who, if anyone, will start speaking. 'Trust the group' said Foulkes. Resisting the impulse to be a welcoming good parent is in itself exhausting. To wait, to observe, to listen can be tense in individual therapy both for the patient and the therapist. Much more *collective* anxiety has to be contained by the group therapist in shouldering responsibility for eight members' psychic welfare.

Therapist's transparency

In the group the therapist moves out of the shadow of the couch into a position of visible equality in the spotlight, sitting in the circle where every move, gesture, expression can and will be noticed. Opinions differ on how helpful therapist transparency is to the group, but when the therapist is personally stressed (for whatever reason) the group is sure to pick this up. Well-functioning groups are generous when they notice that something is clearly going on, and they tend to respond by getting on with their business, by not being difficult, by not making demands, and by somehow creating space for the therapist to get it together. In one hospital group, a very depressed doctor/therapist was 'held' by his group in this way for some time before his state was noticed and he was hospitalised. Then it emerged that the group had been giving him therapy, supporting him in his distress, sitting with him through his tears, fearful that he might lose his job if they told anyone – an example of therapy in the group by the group and of the group.

Difficult patients

These are common to all groups. They may produce a crisis that can rock the group as a whole or rock individual members including the conductor.

The monopoliser needs to be silenced or others will be deluged. The therapist has to look at why the group allows this, at the same time checking whether the patient is hiding his/her true self behind words.

The complainer or help-rejecting patient can produce utter frustration; eventually faith in the group process may suffer and members absent themselves. This kind of patient has highly conflictual feelings about dependency and needs gratification. The members need to be encouraged (often by a fed-up therapist) to provide feedback on what kind of communication helps them to feel closer and what kind pushes them away.

The acutely psychotic patient. Containing a psychotic breakdown in the group and the subsequent hospitalisation of a patient can have a devastating effect and the group may pay a heavy price.

> J, a young man who had a florid breakdown in an outpatient group created an upheaval. The group was left with feelings of guilt, fear of madness and anger about the disruption. They feared they had driven him mad and aggression went underground for a long period as members were fearful of driving someone else mad. One young woman was severely shaken by the ordeal. She couldn't cope and left the group. She was terrified that her own psychic health was far from stable. The therapist, severely tested, struggled with guilt too and with her own incompetence, and endured sleepless nights worrying whether the group would disintegrate.

This kind of event is less stressful in a hospital setting where collegiate support may be accessible.

The seriously disturbed. A manic patient can create a major crisis and the therapist must act. Similarly, a patient who attends high on drugs or drink needs to be dealt with in order to protect the group norms. A disruptive patient can threaten cohesiveness and demoralise other members. Anxiety increases and participation is inhibited. But to remove such a person will not only increase the patient's isolation but also force him into a deviant role and decrease any motivation for treatment. Nitsun (1991) would argue that the antagonistic member is the leader of a different manifestation of anti-group forces, powerful destructive resistance. The group therapist needs to work with this so that the difficult patient might learn and heal through the process. But the patient may have to leave.

Dropouts usually manifest ways of avoiding experience and re-membering but they drain the energy of the group and threaten stability and impede cohesiveness. The group feels devalued implicitly and explicitly as does the therapist, who must explore both the internal and external factors.

Miscellaneous difficulties

Sub-grouping is a high potential risk if there is a conspiracy of silence, but it can produce gain if this is explored openly and confronted. For example, meeting outside the group can produce a crisis if it is not dealt with. It needs interpreting rather than punishing.

Dealing with illness. The fate of a patient suffering from cancer diagnosed while in the group, for example, is a *group* crisis and it is a stressful time for the therapist who needs to use every resource to keep the group focusing on, and not avoiding, whatever feelings arise, while at the same time endeavouring to enable the patient to face the illness.

A breach of confidentiality is always stressful and cannot be ignored. This type of lapse is not confined to patients alone. Therapists must always remember that the group can be damaged by their own carelessness, and everyone can suffer.

Other situations that may provoke stress include:

Hostility/rage/anger. Once a group has passed the initial stage of reliance on the all-caring, omnipotent parent, then hostility, ambivalence, disappointment and rage appear. It is not always open, but often concealed in, for example, complaints about a course, a training programme, or an outside authority. If the conductor remains aloof and disengaged, or repressive, or attempts to deflect attack, defences will be set up and free-floating communication blocked. Attempts to foster a receptive attitude to hostility may have a potentially constructive affect.

Conflict is a general feature of the therapeutic process and is inevitable in group development – a high-risk, high-gain process which can *sabotage* or *facilitate*. It can be oblique hostility, in the form of put-downs, condescension or exclusion of a new member, or it can be directly explosive and threatening; either mode is counter-productive. The therapist's task is to open up the covert material and utilise it to promote interpersonal learning. Direct anger can be destructive when it takes the form of repeated attacks on another member, the therapist, or the group as a whole. Not all groups can tolerate the same level of conflict; the stage of the group's development is a major factor. Therapists have to share the stress but must intervene vigorously to keep conflict within constructive bounds – everyone should be able to learn something from an angry interaction.

Here is an example of systematic aggression and persecution endured by a therapist:

Y was argumentative at the initial consultation, imperiously and arrogantly questioning in a disdainful manner every comment the therapist made. The therapist, X, realising inherent narcissistic injury, swallowed all this and offered her a place in his group. Then began a year of persistent, venomous attack on X – he was the bad father, the stupid father, whom she hated with an intensity that was alarming for some members and also for the therapist. She was intensely competitive – every comment the therapist made was assaulted by her, denigrated with rolling eyes and loud sighs. The group experienced her as very controlling but also at times helpful, and felt she pushed them to the limits of endurance which, importantly, they could survive. (Three had been severely ill and hospitalised in the recent past.) Most were afraid of Y but they recognised her desperation and underlying intense need to be loved. The therapist found her increasingly intolerable and began to dread the weekly abuse and no longer enjoyed his group. In supervision he explored his counter-transference in an attempt to understand what was going on. In a way he liked Y and certainly respected her intellect. The hostility may have contained an important message so he continued to struggle to interpret, to endure and to reach her, to no avail. Y finally said she was leaving. Like a good, well-trained therapist X questioned this decision – he hated to fail. The group questioned too. The group was fine, Y said, X was the problem – stupid, superficial, non-analytic, ridiculously airy-fairy, a thoroughly bad therapist. She left. X was relieved but also upset at failing to contain an unhappy patient. Nevertheless his stress level diminished rapidly!

There are several types of crisis that may arise in the life of a group and which induce stress:

Change of Therapist. A crisis arises when the group therapist has to change, whatever the reason. I have written elsewhere about this process, which is confusing, disturbing and difficult for both the therapist and the group (Sharpe 1991). In general, unplanned change-overs are the most traumatic, and planned ones are just traumatic or difficult. Those unplanned include death and illness. Those which are planned include retirement, resignation and scheduled absences. The loss cycle is repeated at intervals and the therapist who takes over has to survive, to be able to deal with his/her own losses and grief because it is certain he/she will have to help patients endure during their losses and grief.

Death itself is painful enough to deal with. A suicide is a different crisis for a group; feelings of loss, failure, anger, self-blame, lack of responsibility, all flood in. The therapist, under strain, also struggles with personal and professional difficulties over this, but still must continue to steer and support the group. In a hospital setting, I have experienced the *large group* as an invaluable resource in which to air and deal with the multiplicity of responses to tragedy. One hospital always convened a large community group at whatever time of the day or night whenever a catastrophe or a suicide occurred. This containment in, of, and by the community as a whole is significantly stress-reducing, particularly for the group therapist involved, who, in a different situation, would have to contain the distress alone.

Termination, meaning the departure of an individual from the group, may produce trauma and stress for all concerned. The level depends on how the ending is achieved. Ideally in slow-open groups, each person leaves in his/her own time, one member leaves and a new one joins.

Foulkes speaks about the spiral notion of exit (1975): if one exit is not taken, the next one may be a while ahead, hopefully on a higher level of the spiral. This is like climbing a lighthouse tower (you can see more from the window at each level, using the landscape as a metaphor for the psyche) but the 'right' point of exit needs to be recognised, otherwise group dependency may set in. Leaving a group is a matter for the whole group, and has a deep meaning for everyone, not just for the person leaving. Nina Coltart, in *How to Survive as a Psychotherapist* (1992), comments on the uniquely arbitrary way the therapeutic relationship is terminated. It is important that the end should be absolute in order to free the patient from the group.

Another psychoanalyst, John Klauber, writes about a patient always knowing best when he/she has had enough analysis. He says termination by the therapist may produce trauma (in groups too) and only the patient's decision to terminate can preserve the precarious identity he has acquired (Klauber 1986).

There are many reasons for termination that are wrong – for example, fear of anxiety, self-punishment, repetition of old object relations projected on to the group, the therapist or one member. The group may need to get rid of one of its members. Any decision to leave requires extended exploration and analysis. In a stable group there is usually agreement as to when one member should finish. Nevertheless, separation anxieties arise and the group feels threatened; envy often stirs – the one leaving receives special care, understanding and concern. The leaver re-experiences and works through early losses and separations from the past. It is very much a mourning process which involves everyone. 'Ending' itself is an aim that needs to be worked on. It does not take place immediately and might need to be be broached long before the group thinks it is viable.

The following example illustrates an unsatisfactory termination which produced stress in all concerned:

H joined a group at a time when the emotional climate was intense. He felt bleak, overtly depressed, suffered from insomnia, had marital difficulties, hated his work and generally felt he had a black hole inside him. He had had some individual counselling but said it wasn't right for him, so he stopped it. He was an only child of unhappy parents, a non-communicative depressed father and a violent mother. He now had a young child and was understandably worried about how he would cope. In the past he dealt with his depression by drinking and taking sleeping tablets. He seemed well-motivated and was beginning to settle down, although his restlessness was always apparent. Several times he expressed his dissatisfaction with the group and the therapist and underneath his seeming passivity lurked a murderous rage. His verbal dexterity was ably illustrated by his occasional cutting remarks that went straight for the jugular. The group closed for the Christmas break in an uneventful and prepared way. He seemed to be settling down. The therapist returned to find a brief letter from H saying he was not coming back. He was asked to return and discuss this with the group and replied tersely saying that his decision was final. The therapist wrote again expressing regret and inviting him to return in the future if he wished. Another letter arrived saying that he was in individual therapy and he apologised for not saying goodbye. The therapist was upset and and wondered who had taken him into individual therapy without consultation. The group was angry and felt he had kicked them as his mother had kicked him. His manner and timing of departure seemed to be an expression of his rage with his 'mother-group'. It was effective in terms of inflicting pain and of course it was effective in making the group explore their part in this – a need to get rid of him perhaps that he had unconsciously assimilated? There emerged previously un-voiced resentment about his initial entry into the group.

Ending a group – letting it go

A planned ending of a group is a many-faceted and stressful process during which the conductor has to be constantly alert, attentive both to the group and to each individual in it, helping the working and reworking through phases of mourning as described so aptly by Bowlby (1974):

- *Protest* (grief, separation anxiety, denial, sadness, aggression)
- *Despair* (disorganisation, nothing is any good)
- *Detachment* from the lost object (reorganisation)

This loss cycle is repeated at intervals and needs constant attention from the therapist who endeavours to allow this process to happen without blocking it. The therapist also has to let go of the group, like relinquishing a child, and to cope with the stress and pain of very real bereavement. Meticulous attention to this most important event is needed to help the participants to face their new 'group-less' lives creatively.

At the beginning of a year, a long-standing group with a population which had been stable for some years, was reaching a point of decision. Five out of eight members were planning to leave within a short time of each other, all for good reasons. Of those remaining, one had been in the group for eight years and was working on her separation anyway, one planned to leave in a few months and the remaining male was undecided and somewhat ambivalent about the whole process. So here was a group that would slowly disintegrate throughout the coming year. What to do? Of course I could replace each member in turn. That would mean a year of working on starting and ending and a long period of instability for any newcomers. I thought long and hard about it and decided that closing the group forever might be the best decision, allowing members to leave as and when. I put this to the group. Shock and anger gradually dissolved into uncertainty and both positive and negative aspects were endlessly discussed with no decision coming from the group. In March I made the decision and said the group would close at Christmas. This produced some relief and then, one by one, members decided they would stay together and end together in December. Then work began on the long process of separation, loss, and death of the group. Members went through old cycles, symptoms recurred, many seemed sicker, depression returned, with helplessness and rage at the seemingly uncaring parent who was throwing them out – especially from the four foreigners in the group who had found kinship and siblings there. Then, just when I was wondering whether I had been too precipitate, the group mood changed to one of optimism, and new energy began to flow. Members realistically appraised the work they had done, the changes they had made and acknowledged what had to be accomplished in their future groupless lives. We had a good ending; one by one members left the room, leaving me with the empty chairs that these particular people would never fill again. I felt sad. I have not yet replaced that group. Every Wednesday I turn off the lights at 6.15 p.m. and leave. A suitable period of mourning has to pass for a 20-year old group and those who had comprised it and taken part in its life.

LARGE GROUPS

Whilst I do not propose to discuss the particular characteristics of large groups, it is a reality that most group therapists have to cope with or convene large groups at intervals in their careers, and deal with the special sort of stress that they can generate. Pat de Maré pioneered the large group not only in the Health Service but also at the Institute of Group Analysis. He is a pioneer both in the UK and abroad in applying group analytic principles to large groups (de Maré 1991). He stresses the difficulty inherent in the large group about thinking. Feeling tends to dominate. The large group engenders primitive anxiety and splitting, projection, envy, introjection. The group can appear to be terrifying and persecuting even before anyone has opened their mouth. Speakers can be ignored, greeted with hostility or envy or silenced. Staff have to contain all kinds of unmanageable feelings and distortions and at the same time provide a safe container for people to experiment with actually opening their mouths and speaking, often to what seems like a vast empty space. The convenor also has to cope and hold the staff fears and conflicts and distortions as well as personal ones. There is a real fear that large groups cannot contain their own destructive feelings and survive.

In one term of the Introductory Course run by the Institute of Group Analysis, weekly large groups are held, the size of which can range from 130 to 200, including all staff and course members. Having participated in all capacities – as a member, as part of a staff team, and as a convenor – my experience is that this can be a most stressful situation unparalleled in individual therapy or in small group therapy. The pulse rate goes up and one can be frozen in one's seat; the first words uttered provide a temporary relief for all, and then the tension mounts again. It is like a play that is waiting to be created, like music that is often discordant, often outrageous, sometimes gentle, generally always stressful. Common themes in an early large group include discussions about seating arrangements/ latecomers/silent members/who are the insiders/outsiders. These are much worked over, usually as a defence against the sheer anxiety of being in such a setting.

> The night before the first group commenced the convenor dreamt she was having a large party, masses of people were coming and she had no food prepared. She sent a lot of the participants off in a double-decker bus for a mystery tour while she sorted something out. Then two therapists she knew arrived with a huge piece of French paté and bread and she felt considerably relieved.

This obviously indicates anxiety about the first large group and what to provide, with the realisation that others will bring rich food.

A typical large group first session is illustrated in the following example:

> The large group was very full, 90 per cent of the students were on time (unlike their attendance at lectures) – there was an air of expectancy and excited chatter. Gradually a silence prevailed which lasted for seven to ten minutes with latecomers crossing the centre or sitting on the outskirts in an atmosphere of breathless anticipation. The first comment by a member of staff – 'How visible one is as a latecomer' – produced a noticeable relaxation

in the atmosphere. Themes that evolved included Noah's Ark – everyone on it waiting for the rain to start – and the spider's web, referring to the network of communication as one by one people spoke. But where is the spider? Spiders can be dangerous and destructive (the staff?). There was talk of having to concentrate, then of concentration camps in Japan where the children helped the parents. The mood darkened. Hopelessness at the task. What is the production? Who is going to speak up? And how is anyone going to hear? People searched for members of their small groups, familiar faces, to feel kinship, then looked at which area of the large group felt safer, which was the best. Many people watched the door or looked at the ceiling. Last term's 'safe' lecture periods appeared to be more acceptable in retrospect than this large group experience. Several people were not using their first language. Many expressed the fear of being alone in such a crowd. The staff were not making it easy and hostility was in the air: 'The staff are spying on students.' 'The setting makes me feel murderous. I wish I had a gun' said one man.

In a hospital setting the daily free-floating agenda-less large group, providing it is also attended by competent staff, can be the heart-beat of the community. It is an excellent vehicle for the containment of stressful feelings and events which concern the community as a whole, such as rule-breaking, confrontation of staff or patients, a death or suicide. Everyone has the opportunity to be heard, to make a sound, to test out their voices, to communicate and to be respected, any of which may be a rare experience for a severely mentally disturbed person. The staff too can learn how to face and tolerate their own confusion, anxiety and helplessness in a situation where it is more difficult to hide behind a title or role.

ORGANISATIONAL STRESS

Stress management is part of working life whatever one's career. Under the medical model, staff, including group therapists, may need to conform if they want to keep their jobs. In a multidisciplinary unit, responsibility is shared *but* this can also increase stress. There may be no 'boss' to stop the buck. If group patients are lost, or disappear, the therapist has to deal with the crisis, whether feeling up to it or not, since there is often little support or sympathy available in a busy hospital setting.

Psychoanalysts such as Harold Bridger and others from the Tavistock Institute of Human Relations have worked extensively with the dynamics of groups within all types of organisation. Group analysts are now entering the field, although most of the work seems to be described as 'training'. Twenty years ago Dr Fernando Arroyave broke new ground by working closely inside an industrial organisation as a group analyst. (This unique case history is in the process of preparation for publication.) The stresses here were imposed largely by the restrictions of the organisational hierarchy. This sort of setting is generally unfamiliar territory for group analysts and it contains differences that have profound implications for the therapist's experience of power and helplessness which may add to the everyday stress inherent in the job. These differences emerge from the following summarised comparisons of various organisational settings.

In a private practice group

The *group* is the client; the therapist is free of any external influences other than the restraints and ethics of his/her professional association. Stresses are determined primarily by events within the group.

In a hospital or social services group

The client is the *organisation*. If the therapist has an employment contract this will mean consent to the sharing of power over the location, timing and support arrangements for group sessions. Political and negotiating skills become essential to secure and protect the desired group environment. A self-employed group therapist may be able to bargain more effectively than an employee of the body, but ultimately must comply with the client's wishes. Helplessness and concomitant stress can increase because of patients' turnover and their freedom to opt out at no cost. (The client also has limited power over the patients, since they are not on the payroll.)

In an industrial or commercial group

The client has 'paymaster' powers over both therapist and group members. This is a radically different environment from those above:

1 As an independent outsider the therapist may enjoy extra power by virtue of charging fees for special skills which the client is thus

motivated to exploit fully. The organisation is making an investment and group members are more captive in being *obliged* to
attend the sessions and participate (and IMPROVE!). The therapist's additional power, if any, derives from being the client's
agent.

This may partly offset:

2 Greater helplessness which also derives from the agency role. The
work is *primarily* for the benefit of something more important than
the welfare of the group, and, like the other group members, the
therapist is on the payroll and thus implicitly allied to this purpose.
This may be regarded by the group as an anomaly, casting doubt
on the therapist's impartiality. What is going on risks being seen
as something done *to* rather than *by* the group. The group will also
perceive the therapist's inability to exclude interference from the
bosses and may withhold commitment and trust. This can be
extremely stressful for the therapist; it makes an already difficult
task significantly more taxing.

Manipulation is a widespread skill in organisations. The therapist
may at first be treated as 'one of us' as a preliminary to attempts at
enlistment as an ally in group members' everyday conflicts outside.
The group therapist who feels manipulated experiences it as an extra
stress which impedes effective group work.

HOW TO COMBAT STRESS

How do group therapists stay well-balanced emotionally, physically,
spiritually, intellectually? How indeed!

Those of us that venture to take a person into analytic treatment
are undertaking a huge responsibility: a responsibility that demands vision, skill, intellectual acumen, concern and a disciplined
sensibility.

(Khan 1974: 116)

That demanding description of analytic work is itself stress-inducing!
People vary in their resilience under stress. This resilience can be
likened to that of a spring, whose strength determines the distortion
under a given load. If resilience is an inherited characteristic and is
limited there is not much to be done about it except to teach
avoidance and stress-management techniques. These I will return to

later. If it is borderline psychological stress, the individual may react positively to exercises or pressures which encourage them to develop stress-resistant skills.

Stress in itself is of course unavoidable and necessary to a healthy life – the power to resist keeps us alive. But one can have too much of it and that is when to stop 'digging in the dirt' and go into the fresh air.

Group therapists have to learn 'detachment': 'psychodynamically, dissociation is a way to cope with traumatic events leading to resilience' (Early 1993: 7). This is all very well as long as dissociation does not interfere with the therapist's capacity to help the patients. In a his well-researched book the Jungian analyst Early gives a detailed account of his personal approach to psychological trauma based on ten years' work with trauma victims, in groups as well as individually. He vividly describes his stress in working in the USA with Vietnam war veterans: 'At night, at home, I paced the floor, fists rigid, infused with anger. "Since you've been working with vets you've become manic depressive" says my wife' (ibid.: xiii). As an antidote to contamination by association with the emotions of psychological trauma, his hobby of woodcarving provided relief from the grim horror stories he heard daily.

In *The Psychology of the Transference*, Jung wrote:

> When two chemical substances combine, both are altered. This is precisely what happens in the transference. Freud rightly recognised that this bond is of the greatest therapeutic importance in that it gives rise to a *mixtum compositum* of the doctor's own mental health and the patient's maladjustment. . . it is inevitable that the doctor should be influenced to a certain extent and even *that his nervous health should suffer.*
>
> (1954: 171)

The analyst quite literally 'takes over' the sufferings of the patient and shares them with him/her. Group therapists do not always build the necessary space into their life-styles for unwinding and relaxing; their schedules are often too full. At work too little time is allowed for relaxation, or for a walk in the fresh air. They often sit all day and their bodily posture illustrates this. 'Psyche depends on body and a body depends on psyche' (Jung 1954: 4). After conducting several groups in a day the stimulation level needs to drop drastically if one is to do more than just survive. 'Good communication is stimulating as black coffee and just as hard to sleep after' (Lindberg 1992: 99).

Specific problem areas for group therapists to deal with in attempting to reduce stress include:

Conducting too many groups

The number of people who can be retained in the therapist's head has a limit and, beyond this, mental confusion and discomfort take over. It may be more difficult to eliminate this problem in private practice where income depends on the amount of work, but to take on too much is a false economy. A certain way to lose patients is to work in continuous overload, because this risks the therapist becoming careless, exhausted and sometimes indifferent. Zombies do not make good therapists.

Getting the right group composition

This is more than just filling spaces. The right mix reduces stress. Impending vacancies need to be thought through: what does the group need, are any suitable replacements available, what are the therapist's professional needs and financial pressures? A group therapist in a hospital setting with a group vacancy may be better able to resist pressure to fill it with a potentially unsatisfactory candidate on the grounds of cost effectiveness. Taking an unsuitable individual will sooner or later adversely affect the whole group and the therapist.

Administrative support

Whatever the work setting, reliable back-up in the office minimises secondary stressing from without. The group therapist's ability to secure this depends on the politics of the setting, but it is more than just an irritant if phone calls and messages are lost, misdirected or indeed ignored.

Boundary protection

A group needs a stable environment which is quiet in order to flourish. Group therapists can be apt to accept second- or even third-rate standards of accommodation in the firm belief the group will transcend such matters. It may, but the quality of work will suffer. This is where the therapist's personal negotiating skills, particularly in the NHS setting, are important. A surgeon would prefer not to operate in an ill-equipped theatre, and group therapists should not tolerate inadequate accommodation. Moving a group room un- necessarily (which often happens) produces a myriad of responses and ensuing discomfort for the therapist and the group.

A group was warned and prepared about an impending room change. The result was an unsettled group; comments like 'leaving the womb' and 'going into the hostile world' were made, together with expressed thoughts of leaving the group. Memories of other moves from home, country, or schools were evoked. The therapist had also to deal with personal discomfort and distraction because of the change of environment, whilst interpreting the meaning of the change of space, not just for the individual but for the group as a whole.

This example concerns a group that *was* prepared. To have a group room moved with no notice at all is exceedingly disruptive and damaging.

Stability of staff

Co-therapy is the norm in most hospitals, with the exception of some outpatient groups. Careful attention to ensuring complementarity of the therapists' personalities will reduce stress. If they are at logger- heads, personal rivalry and envies will penetrate the group with destructive consequences. Taking 'visitors' into groups is not a good idea, although there is often pressure on hospital staff to do so.

One young group therapist experienced considerable distress and anger by having to endure an aggressive trainee GP as a 'guest' who interfered frequently, took notes in spite of being asked not to, disagreed with the therapist's comments and generally was totally disruptive. When the therapist complained to 'manage- ment', she was not taken seriously and told, 'You can easily manage that.'

Withstanding institutional resistance

To keep the groups functioning whatever, in spite of resistance from other departments and non-analytic staff, is a form of stress which engenders feelings of inadequacy and helplessness. It is quite common for a group conductor (especially if non-medical) to return after a holiday to find several group patients have been discharged without consultation. Thus it is not difficult to feel totally devalued whilst still having to get on and deal with a disabled, even despairing group. Outright institutional resistance and gratuitous hostility from other 'caring' professionals is still a common and a particularly hurtful form of stress which is unavoidable in too many hospital hierarchies.

Professional support groups

Such groups, or self-help groups in which the group therapist can share work problems, may be beneficial. Staff groups can also help, although it is well known that such groups engender their own form of stress. It is exhausting to deal conscientiously with the daily traumas, tragedies and dysfunctions of many patients. Whilst common enough in individual therapy, this pressure multiplies by eight for every group.

Self-defence skills

These may be needed if working with disturbed patients. One student was threatened with a carving knife wielded by an aggressive patient who was angry that she would not provide him with individual therapy. Only quick-thinking physical intervention avoided a catastrophe. The acquisition of skills to deal with hostile physical attacks can increase confidence and alleviate the stress posed by the responsibility for dealing with such events. When violence is imminent the therapist has no option but to intervene immediately for the protection of the group.

Finally, among the most valuable qualities the group conductor needs to cultivate are:

A sense of humour and the ability to play

A paper by George Christie (1994) discusses psychoanalytic aspects of humour. He writes about humour having a generative influence in communication or in the service of manic defence. It can be funny and also cruel and springs from the unconscious. We need to be able to play creatively. He quotes Bion's three possible outcomes to analysis:

1 Success – the patient gets better
2 Failure – the patient gets worse
3 The patient becomes a psychoanalyst

Christie illustrates his thesis by discussing how Winnicott talks about play first emerging in the potential space between the baby and the mother, and that the relationship has to be reliable. Winnicott believed that if a patient has any capacity to play in the clinical relationship then a lot can be done. (There are similar play areas in a group between the therapist and members.) Christie mentions Masud Khan who tries to find the equivalent of Winnicott's squiggle technique in terms of spoken behaviour, and Searles, who says that humour is one of the great avenues by which disillusionment is sublimated in human development and that its appearance during therapy is one of the signs that the patient and the therapist have begun to master and integrate the disillusionment in their relationship.

However, Christie warns that humour's *destructive* potential includes reinforcement of defensiveness in the therapist and the patient; it could be:

- serving narcissistic needs in the therapist;
- a disguise for aggression – confusing the patient; or
- blocking free association.

In the group, play-tools include words, images and thoughts. Peter Lewis (1987) suggests that spontaneous humour might give us access to psychic areas not touched by other approaches. But it is difficult to hold on to a sense of humour when one is overwhelmed by stressful persecutory or depressive feelings. It is difficult to work with a group that does not have a space for humour and play; it is vital to the survival of the therapist.

Here is an illustration from a long-standing group:

X, a 40-year-old serious intellectual suffering from long-term depression had been full of foreboding about the imminent birth of his baby, fearful he would pass on his depression to another generation, as his father had to him. Gradually in the group he learned to play and to respond with humour. The baby arrived and the group rejoiced. One day he walked in with his two-week-old daughter, hugging her closely to him. The group expressed delight and pleasure and he then returned her to her mother in the waiting room. The group continued. Z, another member, arrived, late. He heard about the 'private view' of the baby, was upset to have missed her and said he had seen a pram outside in the corridor. X jumped up and went to get his baby. He quickly returned and said, 'My wife is feeding her but she'll come when she is ready.' The group settled down to normal business. Then came a tap on the door. X leapt up again, the baby was handed to him. He proudly crossed the group to show Z. Turning to the therapist, he laughingly said, 'I don't know what this is doing to the transference!'

CONCLUSION

I have attempted to survey the particular forms of stress which are most likely to beset the group therapist and to distinguish them, where possible, from those which characterise individual therapy. The differences derive from more than just the numbers to be dealt with, though this factor does significantly magnify the load on the therapist, but also from the unique intensity of pressure which groups can bring to bear. On the other hand, it has to be recognised that the group is also able to magnify the emotional satisfaction that comes from surviving its complex dynamics.

I have also tried to make clear that the setting also plays a large part in the nature and mix of stresses which can arise, ranging from the comparative security of a private consulting room to the unstable environment of a hostile, indifferent or controlling organisation.

If only for the sake of the group, the therapist must pay careful attention to keeping in good personal shape, both psychologically and physically. Better management of stress comes with experience and success in dealing with, or at least surviving, the diverse disruptive and destructive forces which the dynamics of a group can make so difficult to work through, and which I have tried to illustrate. Large groups contain particularly powerful and primitive forces which are unique in the extent to which they can test the resources of even the most experienced therapist. But they can also be a source of support in major crises.

As a general rule eternal vigilance is always to be recommended. A certain detachment is also important in maintaining awareness of what is going on, but this must not deteriorate into isolation from the currents running in the group; it is more a question of keeping swimming with one's head clear of the water, rather than trying to scramble ashore.

From my own range of experience in both group and individual therapy I believe that the stresses in group work are often different in kind and degree but at least equally taxing. In one important respect, because members of a group will display a mix of personalities there is usually a better chance of bringing into 'play' the therapeutic power of humour than with a fixated negative individual in one-to-one therapy. Humour and play are perhaps two of the most essential ingredients in maintaining a positive equilibrium in the inevitably stressful occupation of group therapist.

REFERENCES

Bowlby, J. (1974) 'Attachment theory, separation anxiety and mourning', *American Handbook of Psychiatry*, vol. vii.

Christie, G. L. (1994) 'Some psychoanalytic aspects of humour', *International Journal of Psycho-Analysis* 75: 479.

Coltart, N. (1992) *How to Survive as a Psychotherapist*, London: Sheldon Press.

de Maré, P., Piper, R. and Thompson, S. (1991) 'Koinonia – from hate through dialogue to culture in the large group', London: Karnac Books.

Early, E. (1993) *The Raven's Return*, Illinois: Chiron.

Foulkes, S. H. (1975) *Group Analytic Psychotherapy*, Interface.

Jung, C. G. (1954) *The Psychology of Transference*, in *Collected Works*, vol. 16, ch. 7, London: Routledge & Kegan Paul.

Kahn, M. (1974) *Privacy of the Self*, London: Hogarth Press.

Klauber, J. (1986) *Difficulties in the Analytic Encounter*, London: Free Association Books.

Kopp, S. (1974) *If You Meet the Buddha on the Road, Kill Him!*, London: Sheldon Press.

Kreeger, L. C. (1992) 'Envy pre-emption in small and large groups', 16th Foulkes Lecture, *Group Analysis* 25:.

Lewis, P. (1987) 'Laughter and humour: does it have a place in group analysis?', *Group Analysis* 20: 367–78.

Lindberg, A. M. (1992) *Gift from the Sea*, London: Chatto & Windus.

Nitsun, M. (1991) *The Anti-group: The Dialectics of the Creative and the Destructive in Group Analysis*, London: Routledge.

Sharpe, M. (1991) 'Death and the practice', in J. Roberts and M. Pines (eds) *The Practice of Group Analysis*, London: Routledge.

Chapter 13

Stresses in psychotherapists inside the National Health Service

Andrew Skarbek

It should be obvious that a certain amount of tension and stress is present in any situation that involves contact between individuals. Stress is an integral part of a comprehensive adaptation pattern. If it manifests itself in a limited amount it enhances alertness and communication as well as understanding of psychotherapeutic process, but if it becomes excessive it can precipitate an emotional state such as alarm, anxiety, anger, guilt, shame, fear or depression which can be disruptive to therapeutic aims. I shall endeavour in this chapter to present a situation in which excessive stress has affected therapists in various ways and suggest some remedies to deal with these problems.

Psychotherapy is a form of treatment of psychological and emotional problems which patients present to their therapist and which they expect the therapist to help them deal with and solve. In this context stressful situations do exist and do emerge. This is particularly apparent in the NHS because most of the ongoing treatment is frequently undertaken by inexperienced personnel, such as doctors in psychiatric training, medical students during their attachment to a psychiatric department, psychologists in training, psychiatric nurses, and other ancillary workers involved in health care. Occupational therapists, social workers and art therapists also become involved in work which can be seen as psychotherapeutic. Many have not had any formal psychotherapeutic training and enter this field as a result of their involvement with emotionally disturbed individuals. The line between a friendly concerned chat, support, sympathy, counselling and psychotherapy is blurred, and experience and the capacity to work in a psychotherapeutic setting varies significantly in this group of people. More experienced seniors such as consultant psychotherapists or fully trained lay psychotherapists are mainly concerned with supervision of juniors and personnel involved in actual treatment. They also have the responsibility of running psychotherapy departments, managing staff problems and waiting lists, and assessing new patients, as well as dealing with audits and managerial matters, designing training schemes, lecturing and keeping in touch with psychiatric colleagues and GPs. It is their task to convey to referral agencies the advantages and limitations of psychotherapeutic treatment, and what the NHS can provide given its limited resources and the considerable demands for psychotherapeutic treatment made upon them. It is in the context of this scenario that various stresses emerge in our personnel – both senior and junior.

Psychotherapy as a form of treatment does not quite fit into the 'medical model' which dominates the approach to patients in the NHS with its focus on treating symptoms and management within strictly defined boundaries. Management of patients is formulated with the aim of removing offending symptoms, behaviour abnormalities and antisocial tendencies which patients present to their therapist. The therapeutic approach adopted in the training and practice of NHS therapists may have encouraged them to assume a somewhat omnipotent 'professional' stance, treating patients with certain aspects of parental authority, even sometimes requiring unquestioned obedience as a price of cure. This is probably associated with the need of the staff to protect themselves from anxiety associated with the difficult and frequently harrowing task of providing an adequate treatment pattern. This has been discussed fully by I. E. P. Menzies (1961). The change in emphasis which the psychotherapeutic approach demands as a process of facilitation growth and mutual learning induces and precipitates stressful dilemmas in practitioners which I will endeavour to present and discuss in some detail. There is frequently no clear boundary between ordinary human contact, counselling, managing the case by giving well-intentioned and sometimes appropriate practical advice, and assuming a detached exploratory and facilitating stance which psychotherapy attempts to create. A great deal of confusion, stress and helplessness can occur in an inexperienced therapist and this can only be remedied by easily available sympathetic and supportive supervision from a senior member of the team. A clinical vignette will illustrate this problem. A 47-year-old married man with marked obsessive features, depression and a very rocky marriage was referred to our service by a psychiatrist, who had given a certain amount of counselling support without much improvement. The case was discussed at an intake meeting and it was decided to offer this patient a course of exploratory psychotherapy. He was allocated to a young and not very experienced therapist. The patient used the first session to ask the therapist endless questions about what practical steps he should take *vis à vis* his marriage and his job, as well as personal questions which the therapist found very embarrassing. Supervision helped the therapist to establish and convey to the patient the necessary therapeutic boundaries, and to interpret his anxieties in terms of his early insecure childhood. The treatment progressed and the therapist reported improvement.

Stresses associated with the actual psychotherapeutic process frequently lead to frustration and disappointment in most patients and therapists and can lead to the breakdown of treatment. Here the slowness and the austerity of the psychotherapeutic process is at stake. The fact is that it does not produce immediate solutions or alleviate symptoms and above all does not give well-packaged explanations and guidance, but rather depends and relies on the development of mutual understanding and trust between the practitioner and the patient. This leads to a process of discovery within the explorative matrix which facilitates the development of insight and so underpins the process of recovery.

I have already alluded to the problems which some therapists experience associated with the lack of clear understanding of the psychotherapeutic task as well as its theoretical underpinning. Impatient, somewhat impulsive therapists, not used to listening to patients without immediate response and wishing to solve the problems presented, do get frequently stressed and frustrated dealing with patients' emotional problems and their disturbed and sometimes complicated past histories, and they find themselves with few 'remedies'. Those therapists also find theoretical literature about the subject only marginally helpful. The wish to understand, help and encourage the patient is overshadowed by the complex nature of resistance to change, the inability to deal with emotional fixation, and frequently with the patient's past and present life-style.

I shall now discuss difficulties associated with initiating and establishing a psychotherapeutic process. Both therapist and patient entering psychotherapeutic treatment have to 'survive' and use a sometimes unfamiliar experience, and feel able to talk freely and honestly to a stranger. Patients frequently reveal painful, shameful details of their lives. This may all be very confusing and stressful to the therapist who has to deal with and understand the patient's responses to a murky and complicated account, and in particular needs to encourage the individual to make him realise that this experience is worthwhile. The therapist also has to convince himself that he is not wasting his time and that the process will be beneficial to both parties. It is a well-documented fact that only a small proportion of patients who are referred for psychotherapy will enter into it and continue with this form of treatment without running away or expecting a 'miracle' fast cure. The figures from various centres suggests that only about 20 per cent of patients in the NHS finally settle down in an ongoing form of treatment. In a way this is not surprising considering that this treatment frequently has a dubious outcome, is difficult to evaluate and the demands on both the practitioner and patient can be extremely rigorous in terms of emotional involvement, time and encroachment on everyday life. The stresses can be overwhelming if sufficient support is not given to the therapist.

A further vignette will illustrate some of these problems. A very caring but rather rigid female therapist in training was allocated a 26-year-old male professional who was a highly geared, stressed individual suffering from various anxiety problems associated with relationships and his performance at work. The patient was highly ambitious and self-critical. He was brought up by professionally successful parents, and, the youngest of three, was in marked competition with his older siblings. At the intake conference it was felt that he was suitable for exploratory psychotherapy but it was also felt that he might find the situation of a psychotherapeutic encounter difficult to contain and this was subsequently confirmed. The patient found therapy too slow and asked for the therapist's private telephone number, demanding an increase in the frequency of sessions. He found it difficult to terminate sessions when instructed by his therapist, who felt dominated, devoured and drained by her patient to the point of considering termination of treatment. The patient's impact was making her feel stressed which so interfered with her personal life that she developed physical symptoms and had to go on sick leave. The patient had to be taken up by another more experienced and robust therapist.

The nature of transference and counter-transference and how to cope with them in psychotherapeutic treatment, as well as problems of dependence and regression in the course of a psychotherapeutic encounter, seem to be the most difficult and vexed problems facing therapists in the NHS. This is largely because few therapists have themselves experienced a course of personal therapy. Bloch (1982) set out essential qualities necessary for the therapist and I will enumerate them:

1 Warmth – the non-possessive acceptance of and unconditional positive regard on the part of the therapist. In essence, a genuine caring attitude.
2 Empathy – a sensitive and accurate appreciation of what the patient is experiencing by getting into 'his or her shoes'.
3 Genuineness – the therapist's words should touch the patient's feelings, the therapist should be transparently real.

The therapist may be challenging or supportive, authoritarian or permissive, active or passive, detached or involved. Patients are frequently devastated, demoralised, guilt-ridden, and very negative, destructive and envious, and therefore it is not surprising that in the transference the patient will experience anger, disappointment, reverence, dependency, jealousy and seductiveness with regard to the therapist. All those feelings transferred to the therapist can cause considerable stress which may interfere with the establishment of a good trusting relationship and undermine the course of treatment. The ability to develop a psychotherapeutic space in which matters associated with transference and counter-transference can be negotiated, explored and understood in terms of the early experiences of the patient requires particular skill and sensitivity from both parties. This is dependent on the ability to contain both negative as well as positive feelings and prevent acting out in therapy which can, in turn, interrupt the progress of a constructive encounter.

A further clinical vignette will illustrate the points that I have been presenting. A young male college student aged 19 presented with problems of difficult relationships with women at college, a fear of rejection and failure, and a stormy relationship with his parents whom he described as very controlling and, at the same time, indifferent to his problems. His symptoms were mainly severe anxiety and depression with some suicidal ideation. He was intelligent, reasonably insightful and anxious to understand himself. He presented himself to his GP who gave him some support and suggested medication which he prescribed. There was not much response and the GP became alarmed about suicidal thoughts which this patient expressed. He was allocated to a female therapist who was fairly experienced, and was herself undergoing personal therapy.

The treatment started with a great deal of commitment on both sides. The patient was able to use the therapy and was gaining insight. A few months after the start the young man declared his love towards the therapist and became seductive and intrusive; he expressed a great deal of anger and jealousy as well as destructive feelings towards an assumed partner of the therapist. The therapist was alarmed by this, and particularly by the patient's suicidal threats which he expressed. The therapist felt trapped, disappointed, guilty, helpless and intimidated by the fact that she had allowed the development of a close intimate relationship which she could not now handle. She got a great deal of support from her supervisor and private therapist and continued treatment of her patient. She was able to convey to her patient that he saw her as an idealised mother and was expecting in therapy to have something that he never had from his own mother. Gradually insight prevailed and his destructive challenging feelings diminished after nearly two years of therapy. He was able to form a close and more mature relationship with a colleague at college and was also able to form a more distant, less dependent relationship with his parents. It took a further six months to terminate the therapy and acting out stopped. It was only possible for the therapist to continue and complete treatment because she herself showed an ability to respond to the patient with skilful interpretations and concern, at the same time understanding countertransference but keeping it all within the psychotherapeutic boundaries.

Matching suitable patients to suitable therapists is quite a stressful and difficult task. Being able mutually to admit during preliminary exploration that psychotherapeutic treatment is not appropriate may lead to disappointment, anger and resentment in both parties and create a sense of failure. A good match may take time to establish. It is a well recognised fact that even when the therapeutic work starts in a positive and promising way, as time passes and deeper levels of unconscious elements begin to emerge in dreams association and particularly in the intense transference context, powerful feelings are unleashed. Some therapists discover similarities and resonances within their own psyche. I have known therapists say within a supervisory session, 'How can I help this patient of mine? He has such similar problems to mine. It is like the blind leading the blind.' It is only when the therapist discovers that this neutral resonance and mirroring can be made into something more positive and facilitating that the treatment can progress.

It is particularly important in the NHS setting to match patients to therapists so that the case load is reasonably well balanced between patients who are fairly disturbed, acting out or resistant, and those who obviously have more facility to gain insight and are interesting and gratifying to the therapist. Too many difficult, unrewarding patients can cause a great deal of distress to the therapist and hamper his professional progress and lead to disappointment.

Selection of an appropriate form of treatment weekly, more frequent individual therapy or group therapy, matching conditions of suitability for this type of exposure to the availability of suitable facilities, as well as assessment of realistic outcomes of treatment within a possible time-scale, are issues particularly affecting those working in the NHS with a definite term of tenure (such as medical students, SHOs or Registrars). Anxiety and resentment can easily emerge when facilities are limited and the referral rates high, and decisions have been made quickly. Can only a time-limited short course of treatment of 'focal therapy' be offered or perhaps a psychotherapeutic consultation is the only option? Can treatment be planned on an open-ended scale and how intensive should it be? With the pressure exerted by managers and administrators with 'money' in mind, there is pressure from that quarter to treat as large a number of patients as possible to produce 'figures'. This attitude leads to a great deal of stress and anxiety in therapists, particularly in those who are conscientious and committed to doing what is best for the patient. The suitability of some patients is difficult to evaluate in assessment and consultation. It sometimes takes quite a bit of time for therapists to test patients' capacity for treatment and commitment to it. This sometimes leads to patients terminating treatment abruptly, which can be quite a blow to the therapist and may make him feel inadequate, incapable and useless. Although in some centres a type of contract is negotiated and agreed between the patient and therapist, there is however no redress as far as the therapist is concerned. When the contract is broken the patient does not have any financial obligation. This applies even if he does not turn up for sessions without notification and wastes the therapist's time and frustrates his commitment.

A further clinical vignette:

A new Registrar (psychiatric) on a rotational training scheme started his six-month stint in the psychotherapy department and was allocated six new previously assessed patients. Appointments were sent and the Registrar was keen to build up his patient load. Three patients did not turn up, without notification; the other three turned up but after a few sessions only one decided to commit himself to ongoing treatment. This was very disappointing to the therapist who became rather angry and suspicious that as a novice he was being allotted uncommitted patients. However, in due course, with support and supervision he was able to build up an adequate load of patients and at the end of his rotation in the department he continued treating some of his patients. He expressed a great deal of interest and skill in psychodynamic treatment and decided to take further training in this field.

Losing a patient can have a profound and demoralising effect on the therapist because it can easily make him feel that he is inferior to those colleagues who keep their patients, as they may be seen as being more able, gifted and capable professionals. Most inexperienced novices appear to fear losing a patient. Another important factor which is frequently experienced is fear that they may damage the patient – particularly if they feel they are incapable of holding the patient in treatment and themselves fully comprehend and understand the complexity of the psychotherapeutic process. This fear may be associated with fear of making the patient angry, aggressive, homicidal or suicidal. The exploratory nature of the psychotherapeutic encounter can open up and release forces beyond the capacity of the therapist to contain and may lead to a catastrophic end with blame, humiliation and fear of retribution. This will have a negative effect on his professional ambitions. People in psychotherapy, in the hands even of experienced practitioners, do sometimes attempt and commit suicide and this may haunt particularly the inexperienced therapist.

The acceptance that psychotherapeutic treatment can mobilise explosive forces which are directed to the outside or inside can be quite alarming to therapists. It is therefore of vital importance that the therapist dealing with this type of patient has the support of other professional colleagues, as well as himself having the ability and willingness to take steps which will protect him and his patient from a disaster.

The practice of psychotherapy in some professionals leads to the development of rigidity, sometimes to cynicism and therapeutic pessimism. There are a number of studies reporting on 'burn-out' in this group of professionals. I am sure that the NHS with its various restrictions and hierarchical structure provides a fertile ground for this phenomenon. It is therefore very important that practitioners in this field have an opportunity of frequent support through the medium of seminars, scientific meetings and congresses and group encounters which they are encouraged to attend and contribute to in the form of presenting papers, their own research or research of their group, and sharing experiences with other professionals. This involves financial support which is not generally forthcoming from the NHS and this situation may make psychotherapeutic professionals feel undervalued.

The problem of complaints of patients and their relatives about the effect, nature and effectiveness of treatment can cause considerable anxiety. The intimacy of the psychotherapeutic process can easily be exploited and lead to a conflict which can only be resolved through tact, the keeping of professional boundaries, confidentiality, and at the same time a willingness to be available and an ability to confront the problems. Fear of criticism from other professionals, or from one's own colleagues or supervisors, frequently emerges. In this context, what is most important is to be able to contain those criticisms and sometimes learn from them rather than dismiss them or slide into a state of stressful anxiety.

I shall now present a further illustrative vignette. A dedicated, fairly experienced therapist treated a 24-year-old male unemployed schizoid, a depressed and immature individual, for two years with only marginal progress. The patient lived with his parents who were kind and caring but quite intrusive and infantalising. At the same time they resented that their son was progressing slowly and that he did not confide in them what was happening in therapy. They complained to the management. An investigation was set up which dragged on through clumsy, insensitive handling by lay-management fearing legal action. It was only when a meeting was set up between the therapist, his supervisor, the parents and the patient that issues of contention were brought into the open without infringing the confidentiality of the therapist/patient relationship. It took a number of meetings, but gradually conflict and differences of opinion were ironed out. Therapy was salvaged and continued to a satisfactory conclusion. The patient was able to leave home, find a suitable partner and lead an independent life.

Physical illness in the patient or therapist leads to interruption of treatment which creates considerable stress in both parties. There again, a frank explanation of circumstances can go a long way towards alleviating tension which may occur. The existing literature shows that the swing from good physical health in the therapist to illness and back to health is full of inherent traps which affect the psychotherapeutic process. There does not seem to be a consensus about how to handle these clinical situations, but there are some areas of agreement. More depressed patients are supposed to need to know more factual information about the therapist's illness in order to cope with the situation than higher-functioning patients. Therapists affected by a serious illness should not only receive physical treatment for their illness, but should also have psychological help from another independent therapist in order to cope and come to terms with various psychological weaknesses which such an illness can and frequently does reveal. This topic has been extensively presented by Rita W. Clark (1995).

The setting in which psychotherapeutic treatment in the NHS is conducted frequently consists of rather shabby, poorly furnished rooms, basically designed for medical practice, like examination rooms. This is hardly conducive to a relaxed atmosphere. Psycho-therapeutic practice should be conducted in a quiet space without interruption and outside interference. Psychiatric hospitals or psy-chiatric units in general hospitals bring outpatients together with more disturbed patients. This may have a very stressful effect and deter some patients. The therapist essentially is linked to the setting in which he works. Another source of stress which affects the therapist is the difficulty in guaranteeing a continuity in the space used for conducting therapy. Interference in the form of sharing rooms, of noise, or telephone interruptions, can and does obstruct easy uninterrupted communication between the therapist and patient and so undermines the process of healing. Ideally psychotherapy should be practised in a separate building, preferably away from the rest of the hospital, and the rooms should be well equipped so that a friendly, relaxed atmosphere can develop. This is, however, seldom available in the NHS largely because there is still very little understanding, concern and commitment on the part of the manage-ment to this type of treatment, the effects of which are so difficult to evaluate, quantify and establish as an essential and pivotal part of the totality of the Mental Health Service.

REFERENCES AND SELECT BIBLIOGRAPHY

Bloch, S. (1982) *What is Psychotherapy?* Oxford: Oxford University Press.
Capmer, M. and Cattasiano, M. L. (1993) 'Factors affecting the progression

towards burn-out: a comparison of professional and volunteer counsellors' *Psychological Reports* 73 (2) (October): 555–61.

Caunadrio, C. (1992) 'Sex and gender and the impaired therapist', *Australian and New Zealand Journal of Psychiatry* 26 (3): 346–63.

Clark, Rita (1995) 'The Pope's confessor. A metaphor relating to illness in the analyst', *Journal of the American Psychoanalytic Association* 43 (1): 137.

Cox, John L. (1995) 'Consultant images', *Psychiatric Bulletin* 19: 167–8.

Hiscott, R. D. (1990) 'The health and well-being of mental health professionals', *Canadian Journal of Public Health* 81 (6) (November–December): 422–6.

Menzies, I. E. P. (1961) *The Functioning of Social Systems as a Defence Against Anxiety: A Report on a Study of the Nursing Service of a General Hospital*, Tavistock Pamphlet No. 3, London: Tavistock Publications.

Thornton, P. I. (1992) 'The relations of coping, appraisal, and burn-out in mental health workers', *Journal of Psychology* 126 (3) May: 261–71.

van de Ploeg, H. M., van Leeuven, J. J. and Kvee, M. G. (1990) 'Burn-out among Dutch psychotherapists', *Psychological Reports* 67 (1)(August): 107–12.

Whittington, R. and Wakes, T. (1992) 'Staff strain and social support in a psychiatric hospital following assault by a patient', *Journal of Advanced Nursing* 17 (4): 480–6.

Chapter 14

Stress in psychotherapists working outside the National Health Service

Irene Bloomfield

INTRODUCTION

There is general agreement from research into psychotherapy that the relationship between patient and therapist is the most important component of the therapeutic endeavour, and since relationships are unpredictable and subject to a variety of factors, it is inevitable that stresses will arise. Some apply to psychotherapy generally, others are more specific to Health Service or private practice. This chapter will deal primarily with stress for psychotherapists working outside the NHS. There will be consideration of stresses arising from external circumstances such as the setting, referrals, finance, and isolation, and of others arising from the therapeutic relationship and from working with particular groups of patients.

STRESSES ARISING FROM EXTERNAL CIRCUMSTANCES

The setting

One of the first things therapists need to consider after completing their training is the external environment in which they will spend several hours every day. Most people are affected to some extent by their surroundings, such as decor, colours and furnishings, and psychotherapists are no exception. The atmosphere created in this way can be calming, pleasurable and relaxing, or irritating and unpleasant. Anxiety can arise from the conflict between a setting in which therapists feel comfortable and one which reflects too much of their personal reality such as family photographs and ornaments. Some practitioners work from their own homes and can therefore create a setting that suits them, but stresses can arise nevertheless. When patients come to the therapist's home they immediately get a good deal of information about their personal circumstances and taste, and it may feel like an intrusion into their private world. Other members of the family have to be asked to keep out of the way and keep the noise down. This can be difficult with young children who may resent strangers in their home. Answer phones have reduced the aggravation of phones ringing during sessions, but there is generally no secretary to take messages, protect the therapist from unwanted calls, make appointments, or change sessions if necessary. All this has to be done by therapists themselves, which means that there is much more direct contact between patient and therapist outside the clinical context and this can make it harder to establish clear boundaries at the beginning of therapy.

Some of these issues may not arise with practitioners who are well established and have had time to deal with these externals satisfactorily, but for those who are trying to set up in practice, having only recently completed their training, things such as comfortable chairs and couch, a waiting area, a separate toilet, and parking facilities can be quite problematic especially when finances are straitened after the heavy expenses of training, own analysis and supervision.

Working in a single-handed practice can be quite lonely. There is no one to talk things over with, to turn to in a crisis, or to cancel patients in case of emergency such as sudden illness of the therapist.

There is also the risk and fear of violence. Attacks on therapists working privately are not common, but psychotherapists are undoubtedly vulnerable when working on their own without anybody else on the premises. There are practitioners, especially some female ones, who are quite anxious about this and prefer not to put themselves into this situation. In a clinic setting the first contact with a patient is generally via a secretary or receptionist, followed by an assessment carried out by an experienced practitioner. In private practice some patients are referred, but others approach therapists directly. Some very obvious danger signals, such as paranoid attitudes or obvious psychotic thought processes, may readily be picked up, even during a relatively brief telephone conversation or from a letter, but sometimes there is just a feeling of unease without the therapist being able to pinpoint anything specific. It may not be enough to turn somebody down at that point, and more sinister psycho-pathology may only surface in the course of subsequent sessions.

Referrals and assessments

One of the first essentials for newly qualified psychotherapists after setting up their consulting rooms is the matter of getting referrals. This can be quite problematic at present. Until three or four years ago there was no shortage of referrals from more senior analysts or supervisors who generally had waiting lists and were glad to know people to whom they could refer. While many more psychotherapists are being trained there has been a decline in the number of people seeking psychotherapy, partly because of the enormous variety of psychological treatments now available. Furthermore, psychotherapy has not had very good publicity from the media for some time. All of this has made it hard for recently qualified people to get the referrals they need to make a living.

During the therapist's training prospective patients are assessed by an experienced member of staff who will decide about their suitability, so that this decision does not have to be made by the trainee. After qualification, supervisors are generally still available, but the responsibility for taking on patients or turning them down now rests with the 'young' therapist (not as a rule that young as far as chronological is age concerned). Even if such therapists are aware of the possible difficulties with a potential referral, this constitutes a dilemma if they need the work. Moreover, feelings of inadequacy and anxiety about lack of experience are inevitable at the beginning of a new career, and that is where the loneliness of the private practitioner can be particularly stressful.

Containing feelings

Psychodynamic psychotherapists may spend eight to ten hours per day seeing patients, often in the same consulting room, the same chair, looking at the same view. Most of them will be seeing their patients two or three times a week, with patients lying on the couch or sitting opposite. In either case, therapists are exposed to intense emotions from a few individuals who reveal intimate details of their personal lives.

For the patient the fifty minutes spent with their psychotherapist is frequently the most important time of the day, although we may also be in danger of sometimes exaggerating this – but for many it is true. Psychotherapists have to give their full concentration and attention to each individual patient. The ten-minute break between patients which is really needed for getting some space for oneself often has to be used for writing notes, making phone calls or making coffee. All of this can be a considerable physical and emotional strain. Many therapists suffer from back or neck trouble, because of the amount of time spent sitting still and not getting enough exercise. There is also a good deal of emotional strain in having to contain our own feelings, no matter what is thrown at us, and 'of continually offering ourselves to the inner suffering of other people in the hope or faith that there is something we give which may be of therapeutic aid to other people' (Coltart 1994: 94).

There are patients who evoke strong feelings of boredom in the therapist, often when something is being withheld, when emotions are suppressed, or the patient's voice becomes monotonous or inaudible. Until this is confronted within the transference it can be quite hard for therapists to contain the boredom and sleepiness which may result.

Isolation

Psychotherapists working on their own are often quite isolated even though they do, of course, belong to the professional organisations which trained them. They have much less opportunity for formal or informal discussions with colleagues than those working in institutions. This often applies particularly to practitioners living in areas with few other therapists and therefore few opportunities for meetings and informal consultations. Discussions, case conferences and exchanges with colleagues are such a vital part of psychotherapists' satisfaction in their work that without this it can feel like a 'psychological desert', as one colleague described it. Working alone can also mean that it is not easy to get feedback on one's work. 'There are few objective guide-lines in professional literature as to what constitutes successful and mature practice, and therapists therefore have difficulty comparing what they do with what their colleagues do' (Goldberg 1992: 92).

Finance

Money arouses strong and mixed feelings in many patients and therapists, and setting a fee which is right and appropriate for both can be quite a complex task. Most patients accept that if they see a therapist privately they are receiving a service which has to be paid for, and that the therapist has to live, but because the relationship is such an important part of the process, there can be a feeling that it is like 'buying friendship' or even like 'prostitution'. These feelings have to be addressed as part of the therapeutic process, but psychotherapists are not immune from having irrational feelings of guilt about charging for what they offer. This is something they have to work through in their own therapies, but for those who move from institutions where no money is exchanged, it can be quite a difficult adjustment and may cause a good deal of anxiety, especially to therapists who are just beginning and only have the experience of their own therapy or analysis to go on. Charging too low a fee may indicate to the patient that this therapist does not think much of him or herself and can't be much good. Charging the going rate for supervisors and training therapists may seem preposterous and presumptuous and be resented by more senior practitioners. For the established practitioner there is a risk that being able to command excessive fees can encourage greediness and hook into their narcissism and power drive. This is likely to be to their own and the patients' detriment.

STRESSES ARISING FROM THE NATURE OF THE THERAPEUTIC RELATIONSHIP

Transference

The phenomenon of transference is an essential part of analytic psychotherapy, but one which can be hard to deal with. Clarkson writes in the *Handbook of Psychotherapy*, 'In the transference infantile prototypes re-emerge and are experienced with a strong sensation of immediacy' (Clarkson and Pokorny 1994: 33). The therapist can come to represent a number of different significant people from the patient's past, which means that the patient's perception of the therapists and their behaviour can be highly distorted. When the transference is extremely negative, and the therapist has to receive and contain very hostile feelings, verbal attacks, constant criticism and rejection of all interpretations, it can become very wearing and difficult to tolerate, even though we know that the feelings expressed belong to someone else.

Tranference can also be very baffling, especially to a young therapist, just starting. I recall a 25-year-old trainee, Bob, who was seeing Helen, a woman in her mid-forties. She experienced him very much as she had experienced her mother who was an unpredictable person, always making promises she did not keep, being all over her daughter one minute and slapping her hard the next. The student was one of the most reliable of his year, deeply concerned and caring, but Helen felt unable to trust him and was quite convinced that he would let her down. Bob and the other students in the group knew something about the theory of transference, but could not really comprehend how it was possible for a woman of Helen's age to experience a young man – about the same age as her own son – as a mother with witch-like characteristics who misinterpreted and distorted his intentions and behaviour. It was very hard for Bob to reconcile what he knew theoretically with what he experienced. Having such unpleasant characteristics projected on to him which were so out of character was really difficult for him and could only be managed with the constant support of the supervisor and the rest of the group.

Confidentiality

The issue of confidentiality should be quite straightforward, but can in fact be complex and troublesome. All psychotherapists accept that the name and personal details of any patient are sacrosanct and should not be divulged to anybody else, but there are exceptions. We obviously give information to supervisors; the patient's GP may require and be given information, and so will the psychiatrists or social workers involved. All this should only be done with the patient's consent, but it can create problems in the relationship between patient and therapist. Courts can demand that confidential information should be released in spite of objection by therapists, and having to appear in court or having to write a court report evokes the additional stress of having to establish one's credibility which is not guaranteed by the institution. The letter-heading is personal and does not provide the automatic status of a hospital or well-known institution. Moreover, the Patients' Charter requires that patients should have access to the notes written about them. Employers too may ask for information about a patient's progress, especially if they have been instrumental in the referral and contribute to the fees. Most therapists will make it very clear from the outset that such information cannot be disclosed, but different expectations on the part of the referring agency and the therapist can create conflict and distress.

Another dilemma occurs for psychotherapists who would like to use case material in lectures, talks, books or articles. There is fairly general agreement that permission should always be sought from the patient, but this may damage the trust between them. If material is used without permission and is sufficiently disguised to make the patient unrecognisable, it can come across as not truly authentic, but the conceptualising of our work by speaking and writing about it is an essential part of our development as psychotherapists as well as of the profession as a whole. All of this can be exciting and safisfying and facilitate communication between psychotherapists on a national and international level, but it is certainly not without problems, stress and anxiety.

Ethical, moral and legal dilemmas

Dryden and Spurling (1989) quote an American survey which states that legal problems are one of the major stresses experienced by psychotherapists in the USA. UK practitioners have only quite recently become involved with such legal complications, but this trend is changing and legal issues and accusations against psychotherapists have increased steadily. Clarkson and Pokorny state that:

> member organisations of the United Kingdom Council for Psychotherapy (UKCP) must have a published Code of Ethics and all psychotherapists on the Register are required to adhere to the codes of their own organisation, which will have been approved by UKCP.
>
> (1994: 524)

Section 2.11.i states: 'Psychotherapists are required to refrain from any behaviour that may be detrimental to the profession, to colleagues or trainees.' This sounds quite straightforward and self-evident, but situations can arise which create difficult dilemmas and stresses for practitioners. They may not be common, but they occur.

It may emerge in the course of the therapy that a patient is involved in unlawful activities such as taking, buying or selling drugs. The therapist is, of course, perfectly justified in such a case to make it clear to patients that unless they refrain from such activities it will not be possible to continue the therapy, but if something of a therapeutic alliance has been established, however fragile, and perhaps for the first time – as happened with one of my own patients – it can be a hard decision to make and is certainly stressful for therapist and patient alike. Within a hospital setting it is possible to discuss such problems with colleagues who have experience in this field. It is also relatively easy to refer such patients to a drug-dependency unit within the same institution. Without such a referral the therapist can be in danger of litigation.

It is not so long ago that suicide was illegal and suicide attempts were punishable offences, as were homosexual relationships between consenting adults. Fortunately, this is no longer the case, but there are other activities carried out by patients or against them which provide equally difficult dilemmas for practitioners. Patients who fear that they may batter their babies, and those who have in fact done so, do present in private as well as Health Service practices. It is easier to deal with such situations in the Health Service where there are other colleagues to talk to and a better support system, should anything go wrong. Most patients who bring their fear of harming their children do not actually do so, but every now and then there is one who does. This creates a genuine conflict for therapists whose concern is 'to alleviate the suffering of their patients and promote their well-being' (from UKCP Code of Ethics: 521), but not at the risk of harming another human being, especially a child. Therapists may feel that they have to inform the patient's GP or the Social Services Department, but if they tell the patient, as they are expected to, patients may well feel betrayed and the therapy will be in jeopardy, even if the need for such action has been discussed previously. These are moral as well as ethical dilemmas.

Complaints against psychotherapists

Complaints against psychotherapists by patients were quite rare until the late 1970s and early 1980s. More recently there has been an upsurge of such complaints. These can be about a variety of misdemeanours and abuses and can include any behaviour or activity deemed by patients to have been inconsistent with the therapist's organisation's Code of Practice, which covers such issues as terms and conditions of practice, confidentiality, boundaries, competence, and avoidance of any exploitation of patients financially, sexually or emotionally, or terminating therapy prematurely or abruptly.

Whatever the rights and wrongs of any complaint, it can be a nightmare for therapists and is certainly one of the most stressful experiences they can have. Where impropriety of any sort has occurred, sexual or otherwise, it can mean the end of their professional career. Legal proceedings may be put into operation if the charge is of damage to the patient. Even if the charge is completely unwarranted and is part of the patient's transference, projection, fantasy or rage about rejection belonging to an earlier experience, it can be hard for therapists to prove that they have acted within the guidelines of professional behaviour as laid down in the Code of Practice of their organisation.

Being accused of professional misconduct is invariably a tremendous blow to the therapist's self-confidence and self-image, even for one who has been in practice for many years and has a reputation to maintain, but for those at the beginning of their careers it can be devastating, as I found in cases I was involved with in a consultative capacity.

Whilst inevitable, the rise of formal complaints procedures makes the whole process more legalistic and less personal. It can be quite daunting for both parties just to produce the documentation, and both are thrust from what should have been a healing relationship into an adversarial and confrontational one.

If the charges are found to be correct, the sanctions for therapists can be very serious in that they may have their names removed from the UKCP Register and may no longer be able to practise within their organisation. Moreover, false accusations, although rare, do occur, and whatever the outcome of the complaint it is exceedingly stressful and frightening to become an accused person.

Sexual contact with patients

There have been very few surveys and very little research regarding the frequency or the effect of sexual contact between patients and therapists in the United Kingdom before 1992 (Garrett 1986). A good deal of what is known about it therefore comes from work done in the USA, where it has been a significant and recognised problem since the 1970s, and where a large proportion of malpractice deals with allegations of sexual misconduct. The first people who wanted to investigate this were threatened with expulsion from their professional organisations (Butler and Zelen, 1977), and when research was finally permitted, the results were suppressed (Bouhoutsos 1983). It is an issue which causes considerable anxiety among psychotherapists. Evidence shows that practitioners working in the private sector are more vulnerable than those in the public service. It is easier to make allegations when alone with the therapist in a private consulting room than in a hospital or clinic setting.

Serious physical illness of patient

Patients with serious physical illness, especially if life-threatening such as cancer or AIDS, can be very difficult to deal with in therapy and frequently evoke very powerful feelings of helplessness and inadequacy in therapists. Patients who have received a diagnosis of cancer in the course of therapy often feel very angry toward all those who are still fit and healthy. Moreover, they are envious of people who are likely to go on living when their own life is about to come to a premature end. Some of this rage will be directed against the therapist. This is not all due to transference and needs to be acknowledged, accepted and dealt with. It is something most practitioners do not come across very frequently, but when they do, it can be very stressful and also puts them in touch with their own mortality, which is not always welcome.

Crisis for the therapist

Marital difficulties and divorce or serious illness and death of a spouse, child or parent will cause as much pain and distress to psychotherapists as they do to any other person. In these situations the question arises of whether therapists who are in the grip of powerful emotions of their own are able to attend fully to their patients. If they decide to go on seeing patients during a crisis situation, they also have to ask themselves whether it is best to say nothing to patients, leaving them with their fantasies, but also realising that most of them will pick up that something is wrong. Other alternatives might be to give facts which are likely to become known anyhow, such as break-up of marriage, or death in the family, though some psychotherapists would find it unacceptable to do so. There is probably no ideal way to resolve such painful situations, and much will depend on what course of action the therapist feels more comfortable with at that point in time. Information about therapists' personal lives becoming known to patients is often unavoidable if both belong to the same professional organisation or training body, and applies particularly to training analysts/therapists. There are frequent discussions about the advisability of going to meetings which include a social component before or after the formal meeting. Some therapists do not find this too much of a problem, others find it unthinkable.

STRESSES ARISING WITH PARTICULAR GROUPS OF PATIENTS

I am very conscious that every patient is a unique individual with a unique background and experience which accounts for problems and difficulties in the present, and I do not, on the whole, think of people in terms of clinical labels or pathology. There are nevertheless patients with certain conditions or personality structures who generally cause a good deal of stress to most psychotherapists. Those working privately do, of course, have a choice of whether or not to accept such patients, and there is, no doubt, something in each individual which makes them decide on the kind of patients they accept or reject.

Among those who generally evoke anxiety are patients who exhibit self-destructive behaviour – such as substance abuse, anorexia, suicide attempts, self-mutilation – and patients who exhibit aggressive, violent or abusive behaviour towards others. There are also people who are in destructive relationships, people with borderline personalities or with previous psychotic episodes, and people with rigid personality structures and defences such as obsessional and paranoid characteristics.

Talking only in general terms about any of these conditions or giving factual and statistical evidence from surveys would make this a very dull chapter, and although I do not disdain such information and will include it where it has been available to me, I intend to illustrate my contentions with vignettes from my own experience and from that of colleagues, trainees and supervisees. This will make the chapter less scientific, but will, I hope, illustrate more meaningfully what can cause stress to psychotherapists. Names and details have been changed in order to preserve anonymity.

Suicidal patients

Suicide and suicide attempts are probably the most traumatic experience a psychotherapist can have. It is something we do not much like to talk about, and although 'many therapists may have to endure at least one, it is very hard and brings to the fore with singular clarity what a tightrope we are on as we do our balancing act' (Coltart 1994: 94).

During my time in the Health Service 25 per cent of my patients had made previous suicide attempts or were regarded as suicidal at the time of referral, and a few needed to be hospitalised periodically. Since moving to the private sector I have been more wary about taking on patients who were known to have been suicidal. The exceptions were two patients who had seen me previously at the hospital where I had worked, one of whom, Adriana, had gained enough insight and ego-strength not to present much of a risk to herself or to me when she returned for a brief period of further therapy (although one could never be absolutely sure).

Adriana was adamant that she did not want to see anybody else at the hospital, although she did not have much money to spare, and financially it would be hard, even at considerably reduced fees. Having seen her on and off for six years I did not feel I could turn her away. But her very severe depression which in the past had required hospitalisation had contained delusional features, which would have been very alarming had I encountered them for the first time in my private practice. I knew that she had functioned well in the intervening period, being responsible for a major national charity, but it was the demise of the charity and therefore loss of her job which triggered the 'relapse into depression' that she wanted to confront. I felt uneasy about seeing her in my private consulting room, in my own home, and without the receptionist taking phone calls and to greet her as someone well known in the department. Adriana too felt more inhibited, and we had to spend quite a bit of time dealing with the feelings relating to these external changes. If I had not known her so well from her previous therapy with me, I doubt that I would have taken her privately. As it was, I was very aware of the risk involved, but felt it was a justifiable risk to take.

A patient kills himself

Seeing Adriana caused some unease and anxiety, but the actual death of a patient is obviously much more traumatic and depressing than the possibility of a suicide attempt.

Fred was a young musician whom I had also seen briefly during my time in the Health Service. He had tracked me down at my home, and like Adriana he did not want to go back to the hospital where he no longer knew anybody. He was feeling anxious and frightened and could not see where his life was going. I offered him one session to look at the possibilities which were available to him outside the Health Service. I was just about to go on holiday and fitted him in rather reluctantly because he was insistent – which was unlike him.

He had always been a very lonely and isolated man, but since his father's death earlier that year he had become more frightened and unhappy. He was not teaching any more and work as a musician was erratic and required more initiative than he was able to muster.

We looked at the possibilities for counselling or therapy which might be possible outside the Health Service, and I gave him the name of an organisation to approach, but also suggested that it might be a good idea for him to go back to the hospital, where I had first seen him.

On my return from holiday I had another call from him in which he sounded very agitated. I then spent the morning between patients trying unsuccessfully to contact his doctor, and eventually rang the hospital asking for an urgent domiciliary visit, thinking how fortunate it was that I still maintained my contact with the hospital. The duty psychiatrist went to see Fred at the end of his morning session. When he arrived, he found a commotion outside the house. Fred had jumped out of the third-floor window and killed himself.

Fred's death still haunts me. Like most psychotherapists whose patient has committed suicide, I question whether I had done all I could, whether I should have been aware, during the initial encounter, that Fred was heading for a psychotic episode, whether I had been his last resort and had failed him. There are no answers to these questions. There rarely are. We do the best we can, and sometimes it is not enough or not good enough. Some guilt may be excessive and unwarranted, but I believe that in some way I failed Fred by not agreeing to see him again and by not recognising how desperate he was. This is something I have to live with, as do other psychotherapists whose patients have committed suicide.

Access to in-patient facilities, psychiatrists and general practitioners

The experience with Fred made me realise the importance of access to psychiatric or other in-patient facilities for practitioners in private practice, and how difficult it is for psychotherapists who have never worked in the Health Service and have no particular contacts. It helped me to understand the reluctance of many practitioners to accept patients who represent a suicide risk or are likely to go through psychotic episodes. I used to be quite scathing about that when I worked in the Health Service, talking jokingly of those practitioners who only accepted 'healthy patients'. I see their point now, but deplore the situation which makes this caution necessary.

Contact with GPs is clearly important, although the patient's wishes regarding such contact have to be respected. Attitudes to non-medical psychotherapists have changed considerably in recent years since psychotherapy has become established as a profession in its own right, but there is still in many cases quite a variation in the ease with which contact between medical and non-medical psychotherapists and a patient's doctor is established.

When, on a few occasions, I have needed to make contact with the GP, it has been quite difficult to find a time when neither of us was seeing a patient and we could both give the necessary time and attention to an exchange of views, or whatever else was required.

Seeing patients in destructive or sado-masochistic relationships

People stuck in such situations often effect a sort of equilibrium which depends on not confronting the destructiveness of the relationship. They are not able to leave it or to live with it. The cost is often a paralysing depression. If the masochistic partner comes into therapy and gets in touch with his/her underlying rage the situation is potentially explosive.

One patient, Donald, stands out in my mind. His marital relationship was pure hell, but he felt unable to get out of it even though he was convinced that it would end in murder or suicide, and I too feared that some disaster was imminent. I had an overpowering impulse to do something, to make him leave this explosive and dangerous situation, but of course, that is not the psychotherapist's function. I was able to contain my anxiety and fear sufficiently to refrain from telling him what to do, but I suspect that therapists do communicate their hopes and wishes in other ways, even when this is not our conscious intention. The containment of our own strong feelings and impulses is, of course a vital aspect of therapeutic skill and experience, but it is stressful, nevertheless, and the trap of trying to save the patient from getting hurt is one therapists can fall into very easily.

Anorexic patients

Like suicidal and potentially psychotic patients, anorexics too can be at risk, if their weight becomes dangerously low. If that happens, access to the patient's doctor or to specialist services is essential.

Lorna was a gifted art student in her twenties. She had been hospitalised three times because of excessive weight loss, but on each occasion she had put on just enough weight to get her discharge, and as soon as she was back in her own home she started again on her rigid regime of fasting. She showed all the characteristics of the typical anorexic such as the delusional belief that when approaching normal weight for her height and age, she looked disgusting, and that being emaciated was beautiful. She needed to be in control, and controlling her intake of food and her body was the one thing she could be sure of. She was also trying hard to control what she was willing to accept from me, and what I must and must not do.

Her main reason for wanting therapy at that point was that so much time and energy went into thinking about food that her college work was suffering, and her tutor had suggested that she should try and get some help and had mentioned my name. I had worked with a few anorexics in the Health Service and had some knowledge of the particular hassles and difficulties involved and I thought I would see her, even if I had to refer her on. It is often a dilemma, whether to see a patient first for some sort of assessment, knowing that it is unlikely that we will take them on, or just to provide them or the referrer with names. There are advantages and disadvantages both ways: I do not believe that every therapist is right for every patient or vice versa. In order to do some matching, I like to see the patient at least once. That of course has the disadvantage of some transference being established and patients feeling rejected and angry at having to go through their history and presenting problems again. It also makes it harder for the receiving therapist to establish a therapeutic alliance, but making a referral without having seen the patient first seems like a lottery. It may be a kind of omnipotence to imagine that this kind of matching of patient and therapist is really possible or even useful, and different psychotherapists no doubt make different choices. I decided that the stress of seeing someone like Lorna privately without all the support structures available in the NHS was probably too hard and she would have to be referred to someone who had those benefits available to them.

Another stress for me in these situations was having to accept that working privately meant a scaling down of the range of patients I could see. It was a blow to my omnipotence, perhaps quite a useful one, but it also made me very aware of some of the difficult decisions which I had to take on my own without the easy access to colleagues which the hospital setting provided. For practitioners who have only seen two or three selected patients during their training and who have never worked in a hospital where they would see a wider range of people, such decisions are likely to be even more stressful although supervisors may be available for consultation. It may be felt that I have allocated too much space to talking about personal dilemmas with particular patients, and that these would not be relevant to the majority of psychotherapists. It seems to me, though, that the sorts of decisions and choices I have described in connection with these particular patients are issues causing stress to many other psycho-therapist colleagues I have spoken to.

Patients who suffered sexual, violent or ritual abuse

Psychotherapy with patients who have suffered such abuse in childhood can be exceedingly stressful for patients and therapists alike. Although as therapists we are constantly exposed to dreadful accounts of neglect, deprivation and cruelty experienced by many patients, there is something about the experience of severe sexual, violent and ritual abuse of children which is so unthinkable and inconceivable that society and psychotherapists refused to acknow-ledge it until relatively recently.

When psychotherapists began to be faced with patients who reported experience of abuse, often with great intensity of feelings, they found it very harrowing to stay empathically with such patients. Their dilemma was in some cases whether to believe patients, who sometimes found it very hard to believe in their own memories. As children they had often been threatened with dire consequences if they ever told anyone about the abuse. They had convinced them-selves that no one would believe them, and frequently that was the case. Some were quite ambivalent about memories, because they were also attached to the abuser. Psychotherapists found that they had to adopt very flexible methods in order to be of help to these patients. Some found it necessary to extend the fifty-minute hour, others decided to work with a co-therapist, but for all of them the strain of working with this group of people was extreme. Moreover, the former wish not to know has more recently given way to the opposite and has on occasion resulted in false allegations. Some social workers and psychotherapists have been accused of trying to find evidence where it does not exist, or to evoke what have been called 'false memories'.

I was myself very dubious about the existence of ritual or satanic abuse until I saw a young man whose memories of the horrific tortures and sexual degradation inflicted upon him from age 4 were recalled and were accompanied by such detail and intensity of feeling that my doubts disappeared. He frequently went into a trance-like state in which he described what had happened to him. Evidence of the occurrence of such abuse from many highly reliable sources is now available, including an excellent book edited by Sinason (1994).

This is not the place to go into therapeutic procedures, but to look at the causes of stress to therapists, and I now know from my own experience, as well as from that of many other therapists, that the overpowering feeling of helplessness and powerlessness of the abused child have to be tolerated by therapists too when they are confronted with the shame, despair and feelings of utter hopelessness of these patients.

ADVERSE EFFECTS OF THE PROFESSION ON THE THERAPIST'S FAMILY RELATIONSHIPS

Therapists who spend around eight hours a day seeing patients frequently feel emotionally drained at the end of the day and have little emotion left over for family or friends. Some require space and time to recover before they are ready to involve themselves with family affairs, and need their spouses and children to respect this. Others are able to cut off from their work situation quite quickly and do not allow anything to spill over into their private lives. However, marriages are undoubtedly put under strain, and marital breakdown among therapists is high despite our supposedly greater self-knowledge and maturity.

Over-involvement

There is always a risk that we may become over-involved with particular kinds of patients whose pathology triggers some of our own. This can generally be managed through examination of the counter-transference and monitoring of our work, but there are some conditions which tend to evoke extreme reactions. Some of these concern people who have experienced torture in countries where this is common, or have been in concentration camps, or who have suffered violent or sexual abuse and re-experience in therapy what happened to them. It could be said that this is not different from other horrendous experiences which patients bring to their sessions, but it seems that Post-Traumatic Stress Syndrome can have a particularly powerful effect on some therapists who find it difficult to maintain the balance between the observing and the empathic self. This applies particularly to patients who suffered abuse as children, or experienced torture and to therapists who were themselves camp survivors, or refugees and who lost families during the Holocaust.

Sickness and ageing

Being sick and getting old is generally stressful, but in some ways it seems even harder for many therapists to accept that they can be vulnerable, unwell and subject to the effects of old age in the same way as other people. Many therapists find it hard to acknowledge that they are ill or getting old, feeling tired during the day and having to cancel sessions because of ill health. J. C. Norcross and J. D. Guy write: 'Despite our secret fantasy that prominent therapists have found a way to inoculate themselves against the sources of distress encountered by their patients and less experienced colleagues, a careful reading of their biographies proves otherwise' (Dryden and Spurling 1989: 312).

Martin Grotjahn (1987: 249) describes very movingly what it is like to be sick and facing 80. He writes:

> I have been sick with kidney-stones, gall stones, appendicitis – but sickness came and left my life, and I continued more or less as before. Facing 80, I probably have to realise that I am already old, to my surprise. Other people around me got old, but I did not. I never felt old.

One night shortly before his eightieth birthday Grotjahn had an angina attack. He experienced indescribable terror and nameless anxiety. The attack passed, and in the morning he went to see his doctor, but already regretted going. 'I thought it was embarrassing and shameful for a therapist to feel anxiety. The pain of the previous night was almost gone – if there ever was a man with "imagined ill-health" it was I' (ibid.).

Grotjahn describes feelings about illness and ageing which are common to many practitioners. I can certainly identify with them very closely. To be ill and have to cancel patients is very hard. I know it is absurd, neurotic and omnipotent, but the hassle of having to cancel patients for a day or, worse, for longer, seems too great. I also know that it can actually bring up very helpful material in patients' therapy to recognise that psychotherapists are human and vulnerable. Many practitioners deal with illness sensibly and realistically, but it does undoubtedly cause additional stress at the time. It can also be very helpful if patients can subsequently bring their anger and hurt about having been abandoned and neglected or their fear about the possibility of the therapist's death. Sometimes they also feel fear and guilt in case they might have been responsible for the therapist's illness. All of this can, of course, be grist to the therapeutic mill and help with exploration of the transference, but the after-effects of the therapist's illness can be considerable, even if it is not a prolonged or serious one. If the illness is serious and it is difficult to know how long it may last, or indeed whether the therapist will be able to return to his or her practice, it obviously becomes a much more distressing and difficult situation.

Many psychotherapists are quite good at denying that they are getting old and, like Martin Grotjahn, they see their contemporaries ageing but do not readily apply such a term to themselves. We do not have a specified retiring age, and even though we tire more easily, have more aches and pains, and do not remember so well what patients said in the last session, there are quite a number who carry on into their seventies and eighties. Having to give up the profession which met so many needs and gave so much satisfaction in spite of its stresses can be the greatest stress of all.

REFERENCES

Bouhoutsos, J. (1983) 'Literature survey', in P. Clarkson and M. Pokorny (eds) (1994).
Butler, S. and Zelen, S. L. (1977) 'Literature survey', in P. Clarkson and M. Pokorny (eds) (1994).
Clarkson, P. and Pokorny, M. (eds) (1994) *Handbook of Psychotherapy*, London: Routledge.
Coltart, N. (1994) *How to Survive as a Psychotherapist*, London: Sheldon Press.
Dryden, W. and Spurling, L. (1989) *On Becoming A Psychotherapist*, London: Tavistock/Routledge.
Garrett, I. (1986) 'Understanding sexual contact in psychotherapy', in P. Clarkson and M. Pokorny (eds) (1994).

Goldberg, C. (1992) *The Seasoned Psychotherapist*, New York: W. W. Norton & Co, Inc.

Grotjahn, M. (1984) 'Being sick and turning 80', in *My Favourite Patient: The Memoirs of a Psychoanalyst*, Frankfurt am Main, Bern, New York, Paris: Peter Lang.

Sinasson, V. (1994) *Treating Survivors of Satanist Abuse* London: Routledge.

Chapter 15

Stress and psychotherapy: an overview

Frank Margison

'Stress' is an over-used and vague term. Typical of 'dead' metaphors it fails to speak to the reader any longer and we feel we are in the realm of management jargon and out of touch with lived experience. In this situation, as therapists, we might try to breathe life back into the metaphor by allowing space for imaginative play before returning to the way the metaphor has been used in a more formal way.

My first connection with the word 'stress' is a link with the world of objects in the physical rather than the psychodynamic sense. If I were a structural engineer I would be concerned with the ability of a structure and its component materials to deal with the forces which will potentially compress and distort it. The material under stress would have intrinsic properties such as elasticity and brittleness which affect its ability to react to a load. In supporting an external load I would be concerned about how any supporting element might redistribute the load.

My responsibility for the safety of the structure would lead me to set maximum loadings and be aware of any tolerances to allow for exceptional conditions. I would not be showing an understanding of stress and its effects on, say, a bridge if I were unaware of the context in which the stresses might be applied. My awareness of materials science would help me to realise that some elements are more resistant to compressive forces and some to strain forces which pull the elements apart.

The richness of such a metaphor allows me to draw helpful analogies in the world of persons about intrinsic properties and also about the effects of the conditions under which stress is experienced. The ability to use analogical and open thinking is itself one of the first casualties when a therapist is under excessive stress. Alternatively the metaphorical might be mistaken for the real – leading to a rigid, rule-bound existence where people are treated as though they have become physical objects in our internal world.

This book uses 'stress' in several ways: the usage is variable and idiosyncratic. It would not be helpful to reduce this diversity to one common meaning but it may be useful to outline the various underlying views which influence the various authors' analyses. Their views are summarised below:

1 Stress is a *result* – for example, stress can be seen in depression, interpersonal problems, or the 'burn-out syndrome' (see chapters 1, 3, 6, 14 particularly).

2 Stress is the *impact* of certain aspects of the job – for example, its complexity (chapters 4, 5, 6, 7, 12 particularly); its variability or lack of it (chapters 6, 14); its severity (chapters 5, 6, 7, 8, 9, 12, 13); and the total amount of work (chapter 14).

3 Stress is a consequence of *prior vulnerability* caused by previous experience and innate qualities in the therapist (see chapters 2, 7 particularly).

4 Stress is the result of a *mismatch between demand and resources*. The resources might be *internal* (resilience, maturity etc. – see chapters 2, 3, 9) or *external* (psychiatric back-up through to personal support – see chapters 3, 5, 13, 14).

5 Stress is a result of *role conflict* – for example, the tension between two professional roles as doctor or clinical psychologist and therapist (chapters 3, 14).

6 Stress is an *experienced* state which can be understood by re-flection, self-analysis and existential analysis. It can be appre-hended by experiences such as dread, fear, irritability, etc., or by the lack of experience, such as deadness, being cut off, isolation and aloneness (chapters 5, 6, 8, 9, 10, 12, 14).

In this chapter, after an analysis of what 'stress' means and what is known about its adverse effects, methods are given for therapists to analyse their own experience of stress with some suggestions about how stress might be faced.

First, it is useful to reflect on how different authors have con-ceptualised the other key word in the title of this chapter: 'psycho-therapy'. Some authors have dealt with particular modes of therapy (family versus individual, for example); others have dealt primarily with the context (for example, NHS versus non-NHS). Psychotherapy should not be seen as unitary and its diversity needs to be understood before we can generalise from the foregoing chapters.

WHAT IS PSYCHOTHERAPY?

Most contributors have given their own definition, but it is useful to be aware that the term is often used in a broad way to include therapy as an adjunct to other treatments, unstructured 'talking treatments' and structured therapies of various types.

It is useful to describe psychotherapy in terms of:

- *modality or technique* (psychodynamic, behavioural-cognitive, systemic, humanistic/integrative, and others)
- *format* (individual, couple, family, small and large group, community)
- *length* (very brief including crisis interventions, 1–5 sessions; brief, 6–20 sessions; medium, 21–50 sessions; long-term, more than 50 sessions – although these cut-off points are arbitrary)
- *frequency* (for example, several times weekly; weekly; or monthly)
- *'depth'* (depending on the extent to which material previously unremembered by the client is uncovered)
- *degree of structure* (for example, the extent to which aims are defined at the outset; the extent of reliance on a shared 'plan formulation'; the consistency of session boundaries; and reliance on agreed activities such as setting homework tasks)
- *mutuality and openness* (this describes the extent to which the therapy approximates to an equal and symmetrical relationship and specifically how open the therapist is about his or her own experiences in the session)

In this book there is a wide range of these descriptive elements represented by the various authors who try at various points to draw attention to particular elements. For example, Barker and Sharpe draw particular attention to the added complexity of working with several clients simultaneously in family and group therapy respectively.

Psychotherapists themselves are also seen as contributing to the way that the therapy should be described. The *developmental stage* of the therapist is important for several authors. Cushway deals explicitly with beginning or trainee therapists, whereas other authors deal with later stages (the transitional phase between trainee and fully-fledged practitioner; the mid-life therapist; the therapist approaching the end of his or her working life). The different life-stages bring different strengths and vulnerabilities with them into the therapeutic space.

The *organisational setting* is dealt with explicitly in three chapters: the NHS and non-NHS in chapters 13 and 14; and the ministry in chapter 10. The different professional groups involved in therapy are mentioned explicitly by some authors (psychology and psychiatry by Cushway and ministers of religion by Marteau) and the importance of the team setting is shown to be crucial in work with children (Dale) and with adolescents (Hyatt Williams), and in a different context in the contributions of Sinason (working with the learning-disabled) and Wallbank (working with the bereaved, often with links to hospital and hospice practice).

The authors are also dealing with very disparate *client groups* including the extremely demanding work such as happens with borderline patients. These are mentioned by several authors because that client group has a unique ability to penetrate the normal defensive structures of the therapist. An overlapping clinical group causing particular stress is that of patients who are actively suicidal. We could add the particular difficulties of working with patients who are psychotic or who have experienced abuse or torture, and indeed any clinical state which challenges our basic feelings of security.

Different contributors take a different '*distance*' in their accounts of stress at different points in the narrative. For example, Cooper (chapter 6) and Marteau (chapter 10) both take a very personal stance in their accounts, whereas other authors have stressed what is known from the wider literature. The first approach is personal and direct and allows us as readers to identify, but at the same time we cannot generalise from the accounts in quite the same way as when we are situated firmly in the middle of an authoritative view of the literature on stress.

Sharpe (chapter 12) and Cushway (chapter 3) have both succeeded in walking the tightrope by giving very personal accounts, at the same time summarising and giving a bibliography of other writers on related themes.

The strategies adopted by the writers are perhaps analogous to the various coping strategies used by different therapists: some see therapy as a wholly personal endeavour, whereas others stress the technical and problem-solving approaches which can reduce the pressure on the therapist.

STRESS IN OCCUPATIONAL PSYCHOLOGY

There has been a move towards the development of comprehensive, or at least integrated, bio-psycho-social theories to explain the adverse impact of stress (Leventhal and Tomarken 1987). Within such a model a number of general points have been broadly accepted. The way we conceptualise stressors is based on our underlying theoretical model. Hence, a psychodynamic therapist will be likely to conceptualise stress quite differently from a family therapist. But both will have a similar bias towards a clinical perspective and come up with a different view of stressors than would an epidemiologist. This bias is manifest in the content of this book which emphasises heavily the clinical view of stress, but perhaps understates a more sociological perspective which would look at the general conditions of a therapist's working life.

Individuals differ in their response to stress. The presence of a stressful event does not absolutely determine outcome even for the most extreme conditions. The response will vary according to how predictable, controllable, conflictual and episodic is the stress.

These general characteristics of stress come from an empirical tradition which moves from observation, through correlation to hypothesis testing. In the field of psychotherapy as an occupation vulnerable to stress, we are reliant on very general observations and analogy with other professions such as medicine and clinical psychology.

The generation and maintenance of the stress process is seen as a 'constructive activity' of the organism (Neisser 1967), a process of mediating meaning in the human context. Stressors (Leventhal and Tomarken 1987) are divided into (a) discrete events (for example, Holmes and Rahe 1967), (b) ongoing role strains (Pearlin 1983), and (c) 'daily hassles' (Lazarus and Folkman 1984) – with additional attention paid to (d) 'contextual factors' (Brown and Harris 1978) and (e) the 'life-style' in which stressful events are embedded (Kasl 1983).

The work on stress in psychotherapists needs to be seen in this broader context so that conclusions are not reached prematurely. In research terms we are still at the observational level prior to the correlational stage and still further from meaningful hypothesis testing. Sussman (1995) uses the descriptive level as a point of departure encouraging his contributors to describe the 'hazards of psychotherapy' from a very personal perspective (see particularly chapters by E. Tick, E. W. L. Smith, M. Berger, M. F. Myers, and M. Stark in Sussman 1995). Similarly, Guy (1987) gives a personal and practical account of burn-out but his classification of stresses is *ad hoc* rather than empirically derived.

Practical and descriptive accounts, which form the main method in this volume, should not be undervalued. Jenkins (1989) writing on the hazards of psychiatric practice gives a very sobering, practical account of dealing with counter-transference, harrassment, violent patients, assaults on the therapist, suicide, malpractice, sexual contact, therapeutic impasses, confidentiality and issues of consent. He covers several issues facing practitioners which are rarely covered during training, and writes what is in effect a 'survival guide'.

THE EFFECTS OF STRESS ON THERAPISTS – 'BURN-OUT'

Perhaps the commonest condition described as a consequence of stress is the so-called 'burn-out' syndrome (Margison 1987), originally described by Freudenberger and Richelson (1980). Freudenberger described a particular constellation of affective responses which was then linked to analytic practice (Freudenberger and Robbins 1979). They pay particular attention to the difficulty for the therapist of 'holding' feelings of 'hurt, anger, joy and sadness that he must share but is unable to share with anyone, especially not his patient'. As Farber (1983) and Fisher (1983) have pointed out, the narcissistic aspects of burn-out are crucial to their psychodynamic understanding and treatment. Freudenberger and Richelson (1980) comment that burn-out is a particular dynamic constellation with 'fatigue or frustration brought about by devotion to a cause, way of life or relationship that failed to produce the expected reward'.

This implies that the survival of a part of the self is invested in something or someone external. The therapist is reliant on the survival of a sense of identity as a therapist, which in turn has been idealised. As Kohut (1977) recognised, the survival of the self can be linked to self-objects which either mirror back a good and solid sense of self or provide an externalised ideal to which the therapist can aspire.

In therapist burn-out there is an increasingly desperate attempt to revive such an experience by ever more frantic efforts. During this process the therapist loses reality-testing to the extent that he or she cannot see that their work is steadily deteriorating as exhaustion inevitably sets in. This formulation explains why the therapist might be particularly resistant to explanation or suggestions that he or she 'takes it easy'; the therapist feels that personal survival is at stake. Farber (1983) suggests that a helper might be best advised to empathise with the heroic efforts in an unyielding world rather than challenge the defensive structure. The empathic strategy often leads to an opportunity for the burned-out therapist to feel his or her narcissistic dilemma is recognised and can trust the helper to share some of the underlying state of depletion and misery.

A quite different approach is taken by Pines and Aronson (1981) who describe a syndrome which is clinically indistinguishable from depression, but state that the cause may be a unique combination of pressure hitting an exquisite vulnerability in the sufferer.

The effect on the client or patient when a therapist is burned-out is the approach taken by Maslach (1976) who points out that therapists 'lose all concern, all emotional feeling for the people they work with, and come to treat them in a detached or dehumanised way'. Edelwich and Brodsky (1980) make similar points about the effects on the therapist who suffers a 'progressive loss of idealism, purpose, and concern' but they see it as a specific result of conditions under which the therapist works.

THE RISKS OF STRESS

There is no work published on the actual morbidity and mortality of stress on psychotherapists, probably because psychotherapy does not exist as a separate occupational category. In contrast, there has been extensive work on the effect of stress on other health workers (Firth 1986; Payne and Firth-Cozens 1987; Margison 1987; Rich and Pitts 1979; Rose and Rosow 1973; Ross 1973). Doctors have particularly high rates of disorder, after allowing for social-class differences, and, among doctors, psychiatrists are a particularly high-risk group for depression, alcoholism and suicide.

It is not appropriate to generalise from this professional group to psychotherapists and there is simply insufficient information to draw conclusions about the specific risks to psychotherapists. However, it is probably fair to generalise about the *types* of disorder to which we should pay special attention. Turning to substances for relief of anxiety and depression is a known risk in doctors, and psycho-therapists bear personal responsibility for patients who themselves are frightened and in despair. The other principal risk – of the psychotherapist committing suicide (largely related to depression which itself is often inadequately treated) – is rarely discussed at professional meetings and there is no data on its prevalence among psychotherapists. This is partly a technical issue as, even if the number of suicides *were* known, it would be impossible to establish a relative risk because we do not know how many psychotherapists there are in the population.

Another important problem which may be linked to stress in the therapist is the transgression of professional boundaries, particularly through sexual contact with a client or patient (Holmes and Lindley 1991; Gartrell *et al.* 1986; Holroyd and Brodsky 1977). Although sometimes a retrospective justification, therapists who have admitted sexual contact often state that they were under intense stress at the time.

The therapist's life also has an impact on the family. Although, again, few studies have estimated the actual rates of marital and family breakdown in the families of therapists, there is every reason to assume that these might be important effects of stress. Family disruption might be particularly important for those therapists who have difficulty in limiting their commitment to work and cope with stress by spending even more time at work.

HOW CAN THERAPISTS ASSESS THEIR OWN PRONENESS TO STRESS?

The first step in the assessment of stress-proneness is to be able to be dispassionate in analysing our jobs. All therapists seem to develop particular blind spots for aspects of their work which they conceal even from themselves. For example, in clinics which profess to offer short-term therapy there are clients who have been coming for several years but are somehow 'hidden' in the system. Work writing papers, refereeing articles, writing supervision reports, advising colleagues about training are all 'invisible' parts of the job which seem to be discounted when we analyse our role.

Traditionally there have been informal methods for reviewing our work. For example, many therapists have taken time for personal reflection. This might be time alone; time with a trusted colleague, perhaps with a former therapist, mentor or supervisor; or time away at a retreat or workshop which might be focused on personal reflection as such or provide opportunities for reflection through group work and exercises.

The opportunities for these experiences are probably reduced, at least for those working in organisations, as study budgets are increasingly committed to management and statutory training rather than personal development. Some therapists may go back into a further period of personal therapy, commonly at a point where they are facing a personal crisis at work or within the family. Awareness of the imbalance between work life and personal fulfilment (including close relationships) is a very common outcome of such periods of reflection.

Clinically, we need to be alert to signals of excessive burden in ourselves in the way that we might when working with a client. With time it is possible to learn early warning signals. These are often in the form of 'too much/too little' messages. Increasing alcohol consumption, weight, comfort eating, or use of drugs, or decreasing exercise, holidays or time spent on interests should be obvious to therapists who are trained to be self-aware as part of the job. Nevertheless it is a common experience for therapists working with other therapists that these simple indicators are ignored; indeed, sensitivity to such warning signals is probably one of the early casualties of excessive stress.

Having been made aware of an imbalance, the therapist may well be exhorted to 'get extra support'. As mentioned in the structural engineering metaphor earlier, we would not merely ask for 'extra support' for a bridge facing excessive loads, we would analyse the nature of the excess load and define more precisely what extra structures were needed, or if necessary we would restrict the flow of traffic to allow for the reduced load-bearing capacity whilst repairs were carried out.

WHAT IS SUPPORT?

From a research perspective, the concept of support is seen as important but highly problematic (Payne and Jones 1987). The main instruments used to measure support have problems with both reliability and validity. There are also general questions about the way in which support might protect health. There are three main possibilities. There might be a direct effect on health (for example, comfort might reduce symptoms or the lack of human contact might reduce health because a basic human need is not being met). Support might however have an effect on reducing the stress (by offering advice, solving a problem or directly removing the stress). Finally, support might influence the relationship between stress and health. This is usually referred to as 'stress buffering'. This is largely a research concern at present, but there are implications for how we set up and target support systems. Under the direct effect model, extra support will always have a beneficial effect, whereas in the buffering model the presence of support only becomes critical at times of high stress. The buffering model does still rely on some mechanism of action and House (1981) suggests dividing support into four types which might be effective in different situations. He distinguishes emotional, instrumental, informational and appraisal forms of support (see later for links with the concept of 'coping').

It is helpful to be more precise about what elements there might be to support in the therapeutic context. Clearly, we need to pay some attention to reducing the load, but it is difficult to do this if we are not aware of which aspects of the job are stressful and which are supportive. Moreover, there is the added problem that the therapist might have become reliant on excessive workloads as a last-ditch defence to maintain self-esteem and would feel further undermined if the possibility of escaping into work were suddenly removed.

At a personal level, different therapists have different needs. *Affirmation* in the sense of acknowledging the value of what has been achieved may be sufficient for some. Others may actually be hungry for *admiration* which goes further than affirmation and reflects back an enhanced sense of self. The need for high levels of these narcissistic supplies may be part of the therapist's underlying character or it may be a temporary effect of depletion and depression. Both affirmation and admiration are subtly different from *being loved* which implies, among many other things, that the person is still valued despite his or her failings and weaknesses. Without the right balance of these personal supports it is very difficult to reduce the load placed on the therapist without worsening the sense of personal inadequacy.

Professional needs are also important. *Diffusion of responsibility* by sharing a specific aspect of the load may be required, for example when as a colleague you offer a second opinion with sensitivity to the therapist's vulnerable self-esteem, or provide material support by, for example, facilitating an ill patient's emergency admission in a crisis.

Redirection is a mixture of the personal and the professional, by listening and drawing attention to something that has been overlooked. This might occur in a supervisory setting, but might be an informal comment that you have not seen your colleague socially for some time. Social isolation is one of the most helpful indicators that something is going wrong for a colleague, but by its very nature it is easy to miss.

Support, as mentioned earlier, might be through the provision of *space to think and reformulate*. Unfortunately, managers have confused the aims of so-called 'support groups' for staff teams. In some specialised settings it is useful to have a personal group led by an outside facilitator to discuss the complex tangle of projection, projective identification and splitting in a team and its clients. These can support a team in its work but are not intended to provide personal help for the members (although this is sometimes a by-product).

In contrast, another model of support group is intentionally task-centred, usually with a structured format to allow resolution of problems (Scully 1983). These can be effective even when all staff cannot be present at each meeting if the structure makes that inevitable, for example for nurses who work rotating shifts. However, the intention of such groups is again to improve the working capacity of a group rather than to provide personal support.

In addition to the support group at work there is the need for staff to be able to reflect on their work as individuals rather than as elements of a team and the *retreat* model may then be more appropriate. The contrast between the work environment and the 'free space' can itself be a source of pressure and sometimes a *consultancy* model is preferable. In this, a consultant helps the therapist to analyse his or her own support structure and stresses in a more systematic way.

SYSTEMATIC ANALYSIS OF STRESS AND JOB STRUCTURE

Management theory is, perhaps, an alien discipline for many practising psychotherapists, but the tools for job analysis are directly relevant to the amelioration of job stress. There are many courses drawing on management theory. This brief account acknowledges the influence of the Open University, NHS Training Directorate, and Institute of Health Services Management course 'Managing Health Services' (Open University 1993). Their Management Education Scheme by Open Learning (MESOL) works on the assumption that practitioners learn best by applying theory in the practical context of their own working lives.

In this spirit, the next section offers a few ideas for how therapists might usefully analyse their own situation, with follow-up references where appropriate. The first step is to understand the nature of the job we do. This involves five subsidiary questions (based on Open University 1993):

- What are we doing?
- Why are we doing it?
- What demands does this make?
- What constraints are placed on me?
- What choices are open to me?

Each of these questions can be answered with respect to the actual job of being a psychotherapist; with regard to any team of which we might be a member; and to our 'organisation'. The latter often generates divided loyalties between an employing organisation, our professional affiliation and any training organisation with which we might have an allegiance.

Answering '*what we do*' depends on us being able to analyse time into meaningful categories such as direct therapy, supervision, teaching, etc. and then sampling a couple of weeks' activity using a diary.

'*Why*' provokes more difficult conceptual questions, but one approach is to examine the roles we take on. Mintzberg (1971; Pugh and Hickson 1989) suggests that we divide work into three domains: **interpersonal**, **informational**, and **decisional**. He sub-divides these categories further into categories which are more explicitly managerial, but the essential elements are useful in analysing the therapist's role.

The **interpersonal** roles are of *figurehead*, *leader* and *liaison*. The tension of being a 'figurehead' with its position and authority is uncomfortable for many therapists who stress the equality of the therapeutic relationship at the expense of the asymmetry (Hobson 1985). The 'leadership' function is similarly problematic in that it highlights the tension between the needs of a particular client and the needs of the organisation, whereas the 'liaison' role generates different role tensions when confidentiality is under threat.

The **informational** role involves *monitoring progress*. At an informal level this is usually non-stressful, but conflict arises when the monitoring is required for external agencies.

The final heading of **decision-maker** is probably the most conflictual for a therapist. The *entrepreneur* role in this context refers to the responsibility on the therapist to decide to change tack if there are changed external circumstances, whereas the *disturbance-handler* role refers to managing conflict within the therapy. *Allocating* *resources* is very difficult for a therapist who sees his or her responsibility exclusively to the client currently in therapy. Similarly the *negotiator* role is a source of conflict within the therapeutic relationship when there is a tension between what the client explicitly wants (for example, to be seen indefinitely) and the therapist's broader responsibilities.

This way of analysing a therapist's job may seem uncomfortable and distant from the usual concerns of therapy, but it can highlight which roles are particularly conflictual for an individual.

A similar analysis can be carried out for the *demands, constraints* and *freedoms* of the therapist's job as suggested by Stewart (1982). One surprising result for many therapists is that there is a high degree of constraint resulting from breaking the working week into session-size segments and committing many of these sessions to invariant activities. There are also unusual demands for consistency which provide stability but also constrain therapists. The apparent freedoms even within private psychotherapy practice are limited compared to most professional jobs.

Time management is a skill frequently offered on stress management courses. Typically the participant is asked to keep a detailed time diary broken down into tasks which are given different priorities. The concept of 'time wasters' (that is, activities, such as telephone interruptions which distract from the most valued activities) is often well-managed by therapists. However, the strategic management of time is much more difficult for therapists who typically will not have set themselves formal objectives (such as how many papers to be published annually), which makes it difficult to keep track of the overall shape of the job.

There are specific conflicts related to delegation as a way of managing time. For example, a therapist may feel a conflict of loyalties when handing on a patient after assessment, particularly if a close bond has formed at that initial contact. The conflict of 'trust versus control' faced by managers is faced day-to-day by therapists when they supervise or allocate patients.

JOB DESIGN AND JOB SATISFACTION

There is an extensive literature on what makes jobs satisfying and how staff can be remotivated (Alderfer 1983; Hackman and Oldham 1976; Handy 1993; Herzberg 1968a; 1968b; Maslow 1970; Open University 1993). Maslow's (1970) hierarchical approach will be well known to therapists with its emphasis on meeting survival needs before growth needs. He delineates physiological, safety, social and 'ego' needs which must be met before 'self-actualization' can occur. Despite this being known at a theoretical level, therapists do not always apply this as knowledge in action, as can be witnessed by neglecting meal breaks, recurrent back problems caused by maintaining a constant sitting position, seeing potentially dangerous clients in deserted premises, social isolation and masochistically putting the client's needs first.

Alderfer (1983) has produced a useful summary of these levels with the mnemonic ERG for 'Existence, Relatedness, and Growth' as the three main factors to be provided within a job.

Herzberg (1968a; 1968b) takes a different approach and distinguishes so-called 'hygiene or maintenance' factors (by which he means removing those factors causing dissatisfaction) from a quite distinct group of factors which positively enhance the job. Interestingly, he found that some motivators were surprisingly short-lived (for example, having one's contribution recognised), whereas a sense of 'responsibility' for seeing a task through maintained motivation for long periods. In this respect the strong sense of personal responsibility of most therapists will promote and maintain job satisfaction.

'Job enrichment' and 'job design' are the terms used to apply the above when enhancing an individual's job to reduce the risk of demotivation and resulting stress. Herzberg (1968b) suggests the following steps to enrich a job:

- reducing unnecessary controls whilst retaining accountability for one's own work;
- dividing the job into natural units;
- increasing the individual's authority;
- reporting direct to the worker rather than to the supervisor;
- introducing more complex tasks;
- allowing individuals to become 'experts' by taking on new tasks.

Clearly, some of these constructs apply to a very limited extent to the therapist's job which will already have a high degree of autonomy and a line of accountability which does not fit Herzberg's model. Nevertheless, his comments can be used to reflect on the factors which promote motivation: the task is divided naturally, we can become experts, and we are accountable for our own work.

There are important exceptions to this analysis, usually within an organisational culture which wants to reduce individualism and set narrow performance targets. (For a fuller discussion of the clash of organisational cultures see Handy 1993, Chapter 7, 'On the culture of organizations'). For example, in some NHS psychotherapy departments the 'contracts culture' is seriously distorting the personal nature of the therapeutic contract at the expense of the more formal contract between so-called 'providers and purchasers'.

'Job design' refers to the empirical work on what constitutes a 'well-designed' job. The job should form a whole rather than being fragmented; it should be perceived as meaningful and worthwhile; should allow all relevant decisions to be made by the individual; give direct feedback; and provide fair rewards (Open University 1993).

Such a job design is said to maximise *intrinsic* motivation (sense of achievement, self-respect, and the feeling of having learned whilst doing a worthwhile job). In this sense unemployment is more stressful than even the most exacting job, because the unemployed are starved of these motivating factors derived from work.

A similar view is taken by Hackman and Oldham (1976) who link their version of the core job dimensions (skill variety, task identity, task significance, autonomy and feedback) with 'critical psychological states' of 'meaningfulness, responsibility, and knowing what was achieved'. In turn these states are said to result in positive personal and work outcomes (high internal motivation, quality work, satisfaction and low absences from work).

It may be a surprise to see how far psychotherapists are from having well-designed jobs. For instance, the job of a therapist is often fragmented and develops *ad hoc* as patients or teaching roles are offered; decisions are often outside the control of the therapist when funding is in the hands of a third-party payer such as a Health Authority; the patient offers idiosyncratic feedback and what does occur is often distorted by transference and counter-transference forces; and rewards are often meagre, particularly for therapists who work independently. Luckily, the experience of the job being meaningful and worthwhile offers considerable compensation under most conditions.

The contribution from management theory to the understanding of stress is by no means a one-way flow. There has been considerable work from the Tavistock Institute of Human Relations in London focused on a psychoanalytic view of organisations and the contribu-

tion of unconscious dynamics to work-related problems. Menzies
Lyth (1988) in a series of essays dating from her action research in
various health and other settings provided a rich understanding of
the institutional defences against anxiety. In a classic study of
anxiety in nursing staff she pointed out that organisational defences
reduced the quality of care available for the residents in a long-stay
hospital. The diffusion of responsibility and fragmentation of care
led to insuperable difficulties for the residents in becoming attached
to secure care-takers.

In the light of the work cited above, however, such defensive
fragmentation also led to less satisfying conditions for the nurses. In
'The functioning of social systems as a defence against anxiety'
(Menzies Lyth 1959) the high levels of tension, distress and anxiety
experienced by the nurses were noted. There were also high levels
of staff turnover and absenteeism. Rather than accept that such
anxiety was an inevitable part of intense therapeutic work, she
suggested that the nurses could be supported in their role once the
nature of the anxiety had been understood.

The objective situation confronting the nurse bears a striking
resemblance to the fantasy situations that exist in every individual
in the deepest and most primitive levels of the mind. . . .

Because of the operation of aggressive forces, the inner world
contains many damaged, injured or dead objects. The atmosphere
is charged with death and destruction. This gives rise to great
anxiety. The infant fears for the effect of aggressive forces on the
people he loves and on himself. He grieves and mourns over their
suffering and experiences depression and despair about his inadequate ability to put right their wrongs. . . . The nurse projects
infantile fantasy situations into current work situations and experiences the objective situations as a mixture of objective reality
and phantasy.

(Menzies Lyth 1988: 46–9)

This work was based on the overtly threatening nature of physical
illness, but a similar analysis is helpful in understanding the confusion experienced in psychotherapy work settings which may feel
charged with immense anxiety.

Her description of the defences mobilised by the nurse could
equally be applied to the therapist. She describes:

- the organisation disrupting the essential nurse–patient relationship;
- depersonalisation, categorisation and denial of the significance of the individual;
- detachment and denial of feelings;
- elimination of decision-making by ritual task-performance;
- using checks and counterchecks and collusive social distribution of responsibility;
- purposeful obscurity in the formal distribution of responsibility;
- delegation to superiors to reduce impact;
- avoidance of change;
- idealisation to underestimate personal development possibilities.

Menzies Lyth's analysis is the prototype of a Kleinian model for analysing work and organisational stress which has been replicated in many industrial and public sector settings (Jaques 1955). Oddly, this method has been used infrequently to look at the work conditions of psychotherapists as such.

A related approach drawing on the tradition of seminars instituted by Michael Balint (1957) was developed by Main (1978). He described characteristic ways that doctors develop to deal with stress which he, like Menzies Lyth, saw as originating in the internal world of the professional. He related the stress on the doctor as analogous to facing war:

All analogies eventually become strained, but mine can be pursued a little longer. Medicine and war are both serious, with issues of crippledom and loss, sadnesses and terrors about external dangers; and both also complicated by anxieties from the inner world, unconscious fantasies of primitive sadism, punishment and so on. [The front-line officer and the general practitioner] [b]oth need professional egos (to use Enid Balint's term) that are strong enough to withstand and not be overwhelmed by major tensions and that can simultaneously preserve full commonsense and professional skills; all this without resort to pathological defences.

(Main 1989: 206)

Given that this was an address to the Balint Society, it is unsurprising that Main was advocating the systematic use of seminar groups to explore the doctor–patient relationship in a way which would minimise the impingement of pathological defences.

We need not be surprised therefore . . . if doctors seek ways of limiting their subjectivity and of alleviating the strains of uncomfortably close encounter . . . if they adopt and institutionalize as a profession various defences against the dangers of becoming helpless and stupid. . . .

(ibid.: 213)

Main's advocacy of the detailed exploration of defences in what are often now called 'Balint Groups' suggests a way of offering support whilst simultaneously improving practice.

The salutary warning from Main leads naturally to the last section which concerns some of the other practical ways in which therapists might analyse their own stress and find ways of alleviating the resulting tension without resorting to pathological defences.

ANALYSING STRESS IN THE WORKPLACE

Therapists are not always articulate about the nature of their difficulties (Grosch and Olsen 1995). A useful approach to the elucidation of stressors comes from the work of a research group based in Warwick University (Davis et al. 1987). They developed a taxonomy of 'difficulties' based on the experience of the therapist. Their work can be applied as part of clinical training (Margison 1991). This involves the therapists writing down an account of an incident which they found difficult or stressful, then stating their feelings at the time, and, finally, what they did to cope. The therapists work in small groups using the taxonomy developed by Davis and colleagues and later discuss their feelings and their ways of coping.

The list of difficulties helps therapists by giving a framework for understanding the problem and by communicating that such experiences are not unique! They describe difficulties of painful feelings being evoked (incompetence, being damaging, puzzled, threatened, out of rapport, stuck or thwarted); having personal issues triggered, facing a painful reality (such as terminal illness); and facing an ethical dilemma with conflicting loyalties.

This work has now become part of an ongoing international collaborative study looking longitudinally at therapist development (Davis et al. 1995). This recent report suggests that there are three stable sub-scales of therapist difficulties in the 'difficulties' section of the Common Core Questionnaire of the international study: difficulties located in the patient; in the therapist; and in external issues such as moral, ethical and existential issues. The difficulties located in the therapist seem to be attenuated by experience–unlike the other two factors (Davis *et al.* 1995).

The exercise of exploring therapeutic difficulties can act as an introduction to a further training method using role play. This is based on Kagan's work (Kagan 1980; Margison 1991) which assumes that therapists deny their anxiety through the adoption of 'feigned clinical naïveté', by which he means a deliberate pretence that the therapist has not recognised a distressing feeling in case, for example, 'she might cry if I told her I knew she was "hurting" and then I would feel I had made her cry'.

Through structured peer-support and self-scrutiny Kagan minimises the potential 'narcissistic injury' to the therapist who can then explore the four basic paradigmatic fears: fear of engulfing or being engulfed; and fear of attacking or being attacked. He suggests that each therapist is pre-set to be vulnerable to different paradigms and that the defensive reaction to this stress leads the therapist to behave disingenuously, 'like a diplomat'!

There are numerous tailor-made stress inventories. An example is a simple checklist developed by Dailey (1985) called 'The Burnout Test' which has fifteen items which in fact cover in a somewhat confusing way issues related to job structure, coping strategies, symptoms and suggested solutions. His checklist, however, is worth summarising as a helpful *aide-mémoire*:

- Do you take your vacations?
- Do you schedule personal time?
- Do you eat regularly and take meal breaks?
- Do you take care of yourself?
- Do you still get pleasure?
- Are the staff–patient ratios balanced?
- Do you feel indispensable?
- Can you manage time?
- Do you relieve stress by contacting others?
- Do you still laugh?
- Are you over-responsible for the behaviour of others?
- Do you take on a personal role for the patient (e.g. missing spouse)?
- Are you a perfectionist?
- Do you have a grandiose self-view?
- Do you 'have the solution'?
- Do you set unrealistic deadlines?

The unusual mix of items, such as asking about sense of humour, helps the therapist to 'think again' about stress, but it does not pretend to methodological rigour.

COPING AND STRESS

Having examined stress and support and the impact of the way we construct our working lives, we end with the concept of coping. In the lay sense this means 'getting by' but in the literature on stress there is more emphasis on the styles by which we cope.

A critical analysis of the literature on coping is given in a review by Cohen (1987). She points out that the conceptualisation of coping is as subject to underlying theoretical assumptions as is the concept of stress. Essentially, coping is seen as both action-oriented and intrapsychic and hence has two types of outcome: problem-solving and emotional regulation (Hamburg, Coelho and Adams 1974; Lazarus 1975). Coping can also be seen as an enduring aspect of the person (a trait) or something which is more specific to particular types of episode.

Although the distinction between problem-focused and emotion-focused coping is still widely accepted and embedded in many measurement tools (Joffe and Naditch 1977), there is good evidence that most people use both strategies together most of the time (Folkman and Lazarus 1980). Indeed, it is evidence of healthy coping to manage feelings whilst also being able to take action.

There has, perhaps, been an unhelpful stereotyping between the therapists who specialise in staying with feelings (for example, the psychoanalytic concept of 'negative capability') and those who specialise in action (for example, the active approaches seen within some behavioural treatments where the therapist might prevent an obsessional ritual). An unrecognised source of imbalance for therapists might be that they stay day in and day out within one restricted coping style and then apply the same strategy unthinkingly in their own lives.

From an empirical perspective, Cohen et al. (1986) distinguish five main coping strategies:

- seeking more information;
- acting directly;
- inhibiting action;
- using intrapsychic processes;
- turning to others for support.

However, these are useful mainly for research and are not easy to translate into remedies for stress, nor for assessing the possible imbalance in our coping repertoires.

The description of coping factors has been developed into a more directly useful schema which can be understood in terms of emotional distance, relationships and self-management. Folkman *et al.* (1986) describe eight basic coping strategies:

Distance

- confronting
- distancing
- escape/avoidance

Self-management

- self-control
- positive appraisal
- accepting responsibility
- planful problem solving

Relationships

- seeking social support

The study of therapist difficulties discussed earlier (Davis *et al.* 1987) also examined therapists' use of coping strategies and developed a taxonomy which is consistent with the empirical work of Folkman and colleagues. The coping strategies are divided into two main groups: turning towards a resource and turning against the problem (or ultimately the patient). The taxonomy does not explicitly state any values, but the discussion soon differentiates between adaptive 'turning towards', such as towards self for reappraisal or self-management, or towards the patient to share resources in dealing with the difficulty; to others for consultation or education; or towards practice by various different types of intervention or even deciding to change tack. In contrast, 'turning against' clearly implies avoidance of the problem or the patient, ultimately through terminating contact.

An alternative approach to examining coping style is to use for ourselves as therapists the questionnaire designed as part of the repertoire of methods of Cognitive Analytic Therapy (Ryle 1990). The Personal Sources Questionnaire clarifies from where the respondent obtains support, and by implication from the negative responses it is possible to work out areas of lack of support or vulnerability. The choice of supports then leads to an understanding of our preferred coping style. This model suggests that we have a repertoire of styles which we can tap under different conditions. The *flexibility* of such changes in strategy is seen now as being at least as important as the coping strategies themselves, although no satisfactory measure of flexibility has yet been developed (Cohen 1987).

CONCLUSIONS

This chapter takes a step back from the detailed accounts of stress and coping given from a wide range of therapeutic modalities and work settings. The literature on job structure, motivation, stress and coping is now very extensive. This chapter merely dips a toe into a new pool of ideas which put the stress experienced by therapists into a wider context.

However, psychotherapists themselves have made a considerable contribution to understanding stress in organisations and within individuals and this is seen here within the context of the broader literature.

Many models of psychotherapy rely on enhancing knowledge – both self-knowledge and knowing how to change unhelpful conditions. The use of some of the analytic methods described here will lead to an awareness of what needs to be changed in the environment or at times in ourselves.

REFERENCES

Alderfer, C. P. (1983) *Existence, Relatedness, and Human Growth: Human Needs in Organizational Settings*, New York: Free Press.
Balint, M. (1957) *The Doctor, his Patient, and the Illness*, London: Tavistock.
Brown, G. W. and Harris, T. O. (1978) *Social Origins of Depression*, London: Tavistock.
Cohen, F. (1987) 'Measurement of coping', in S.V. Kasl and C.L. Cooper (eds) (1987).
Cohen, F., Reese, L. B., Kaplan, G. A. and Riggio, R. E. (1986) 'Coping with the stress of arthritis', in R. W. Morowitz and M. R. Hang (eds), *Arthritis in the Elderly*, New York: Springer.
Dailey, A. L. (1985) 'The Burnout Test', *American Journal of Nursing* 85: 270–2.
Davis, J. D., Elliott, R., Davis, M. L., Binns, M., Francis, V. M. and Kelman, J. E. (1987) 'The development of a taxonomy of therapist difficulties: initial report', *British Journal of Medical Psychology* 60 (2): 109–20.

Davis, J. D., Schroder, T. A., Davis, M. L. and Orlinsky, D. (1995) 'Where do therapists locate difficulties in their therapeutic practice?' Panel Presentation, 23 June, Annual International Scientific Meeting of the Society for Psychotherapy Research, Vancouver, Canada.

Edelwich, J. and Brodsky, A. (1980) *Burnout: States of Disillusionment in the Helping Professions*, New York: Human Sciences Press.

Farber, B. A. (ed.) (1983) *Stress and Burnout in the Human Service Professions*, New York: Pergamon.

Firth, J. (1986) 'Levels of stress in medical students', *British Medical Journal* 292: 1177–80.

Fisher, H. J. (1983) 'A psychoanalytic view of burnout', in Farber (ed.) (1983).

Folkman, S. and Lazarus, R. S. (1980) 'An analysis of coping in a middle-aged community sample', *Journal of Health and Social Behaviour* 21: 219–39.

Folkman, S., Lazarus, R. S., Dunkel-Schetter, C., De Longis, A. and Graen, R. J. (1986) 'The dynamics of a stressful encounter: cognitive appraisal, coping and encounter outcomes', *Journal of Personal Social Psychology* 50: 992–1003.

Freudenberger, H. J. and Richelson, G. (1980) *Burnout: The High Cost of Achievement*, Garden City, NY: Anchor Press.

Freudenberger, H. J. and Robbins, A. (1979) 'The hazards of being a psychoanalyst', *Psychoanalytic Review* 66 (2): 275–96.

Gartrell, N., Herman, J., Olarte, S., Feldstein, M. and Localio, R. (1986) 'Psychiatrist–patient sexual contact', *American Journal of Psychiatry* 143 (9): 1126–31.

Grosch, W. N. and Olsen, D. C. (1995) 'Prevention: avoiding burnout', in Sussman (1995).

Guy, J. D. (1987) 'Burnout among psychotherapists', in *The Personal Life of the Psychotherapists*, New York: Wiley.

Hackman, J. R. and Oldham, G. R. (1976) 'Motivation through the design of work: the test of a theory', *Organizational Behaviour and Human Performance* 16: 250–79.

Hamburg, D. A., Coelho, G. V. and Adams, J. E. (1974) 'Coping and adaptation: steps towards a synthesis of biological and social perspectives', in G. V. Coelho, D. A. Hamburg and J. E. Adams (eds), *Coping and Adaptation*, New York: Basic Books.

Handy, C. B. (1993) *Understanding Organizations* (4th edn,) Harmondsworth: Penguin Books.

Herzberg, F. (1968a) *Work and the Nature of Man*, London: Staples Press.

—— (1968b) 'One more time: how do you motivate employees?' *Harvard Business Review* 46: 53–62 (cited in Open University 1993).

Hobson, R. F. (1985) *Forms of Feeling: The Heart of Psychotherapy*, London: Tavistock.

Holmes, J. and Lindley, R. (1991) *The Values of Psychotherapy*, Oxford: Oxford University Press.

Holmes, T. H. and Rahe, R. H. (1967) 'The social readjustment rating scale', *Journal of Psychosomatic Research* 11: 213–18.

Holroyd, J. C. and Brodsky, A. M. (1977) 'Attitudes and practice regarding erotic and non-erotic contact with patients', *American Psychologist* 32: 843–9.

House, J. S. (1981) *Work, Stress and Social Support*, Reading, Mass.: Addison-Wesley.

Jaques, E. (1955) 'Social systems as a defence against persecutory and depressive anxiety', in M. Klein, P. Heimann and R. E. Money-Kyrle (eds), *New Directions in Psychoanalysis*, London: Tavistock.

Jenkins, P. L. (1989) *Hazards of Psychiatric Practice*, Chicago: Year Book Publications.

Joffe, P. E. and Naditch, M. (1977) 'Paper and pencil measures of coping and defence', in N. Haan (ed.), *Coping and Defending: Processes of Self-Environment Organization*, New York: Academic Press.

Kagan, N. (1980) 'Influencing human interaction: eighteen years with IPR (Interpersonal Process Recall)', in A. K. Hess (ed.), *Psychotherapy Supervision: Theory, Research and Practice*, New York: Wiley.

Kasl, S. V. (1983) 'Pursuing the link between stressful life experiences and disease: a time for reappraisal', in C. L. Cooper (ed.), *Stress Research*, New York: John Wiley.

Kasl, S. V. and Cooper, C. L. (eds) (1987) *Research Methods in Stress and Health Psychology*, New York: Wiley.

Kohut, H. (1977) *The Restoration of the Self*, New York: University Press.

Lazarus, R. S. (1975) 'The self-regulation of emotions', in L. Levi (ed.), *Emotions – Their Parameters and Measurement*, New York: Raven Press.

Lazarus, R. S. and Folkman, S. (1984) *Stress, Appraisal and Coping*, New York: Springer Publishing Co.

Leventhal, H. and Tomarken, A. (1987) 'Stress and illness: perspectives from health psychology', in S.V. Kasl and C.L. Cooper (eds) (1987).

Main, T. (1978) 'Some medical defences against involvement with patients', *The Journal of the Balint Society* 7: 3–11 (reprinted in T. Main (1989) *The Ailment and Other Psychoanalytic Essays*, London: Free Association Books).

Margison, F. R. (1987) 'Stress in psychiatrists', in R.L. Payne and J. Firth-Cozens (1987).

Margison, F. (1991) 'Learning to listen: teaching and supervising basic psychotherapy skills', in J. Holmes (ed.), *Textbook of Psychotherapy in Psychiatric Practice*, London: Churchill Livingstone.

Maslach, C. C. (1976) 'Burned out', *Human Behaviour* 5: 16–22.

Maslow, A. H. (1970) *Motivation and Personality*, London: Harper & Row.

Menzies Lyth, I. (1959) 'The functioning of social systems as a defence against anxiety: a report on a study of the nursing service of a general hospital', *Human Relations* 13: 95–121 (reprinted in Menzies Lyth 1988).

Menzies Lyth, I. (1988) *Containing Anxiety in Institutions: Selected Essays*, London: Free Association Books.

Mintzberg, H. (1971) 'Managerial work: analysis from observation', *Management Science* 18 (2): 97–110.

Neisser, U. (1967) *Cognitive Psychology*, New York: Appleton-Century-Crofts.

Open University (1993) *Managing Health Services*, Milton Keynes: Open University Press.

Payne, R. and Firth-Cozens, J. (1987) *Stress in Health Professionals*, New York: John Wiley.

Payne, R. L. and Jones, G. (1987) 'Measurement and methodological issues in social support', in S.V. Kasl and C.L. Cooper (eds) (1987).

Pearlin, L. I. (1983) 'Role strains and personal stress', in H. B. Kaplan (ed.), *Psychosocial Stress: Trends in Theory and Research*, New York: Academic Press.

Pines, A. and Aronson, E. (1981) *Burnout: From Tedium to Personal Growth*, New York: Free Press.

Pugh, D. S. and Hickson, D. J. (1989) 'Henry Mintzberg', in *Writers on Organizations*, Harmondsworth: Penguin Books.

Rich, C. L, and Pitts, F. N. (1979) 'Suicide by male physicians during a five-year period', *American Journal of Psychiatry* 136 (8): 1089–90.

Rose, K. D. and Rosow, I. (1973) 'Physicians who kill themselves', *Archives of General Psychiatry* 29: 800.

Ross, M. (1973) 'Suicide and the psychiatrist', *American Journal of Psychiatry* 130: 937.

Ryle, A. (1990) *Cognitive-Analytic Therapy: Active Participation in Change: A New Integration in Brief Psychotherapy*, Chichester: John Wiley.

Scully, R. (1983) 'The work setting support group: a means of preventing burnout', in B.A. Farber (ed.) (1983).

Stewart, R. (1982) *The Choices for the Manager*, New York: McGraw-Hill.

Sussman, M. B. (1995) *A Perilous Calling: The Hazards of Psychotherapy Practice*, New York: John Wiley.

Index